RESTORATIVE JUSTICE:
Healing the Foundations of Our Everyday Lives

Second edition

by

Dennis Sullivan
Institute for Economic and Restorative Justice

and

Larry Tifft
Central Michigan University

Willow Tree Press, Inc.
Monsey, New York
2005

ISBN: 1-881798-63-1.

CONTENTS

DEDICATED TO

David Gil

Who has worked tirelessly
For the good part of a century
To alleviate the pain and suffering
Of human beings everywhere

and

Richard Quinney

Who has continuously searched
To understand the human condition
And who has inspired many to witness injustice
And pursue peacebuilding

Preface to the Second Edition

When talking with people, young and old alike, about how conflict was handled in their families when they were growing up and even to this day, a real conversation-stopping question is: What kind of mechanism or process existed, or now exists, for responding to harms or conflict in your family? Suppose you saw your younger sister, who had been teased and belittled for years by your older brother, reach her boiling point one day and haul off and smack him in the face? What if you had been terribly upset by this situation all along, but this was the last straw, and all the frustration and pain you had been feeling came to the surface? Did your family have a process which you could initiate so you could talk about your feelings and thoughts about this violence, and to which you could invite your brother and sister and the rest of the family to talk about their perspectives and feelings? And similarly, what if you saw your father mistreat your mother in a way that deeply affected you because you saw your mother close down emotionally for a fairly long period of time? Was there, is there, a forum in place wherein you might begin to tell your story of hurt feelings and ask everyone who was still smarting over this conflict to talk about the underlying or precipitating issues so that your mother's and father's needs could be better met and their emotional and relational well-being restored?

When we ask these kinds of questions, we often notice that there is a moment of silence. You can see people thinking with their eyes, thinking not only about how their families handled such matters in the past, but how such a process might work. Many have never before entertained such a question and this is true even if they have heard of restorative justice, for far too often restorative justice is presented, discussed, and practiced as if it were solely an alternative to the criminal justice system's response to crime, something solely external to family life, something solely external to you.

As the authors of the exploration that follows, we are continuing with what has been our main interest for the past 33 years as we have collaborated in teaching, activism, and writing. That is, we have been looking for ways that we, the human community, might organize our lives together or create ways of relating with one another that would better meet people's needs and, as we have said time and time again, meet the needs of all. And we have been especially interested in social situations when someone has harmed another, looking for how we might invent ways to help all those affected by the harm find some relief from their pain and suffering. We include in our search, of course, not only an application to individuals whose lives have been turned upside down but also applications to groups, communities, and nations of people.

So we have an interest in the young woman who was traumatized by the slap her sister gave her brother, and by his constant belittling and, before that, the pained bickering that had frequently taken place between them. Her life, perhaps all their lives, had been up-ended. But what if there was no way for her to tell her story, no process to which she could have recourse to ask all the members of her family to come together to deal with what she found so very troubling? The Navajo have such a process; it is called "peacemaking." It is a process where someone who is troubled, upset, or harmed for one reason or another, can call upon relatives, elders, or the community as a whole to help them resolve peacefully what is eating away at them. It might be the alcoholism of a spouse, a battering or sexual abuse situation, a feeling of being excluded, or the loss of one's positive identity. But whatever the trouble or harm, they have a mechanism they can activate, a process for storytelling, for telling others about their pain and suffering and their desire to have their needs attended to. Moreover, they come to this peacemaking process not simply to be heard but to listen to others and hopefully reach some level of reconciliation, achieve some sort of reconstruction of their lost sense of self. The Navajo had such a process in place for centuries until the U.S. government dramatically invaded their lives and forbade them to engage in it.

Our interest here is in processes of justice like those of the Navajo that help restore people to their former selves, well aware that no one can ever be the person they were before a devastating harm entered their lives. But, as we said, we are interested in restorative processes at all levels of social organization: the global political-economy level, the level of the nation-state, the level of the community or neighborhood, the level of personal relationships, and the level of self. We linked up with restorative justice because we saw restorative justice as a process of responding to harm from a needs-based perspective. Because our main area of interest for these past decades has been needs-based justice, we thought we might have a contribution to make to the restorative justice community once we opened ourselves up to the many gifts its members had to offer us.

But because our interest has been in broad social-structural change, the kind of change through which the needs of all are taken into account, we have been primarily interested in structural change in people's lives, in the foundations of our lives. In 2000, we put together a 46-page booklet called *Restorative Justice as a Transformative Process: The Application of Restorative Justice Principles to Our Everyday Lives.* Our desire there was to call attention to the tremendous possibilities of restorative justice, for sure, but it was also to expand the boundaries of restorative justice to include harms and conflicts in all areas of our lives: our families, our schools, our places of worship, where we work. And, as you will see in this much longer version, our interest is not simply in establishing restorative measures in these social institutions after someone has been harmed but also, and perhaps more importantly, in structuring these institutions according to needs-based, restorative principles. When used in this way, restorative justice principles possess a great capacity for preventing harm. However we also know that the farther restorative practices move away from a needs-based foundation, the less restorative these practices become. Needs-meeting is the bellwether of true restorative justice practices.

When we first shared our booklet with friends who are teachers, writers, activists, and practitioners of restorative justice, many said that what we had written had resonated with them, some deeply. But a large number of these folks said they would be interested in hearing more about the application of restorative justice to our daily lives, especially how its principles were related to meeting the needs of everybody who was involved in a particular harm situation. They also asked for more "real life" examples to more thoroughly illustrate the concepts we were talking about. We were pleased to respond to their requests with a much longer essay, which turned into the first edition of this book.

The many people who read the first edition and used it in prison ministry or in their classrooms with young students were kind in their remarks about what they had read but, at the same time, they asked for even more illustrations and further explanations of the concepts which, though written in plain language, were largely unfamiliar and therefore difficult to grasp. We have responded with this second edition of the book.

This edition contains many more illustrative examples than the first. It also contains a much expanded and detailed explication of the concepts. Furthermore, it incorporates, to the extent we were able, the best of the most recent research, concepts, and analyses contained in the many fine books, original essays, and anthologies that have been published since 2001. We thank our colleagues who are traveling a path similar to ours for their contributions to this work.

* * *

To the reader, we urge patience with us and with yourself

as you begin on a path that will present new vistas, vistas that will challenge your values and principles, who you are, and how you relate with others. Whether you agree with what we say (fully or partially), we believe you will walk away from these pages with deeper insights into the foundations of your life, into the human condition. You will find yourself to one degree or another enriched and restored. At least that is our wish.

Larry Tifft,
Mt. Pleasant, Michigan

Dennis Sullivan,
Voorheesville, New York

January 31, 2005

ACKNOWLEDGMENTS

As we were preparing the first edition of this book, the pamphlet that went before it, and now the second edition, many people have shown unfailing enthusiasm and support for what we have done.

We would like to thank Jim Acker for being one of the catalysts for moving us to first publish these ideas in pamphlet form in 2000.

We would like to thank as well Bill Cuddy for using the pamphlet in training courses with his colleagues at the Syracuse Jail Ministry. Father John Weygand, Mary Farrell, and Father Timothy Taugher offered kind words to us about the pamphlet which encouraged us to expand it into a book.

Our friend and colleague, Harry Mika, has been a continuing source of encouragement, as well as friends Larry Siegel, Kathryn Sullivan, Peter Sanzen, and Pat Shields.

Generous and continuing support has also been offered by our Albany Catholic Worker friends, Fred Boehrer and Diana Conroy; and Jane Sammon of the New York City Catholic Worker invited us to discuss these ideas at one of the Catholic Worker's legendary Friday night meetings for clarification of thought. Thomas Vecchio, now of Twin Oaks Community, was part of that effort as well.

Our long-time colleague and supporter, Doug Thomson, organized a "readers meet author" conference session in Chicago last year at which he, Dragan Milovanovic, and Diane Schaefer offered many insights and thoughtful suggestions for revising the first edition. Similarly, we would like to thank Shadd Maruna, Walt Chura, Andrew Wolford, Sarah Eschholz, Anne-Marie Marshall, and John Wozniak for writing published reviews of the first edition and offering substantial support and critique.

In addition to Shadd Maruna, our thanks go out to Noam Chomsky, Dan Berrigan, John Braithwaite, and Howard Zehr, who were kind enough to read what we have written and to offer comments for the back cover of the book.

We would also like to thank the many teachers who used the first edition in their classrooms and the many students who engaged each of us in thoughtful conversation about the ideas we have expressed. We saw such great wisdom and intelligence on the part of dear friend Hal Pepinsky's graduate students at Indiana University, who engaged us in enthusiastic and inquiring on-line discussions.

With respect to resources, we would like to thank Mark Yantzi for sharing materials on the early development of victim-offender reconciliation programs in Canada. Voorheesville reference librarians, Lorraine Smi and Suzanne Fischer, were also invaluable in helping us secure many needed reference materials, meeting the challenges offered them with a spirit characteristic of the best librarians.

And, we cannot fail to thank Rich Allinson, publisher of Willow Tree Press, for taking on this project. He saw the heart and soul of the project when we first presented it to him. Plus his editorial insights have been invaluable.

Finally, Georgia Gray and Lyn Markham were also invaluable readers and editors in the preparation of this manuscript as well as its earlier versions. To them we would like to express our gratitude for being our partners, our day-to-day foundations, showing that needs-based egalitarian relationships are possible.

FOREWORD

by Harry Mika

Images of justice are contested property of the agent and the victim, the professional and the citizen, the friend and the enemy, the neighbor and the stranger, and the partner, child and self. Though this should be one of the oldest lessons, it remains largely unlearned and we remain resolutely condemned to reproduce its agonies as we flail about in search of the just community. With some effort, we may come to appreciate these many faces of justice. With considerably more introspection, we may arrive at an image that includes our own face. These authors seek to engage us in such a personalist view of justice. But what is the nature of their seduction?

Justice as Ritual

Justice is an organization of everyday life, seemingly without political stripe, that is ritually constructed, deconstructed and reconstructed. Its rhythms fix a fluid world, and allow us the strategic control with which to make sensible and routine violence, despair, harm, power, and the patterns of exchange and distribution that produce them. Ideas of justice divide the natural from the imposter, desensitizing us to possibilities, enticing our acquiescence to an order of social relations that appears incontestable and beyond reproach. These truths are comfort food for the mind, the heart and the soul.

Searching for images of justice that are not so uniquely tailored to us personally is a decidedly uncomfortable task, seemingly a betrayal of the natural order of things. However, the exercise – divesting the armour of soothing justice mythologies – is an elemental step in the direction of self-critique and transformation. It is nonetheless troubling, and often deeply so, to reflect on the ease with which we assume to know the nature of victim, harm, offender and community, only to be confronted with disturbing alternative realities. Four justice vignettes both suggest the extent of my own arrogance, and the mayhem in our thinking that is assured if we peek behind the political discourse and contemplate the situation of the other.

Justice Is Oblique

This was not, in my experience, the standard fare of neighborhood mediation. We had some time ago stepped well outside of the box. Among the twenty or so seated around these tables were men recently arrested and jailed for beating each other with pieces of lumber in the street, contesting the right of the other to park their cars in particular places. Their "voluntary" participation was encouraged by the referring Justice of the Peace who gave the principals in the case a choice between further jail time for successive violations of court orders, or community mediation.

Over several weeks, the group had aired a mountain of grievances.

We had listened intently as one woman described her unsuccessful efforts to strike neighborhood children with her car, children she had said who had run through her flower garden.

A man who had leveled a loaded shotgun in the direction of neighbors seated at a picnic table did so, he said, because other men in the neighborhood thought him less of a man since he had quit drinking, they had lusted after his daughter, they had called his son a "fag."

Another man admitted that he did not often pay close attention to the concerns of his neighbors, but one afternoon, when someone walked across the street and put a pistol to the side of his head, he began to listen more carefully. He was thankful, he confessed, for that epiphany.

Many in the group described how calling the police on each other was the local sport, an essential weapon in their arsenal of trouble.

Certainly not to be outdone, during a particularly difficult moment the previous week when we were at loggerheads, I had remarked how thankful I was not to live in their neighborhood, with them. It was a cheap trick, and 'bought' us another spirited and largely productive hour of dialogue. But I was determined this week to apologize to everyone for my comment, and to assure them that as long as my involvement was productive, I was committed to staying on.

During a mid-morning break, I approached the woman whose husband was acknowledged to be the chief protagonist in this ten year neighborhood conflict. He was a hard man, who had served a prison term for manslaughter. He had been literally driven, with his family, from an adjacent neighborhood for his antics years before.

I thanked her for her involvement and for encouraging her husband to participate. These matters, I said, could not be resolved unless he was intimately involved.

She looked up, bemused. No, I am thankful, she said. As long as he is fighting with the men in the neighborhood, none of their women will open their doors to me. And when he beats me, I will have no place to go.

Justice Is Hard

Frankie is twelve years old and lives in a Protestant working class area of Belfast. Like his brothers before him, Frankie is well known locally for breaking into the homes of senior citizens and for stealing from local merchants. Paramilitaries, who function informally as the local police, have previously beaten Frankie for his antisocial behavior, which has nonetheless continued unabated. The punishment tariff system promises that Frankie is soon to be beaten again by paramilitaries, or perhaps this time shot in the legs.

A new community-based justice program seeks to end punishment violence by offering an option to local paramilitaries who feel pressured by the community to beat and shoot boys like Frankie. A referral is made to the program, and a somewhat reluctant Frankie is persuaded to participate.

Over many months, he makes amends to the senior citizens he has terrorized, and logs hundreds of hours working for the local shopkeepers. He has begun to change himself as well, attending counseling sessions and daily tutoring lessons.

Frankie, who initially told program staff that he aspired to be an ex-prisoner, now speaks of his special talents to reach other young people caught up in trouble like he was. Indeed, program staff treat Frankie as their poster child, and when international visitors or the media come to size-up this innovative program, Frankie often volunteers to say a few words about his transformative experiences in the program. It is a real show stopper.

One day, after yet another command performance, Frankie meets up with me in the back kitchen. We are alone.

I was lying, he said. *Oh?*

Yea, I would have rather been shot than go through this program. It is too hard.

Apparently, the punishment, and not the program, is soft on crime.

Justice Is Blind

The most likely scenario for victim offender mediation is a first time offender, a young male, negotiating restitution for a property offense involving a single victim. The routine of such cases in some jurisdictions is numbing. So this mediation, involving a well scrubbed (and I suspected, a well rehearsed) ten year old boy, his parents, and the old woman whose window had been broken, seemed unremarkable.

The boy said he went outside after dark to the park, and began to throw apples from under a tree at the old woman's house. When he heard a window break, he ran home.

He said he didn't know why he did it.

His father said he didn't think his son could throw that far.

His mother whispered an apology across the table.

I asked the old woman to describe what had happened. In a sad and tired tone, she said that she was watching television when she heard a very loud crash. She turned off the lamp next to her chair, and switched off the TV. She sat petrified and motionless for a couple of hours. After she could summon the courage, she turned on the lights and went into the next room where she found the broken glass, and later, the apple.

She talked about living in this house for so many years, and how the park and the neighborhood had changed, how the young boys antagonized her, and how the teenagers in the park, who stood between her house and the grocery, intimidated her. She felt trapped.

(I doubted that the young boy understood.)

The matter of the broken window was resolved with dispatch. All agreed that the replacement cost was fair. The parents would write a check to the court, who would in turn pass it on to the old woman. For my part, I had to type an agreement for the parties to sign. The court would accept this, and the pending case would disappear.

Sitting at the typewriter, I had a ten year old talking in my ear. It was mostly chatter, until he asked me why this was such a big deal. I stopped typing, and asked him if he had heard how afraid the old woman was. Sure, he had heard that.

More typing and more chatter, and the boy remarked that he couldn't believe how much trouble he was in with his parents. I stopped again, and started to talk about my own boys, and how I wanted them to treat other people, and not get into trouble.

But why, he said, is he in trouble for hurting that bitch? *That bitch?*

Was not this ten year old (the one in trouble) doing precisely what most of us want, modeling the attitudes and values of his parents (the ones not in trouble) towards *that bitch?* Obviously, we had not even begun that day to talk about the poisoned apple that broke the window, that broke the back, that broke the heart of the old woman who lived in the house by the park...

Justice Is Intimate

I had specifically requested that the local mediation center, with whom I was conducting a program evaluation, direct me to individuals who had refused to refer any cases or participate with the program. So as I sat waiting for the local prosecutor, in this politically conservative part of the state, I thought I knew what to expect.

He rushed into his conference room, and curtly shook my hand and apologized for being late. He had spent the morning, he said, listening to recorded telephone conversations between a woman and her partner who beat her.

Without so much as taking a breath, this thirty-something prosecutor launched into a diatribe about the challenges of doing *real* justice, and the meddling, liberal, knee-jerk "justice" of community mediation. Amateurs, he said, haven't got a clue.

I can put men in jail, I can put them in prison, I can try to tie them in knots with protective orders, but no judge or victim advocate or prosecutor can keep these women from taking abusive men back into their homes.

As he went on, his voice started to crack and it became more shrill.

He began to describe the strategies, the threats and the punishments he intended to met out now to the women who would not cooperate with his office.

He had started to cry.

Did I have any idea, he said, what it is like to listen to your own sister plead with a man over the phone, a man who beats her with impunity, to come home? Everything is going to be alright, she promises him. No more trouble. Please...

No, I had no idea about what that was like.

Justice on Galapagos

There is a popular view of the development of restorative justice, idyllic and soothing, and full of synergy. It will not be betrayed by data. There is lovely visioning, creative modeling, the angst of implementing, and finally courageous evaluating. The evolution of the great good thing. Another version of its appearance is less eloquent and reveals decidedly darker images. Here, restorative justice is disembodied and wrenched from its historical antecedents, including the social forces that give it meaning and character ... **justice as spectre**. Restorative justice becomes the grist of the new justice wars on all the continents, a deep seated contesting of ownership between state, community and self interests, of marking and defending territory ... **justice as combat**. In the name of restorative justice, obscured by the deafening regaling in its name, practice soon becomes alienated from immutable values, diluted and fading away ... **justice as entropy**. With numbing predictability, instantly recognizable by the long-suffering advocates of withered incarnations of alternative justice schemes, restorative justice rolls headlong into retributive impulses, appetites and concessions ... **justice in harm's way**.

Justice as Transformation

As justice merely evolves – like an old man and his old dog – it comes to resemble its antithesis, injustice. The challenge has always been to locate the source of a counter-violence, a process that might destabilize the historical forces that conspire in this time and place to betray human growth and potential, and peace. Surely, there has always been very interesting speculation about rapture, or revolution, or any manner of grand manipulation. But at the end of the day we may find, quite unremarkably, that the transformative potential of restorative justice is entrusted to us, as a personal mantle and mission for how we conduct our daily lives.

Dennis Sullivan and Larry Tifft have struggled to take us down this road before. They are journeymen provocateurs, unrelenting and unrepentant. If preservation of criminal justice as punishment industry and professional practice – including its newest flavors such as restorative justice – is penultimate, then their marginality to the contemporary discourse on crime and justice is richly deserved. The following pages will do little to change that.

But they intend this to be a very different excursion. Theirs' is a passionate advocacy for a non-oppressive world, molded by new patterns of actions, interactions and social relations that become the basis of a new political economy of just relationships, in all arenas and in every dimension of our lives. The standard fare of a restorative justice anchored exclusively to harms-based situations will not do. Rather, the authors insist that restorative justice – if it is to evidence its transformative potential – must flow from needs-based relationships, an architecture of justice that is embedded first and foremost in "that part of our inner being where the roots of restorative community thrive." That is the long gauntlet of their personalist vision. That is the nature of their seduction.

CHAPTER ONE.
The Emergence of Restorative Justice

The Work of Healing in the Face of Harm

Toward the end of the Tim Robbins movie, *Dead Man Walking*, a Roman Catholic nun, Sister Helen Prejean, portrayed by Susan Sarandon, speaks with the father of a boy who had been brutally murdered by two young men. The conversation takes place alongside a road in a cemetery close to the burial site of one of the killers, who had been executed the day before by officials of the state prison system of Louisiana. Sister Helen, who had been the spiritual advisor of the executed prisoner, approached the father of the murdered boy and thanked him for coming to the burial service. All the father could say was, "I don't know why I am here. I got a lot of hate. I don't have your faith." But Sister Helen, both worldly-wise and as merciful as anyone of us can be, told the man that in dealing with such loss, "It's not faith. I wish it were that easy. It's work. Maybe we could help each other find a way out of the hate." But, the hapless father answered, "I don't know. I don't think so."

Although the depiction of this encounter offered by Sister Helen (Prejean, 1993) in her book of the same title differs somewhat from the movie's version, both works point to the reality that one of the most difficult situations we find ourselves in daily is dealing with the pain another has inflicted upon us, especially when that pain is considerable, such as the taking away of our child, our job, or our identity. For most, if not all of us, our most immediate feelings are feelings of anger and revenge. Driven to retaliate, we want to equalize the harm done

– 1 –

by inflicting a counter-harm on the person who hurt us. We want to respond to violence with counter-violence, believing that, even if this violence will not restore our lost well-being, it will at least force the other person to experience pain as we have (Sullivan and Tifft, 1998b). Either directly or indirectly, we say to the person who hurt us, "Here, take this! Now, you can see what it feels like."

And, it seems that this drive to retaliate and the feelings that refuse forgiveness are fueled all the more when those who have harmed us fail to acknowledge their misdeeds and to express remorse for the acts that cause the pain: these two steps, as South African psychologist Pumla Gobodo-Madikizela asserts, are "the most crucial sign" of restorative justice (2003: 97-98; see also Neier, 1990). So when South Carolina shrimp fisherman Jimmy Leland attended a state parole hearing for Ray Brooks, the man who killed his wife while she was working at their hometown post office, he told the board that they ought not to release Brooks because of the great pain Brooks had caused Leland, his family, and his friends. Then, Leland commented especially on Brooks's failure to show remorse not only at the parole hearing but at the trial. "He didn't apologize for anything," Leland said, "He never said he was sorry; he never said he was sorry. Did anyone hear him say he was sorry? He's not remorseful and that's, that's got to be the first step" (Forman and Klug, 1999).

Indeed, in any situation in which we have been harmed, whether at home, in school, at work, or on the street, our hope is that the person responsible for the harm will at the very least acknowledge what he or she did, perhaps recognize the devastating effects his or her acts created in our life, and maybe even offer an apology (Enright and North, 1998). This hope is part of our desire to achieve some level of accountability (Mendez, 1997). Setting the record straight is part of a narrative that helps all involved in a harm situation to begin to reground their shaken lives (Brison, 2002; Mendez, 1991). Though we might find support from family and friends for our misfortune, without some acknowledgment of our diminished self by the one who caused it – and this might include officials of the state as well as members of the community we live in – we find it hard to simmer down; we feel that we are being dismissed, that our needs are being written off, that we don't count (Herman, 1992). We look in the direction of those who refuse to acknowledge what has taken place and, if only with wistful eyes, ask: "Won't you at least admit that you can see how your acts have affected our lives?"

Of course, asking others to acknowledge the harm they have done or are doing to us and to offer an apology or stop what they are doing, grows out of a certain political-economy of relationship (Flanigan, 1992, 1996). It is a political-economy that sees acknowledgment of a harm-done, apology for it, forgiveness offered in return, and perhaps reconciliation as processes that are personally healing for all involved and simultaneously restorative of the community we share or hope to share (Tavuchis, 1991). This was the thinking behind the Truth and Reconciliation Commission that was established in South Africa in 1996 to investigate the multitudinous and heinous atrocities that South Africans committed against each other during apartheid (Truth and Reconciliation, 1998). The aim of the commission was not to seek vengeance, but to create a venue through which all South Africans could find out the story of what took place, a major part of which was getting those responsible for these crimes to acknowledge their involvement (Hayner, 2001; Boraine, 2001; Villa-Vicencio and Verwoerd, 2000). Some speak of this kind of process as an attempt at making moral reparation to those who have been harmed (Duff, 2002). Feelings of grief, resentment, and disdain for the person or persons who caused the harm might persist for "victims/survivors," but what they seek is quite different from the call made by frustrated and furious victims reacting to not receiving legal and public acknowledgment of their suffering and not having their needs acknowledged and addressed in the criminal justice system's processes (Strang, 2004:102).

Moving On from "Victim" to "Survivor"

Of course, experience shows that no matter how conciliatory the call of a "victim" might be, an acknowledgment of the harm done and even an apology can never undo what was said or done. So, we are talking about a restoration of a different sort, one that helps those harmed move from "victim" to "empowered survivor" (Herbst, 1992; Aron, 1992; Cienfuegos and Monelli, 1983). And there is a healthy realism in this move for, as Martin-Baro (1990:185) has noted, "Nobody is going to return to the imprisoned dissident his youth; to the young woman who has been raped her innocence; to the person who has been tortured his or her integrity. Nobody is going to return the dead and the disappeared to their families" (see also Herman, 1992:196). But we also know that once there is public and even legal acknowledgment of a wrong committed, everyone affected by the harm seems to be released or set free from a disabling uncertainty, if only in some small way. And, oftentimes such freedom has to do with very practical matters. When the Mothers of the Plaza de Mayo met each week during the 1980s in front of the Presidential House in Buenos Aires, Argentina, they demanded that the community and government acknowledge the disappearance of 8,960 family members and friends under Argentina's military regime. For years their pleas were not recognized, until in 1994 the government officially acknowledged the harm done to them through the creation of a new legal status, the "forcibly disappeared." This was a victory the Mothers regarded as more important than monetary compensation. On a practical level, the new legal status enabled them to move on, for it provided, as Hayner (2001:177) noted: "the legal equivalent of death for purposes of civil matters, allowing families to process wills, distribute inheritance, close a disappeared person's estate, and other matters, but it stops short of declaring the person dead." Conversely, when a form of acknowledgment such as this does not occur, many people who have been harmed directly or indirectly find it extremely difficult to release themselves from a disabling and continuing victimhood (Barstow,

2003). Never mind having one's needs met, the reality of one's life is not even recognized (Bergman et al., 2003).

However, once we do hear words spoken that acknowledge the pain and distress in our lives, as we experience it, we find ourselves enabled to move on because we are given a psychological base from which to create a more meaningful future. We feel relieved, especially when we believe that an apology made is sincere, because it reflects not simply a promise to change on the part of the person who hurt us, but that a change has already taken place in that person. It is a signal that the mental constructs that sanctioned the harmful behavior in the first place have begun to dissolve, that the person responsible for the harm is not continuing to justify his or her actions, that is, his or her commitment to power and violence (*Bringing Them Home*, 1997). And if the changes made might be in the social-structural or organizational conditions that gave birth to the harm in the first place (Tannen, 2001), these would be radical forms of transformation. For example, family members might begin to relate with one another as equals, respecting each persons' dignity and voice. They may begin to resolve conflicts and make family decisions collectively: that would indicate that a future has been fashioned in which the harmful behavior is no longer possible, that is, where the needs of others have become a more central part of the person's or social institution's life. In terms of persons, they have offered a "guarantee against repetition" because they have begun to grasp what the harmful behavior they inflicted on others feels like (Cunneen, 2001:92-93).

Such change is helpful to those who seek to move beyond their status as "victim," especially those who speak of their deep desire to decrease the centrality of these events in their lives. When Paula Kurland, whose daughter Mitzi had been brutally murdered by Jonathan Wayne Nobles, decided to meet with the Texas prisoner in a restorative mediation session on death row, toward the beginning of their meeting she blurted out in great distress, "I don't know what to do with you, Jonathan. I just don't know what to do with you" (Forman & Klug, 1999; Sheffer, 2001). Clearly Kurland was crying out for some relief from the inner turmoil she was suffering since her daughter's death, that is, for closure. In intimate and familial relationships many people who have been abused by a parent or spouse yearn for an acknowledgment of the harm done by the offending person, believing that this would be a first substantial step in bringing some degree of closure to that part of their lives. Sue William Silverman (1996), in her heart-rending memoir, describes her struggle to reach some kind of closure with her father, who had repeatedly sexually molested her during childhood. As he lay on his deathbed barely able to speak, she tells him she loves him and he says in return, "I love you too" (p. 240). But Silverman says she was praying to hear more, knowing that time was running out. She thinks maybe "he can be redeemed, as if something can be said or done, if not to erase the past, then to diminish it. If he would ask forgiveness. If he would tell me he'd made a terrible, terrible mistake. If he would just acknowledge it" (pp. 240-241). She said she felt "like a stubborn, willful, yet loving child [sitting] by him in his room, waiting for some acknowledgment before he [died]" (p. 241). But it did not come, just as it had not come for Jimmy Leland before he died at the age of 54 in the fall of 2004.

The Illusions of Punishment

We can see why those who embrace a restorative or reconciliatory response to a harm-done believe that punishment and other forms of reactive violence are not capable of fostering the kind of growth that restores personal well-being, much less of helping those affected by a harm to reconnect with members of their families and communities. First of all, for the "victim" who clings to feelings of hatred and revenge, no healing, no moving on is possible because his/her psychological landscape has become a self-perpetuated war zone. Indeed, some "victims" live in terror of their own impulses as their "violent, graphic revenge fantasies may be as arousing, frightening, and intrusive as images of the original trauma. They exacerbate the victim's feelings of horror and degrade her image of herself" (Herman, 1992:189). Ironically, while "getting back at" the other through one's words, thoughts, and imagination, the loss continues, personal stability erodes.

From experience, we all know that punishment is capable of achieving compliance and submission from someone and even of coercing a person to publicly acknowledge shame for certain acts. But because such punitive measures show little concern for the needs of the persons they are directed toward, they create a vacancy or void in those persons (Maag, 1996, 1997). Punishment shuts people down; it incites resentment in them and oftentimes rekindles an allegiance to the justifications for the original harmful acts (Foucault, 1977). Within such a frame of mind, engaging in a process of heartfelt apology, forgiveness, and ensuing reconciliation is nearly impossible because the person being punished is not able to open up her or his heart or soul to begin to envision a new way to be with and among others (Macmurray, 1961).

Part of recovery from trauma of any sort requires creating a safe place in which people can tell their stories, can rebuild their previous social contacts, and begin to build new ones. Some have argued that, at least initially, creating such a safe environment is more important than providing any kind of psychological intervention or therapy (Mimica and Agger, 2000). But, one of the hardest things for many people to recognize – especially those who have been harmed and who cling to feelings of vengeance – is that punishment destroys all possibility of creating such environments. It is hard sometimes for people to see through their justifications, but punishment is a form of violence, a variant of the violence that required corrective attention in the first place, and such counter-violence is always accompanied by justifications identical to those offered by the person responsible for the original harm (Gil, 1999).

When it comes to responding to pain and suffering then, the big question we are continuously faced with is: how can we receive and accept accountability or reparation for acts that are the source of our pain and suffering without acting violently toward those responsible for such loss? How can we foster healing for those harmed without creating a harmful situation for those who have inflicted these harms, without ourselves becoming the source of some new form of violence and, worse, coming to believe that this violence is ameliorative and justifiable? By allowing feelings of vengeance or retribution to narrow our focus on the harmful event and the person responsible for it – as others might focus solely on a sin committed and the "sinner" – we tell ourselves that we are taking steps to free ourselves from the effects of the harm or the sin in question (Consedine, 1995). But, in fact, we are putting ourselves in a servile position with respect to life, human growth, and the further enjoyment of relationships with others. We are locking ourselves into the past and into definitions of self that are further disabling because they allow for no new commitment to the small everyday things in life that provide a context in which the pain and suffering associated with trauma might dissolve.

The late American composer, John Cage, used to say that a measure of our commitment to life and personal growth cannot be found in how hard we work to uphold or live up to a certain vision of how things should go in life. Rather, it is a matter of how long it takes us to say "yes" to no-matter-what event enters our lives. That is, it is a matter of acceptance. When we are harmed in some way, that harm, and the pain and suffering associated with it, have already become part of our life; if we desire to restore ourselves in hopes of moving on, to become that self which we truly are, we must acknowledge all of its dimensions as they unfold, embrace the bad with the good, the losses with the gains (Rogers, 1961; Baumeister and Bratslavsky, 2000). This helps to regenerate our psychological faculties that were damaged by the trauma, including trust, autonomy, initiative, competence, identity, and intimacy (Herman, 1997). On the other hand, acknowledgment, acceptance, apology, forgiveness, moving on with life in the face of adversity – sometimes horrendous adversity – these are the kinds of issues that proponents of restorative justice have begun to raise anew and to open up to the world community to discuss seriously (Gutlove and Thompson, 2003; McCullough et al., 1997). These are questions about what constitutes human well-being, about what promotes personal growth, and about what brings us together in communities of human concern, and, yes, even in the face of the most dire of human circumstances, when blood is shed, when we have shown our most callous sides to one another.

The Justice-Industrial Complex

But here we are raising questions about the possibilities for forgiveness, reconciliation, restoration, and just communities in the early 21st-century United States when our lives are encased by a political-economy which, far from restorative, is responsible for the most massive "justice-industrial complex" the world has ever known (Sullivan, 1980; Irwin and Austin 1994; Tonry, 2004). What is so disturbing about this phenomenon (the greatly increased production and implementation of coercive strategies of social control) is that it does not seem to bother all that many people, nor do they seem to fathom its implications for the quality of life we live (Schlosser, 1998; Burton-Rose et al., 1998). What we must keep in mind is that the violence we do to each other through collective entities, such as the nation-state, and the violence we do to each other directly, are both forms of violence. As Herman (1992) has indicated, by relying on violence to "correct," to respond to harm, we terrorize ourselves as well as those toward whom our violence is directed. And the ramifications of such actions are increasingly clear: more and more of our children are eating their way into fatness or eating disorders; more and more of us are ingesting mood-elevating substances to bolster our spirits, to get us through the day; more and more of us are purchasing consumer goods beyond our means via credit cards to novocaine our pain and deny the structural roots of our personal troubles.

The connection between relying on direct versus indirect violence to problem-solve is indisputable. If we become a person who, as a pattern, batters a partner face-to-face, or one who develops or implements a national strategy to dominate other nations or the world in order to ensure that our or our nation's needs are met, we tend to become a certain kind of person. That is, we become a destroyer of life, a power-monger, a definer and enforcer of the identity of others whom all close by live in fear of and skirt around (Tifft and Markham, 1991). What most of us fail to realize is that when we rely on the state and other agencies of "social welfare" and social control to perform vengeful, violent acts for us – even though we speak of such acts as necessary and in terms of corrections, restitution, and perhaps even restoration – we do not escape the personal consequences of such acts. That we are not involved personally or directly in inflicting the violence makes little difference for we have become a voyeuristic (willing) variant of the person who subdues others face-to-face (Merton, 1961a). By creating and relying on a justice or corrections complex, we also share in the destruction of life by chiseling away at the foundations of the kind of community we say we desire (Sullivan, 1980). The only difference is that we do not see clearly who or what we are becoming and what kind of community we are in fact exhibiting, because the justifications that vengeance, retribution, and deterrence offer us sedate our consciousness. We live our daily lives with euphemisms such as "correctional clients," which refers to warehoused prisoners, and "collateral damage," which refers to children whose arms, legs, and faces have been blown off by rocket mortars. Through such a twist in logic, we lock out the possibilities of a radically different form of existence, one that takes into account the needs of others and which allows us to get out from beneath the weight of our burdensome institutions. We imagine that we are freeing ourselves when in fact we are engaging in our own imprisonment. It is no coincidence then that we have created a society that imprisons more people domestically for the purposes of crime control than any society in history (Mauer, 1990; Clear, 1994). The numbers speak for themselves. The saddest part of this equation is that the U.S. government has exported these atrocities to other nations in aggravated forms. The U.S.-administered prison of Abu Ghraib in Iraq and the detention facility at Guantánamo Bay, Cuba, immediately come to mind. In the latter, an inspection team of the International Committee of the Red Cross has said recently that the U.S. military uses modes of physical and psychological coercion on prisoners that are tantamount to torture (Danner, 2004; Schlesinger et al., 2004; Fay, 2004; Lewis, 2003).

When we look at recent trends in imprisonment in the United States, we come upon other startling statistics. Throughout the first three-quarters of the last century, the incarceration rate in the United States consistently averaged 110 prisoners for every 100,000 people in the overall national population. In the 1970s, this rate was 144 (for those imprisoned and jailed) and began to increase steadily. In the 1980s and 1990s, it grew exponentially to the point that there are now 715 people for every 100,000 population who are in a federal, state, or local lock-up (International Centre for Prison Studies, 2003; Tonry, 2004). This rate of incarceration is not only the highest in the world, but is nearly five times higher than the rates found in other Western countries. By comparison, Canada's imprisonment rate was 116 per 100,000 in 2000. The highest rates in other Western nations in 2000 were around 150 per 100,000 (in Portugal and New Zealand), and most rates were below 100 (e.g., in France, Germany, Italy, and all the Scandinavian countries) (Barklay and Tavares, 2002). In Asia, the incarceration rate in the People's Republic of China was 119 per 100,000. In raw numbers these rates mean that, whereas in 1972 we imprisoned about 200,000 people in the U.S. who were convicted of a crime, in 2001 we imprisoned over 2 million (Beck and Karberg, 2001).

While these facts might be shocking to some, what the numbers do not reveal is the growing hordes of prisoners being warehoused in SuperMax prisons called "Special Housing Units" (SHUs), "Control Units," or "Management Control Units," depending upon the state in which they are confined. Twenty years ago about a half dozen states had built such gulags, but now more than 45 states have committed themselves to this "Marionization" of prison life, as some refer to it, the name coming from one of the first control units established at the federal penitentiary in Marion, Illinois. Two years ago, observers of human rights violations suggested that more than 20,000 prisoners, or nearly 2% of the prison population, were being housed in solitary confinement, but Lorna Rhodes (2004) asserts that the actual number might be closer to 40,000, of whom 15% to 25% are said to be mentally ill.

As most of us know now, in these panopticon gulags prisoners are confined 23 of 24 hours a day, seven days a week. They are allowed 60 minutes for recreation in a cage attached to their cell (about half the size of the cell) with barely enough room to do jumping jacks. Not only are more prisoners developing mental disabilities because of this solitary existence, but more and more mentally and emotionally disabled prisoners are being sentenced to these units. Speaking about the devastating effects of such institutional confinement on the mental well-being of prisoners, former United States Attorney General Ramsey Clark said in a recent interview that: "In these new prisons you're cut off from all what psychologists call 'sensory perception.' You find a crack in the wall and you say 'that looks like the Mississippi River' or something else just to keep your mind functioning" (Sullivan and Boehrer, 1999:7). When these projects of quarantine and social exclusion "are framed in entirely individualistic and non-rehabilitative terms," as Lorna Rhodes (2004:7) queries, "they confront us with disturbing questions about what it means to be a human – a social being."

Concerning the number of mentally ill inmates in these prisons, in 2003 Human Rights Watch (2003) produced a report on the number of such people who are being warehoused in solitary confinement units and in prisons generally. It was estimated that 300,000 men and women, of whom 70,000 are "psychotic," are housed in U.S. prisons. As lawsuits have been brought against various departments of correction in behalf of mentally and emotionally disabled prisoners, many judges have responded with grave concern for the welfare of these human beings. One federal judge, calling attention to the conditions in the Texas prison system said (Ruiz v. Johnson, 1999):

> Whether because of a lack of resources, a misconception of psychological pain, the inherent callousness of the bureaucracy, or officials' blind faith in their own policies, the [corrections department] has knowingly turned its back on this most needy segment of the population.

Part of the lack of concern among most correctionalists regarding the mental health of prisoners is because mental health is treated as if it were an accident of human well-being rather than " a mainstay of life...a need as essential to a meaningful human existence as other basic physical demands our bodies may make for shelter, warmth, or sanitation" (Madrid v. Gomez, 1995). The standard prescription of state and federal correctionalists, then, is to keep the mentally and emotionally disabled supplied with a steady dose of deadening medications. And when it comes to these prisoners being "riddled with staff violence...," as Fellner (2004) asserts, "it is not just that senior officials have failed to control it. They have accepted it as part and parcel of doing business. They may even participate in it themselves." If anything negative can be said about Amnesty International's expansive report on the torture-like qualities of prisons in the United States in 1998, it is only that it was not issued sooner (Amnesty International, 1998).

What inhibits us from developing a clear understanding of the political-economic forces that promote the development of this flourishing punishment industry are the obfuscations and smokescreens that we citizens and public officials alike employ when it comes to speaking about the requirements of justice, especially about responding to people in need. For example, while Mario Cuomo served as Governor of New York (in 1982-1994), he vociferously opposed the death penalty, a position for which many New Yorkers and citizens from around the country gave him praise. They agreed that killing a person for killing a person was a less than moral or human response to even the grossest of crimes. And yet, more prison cells were built while Cuomo was governor than during the administrations of all the previous governors of New York combined, and the state's prison population more than doubled. Sadly, this was a state of affairs that many either thought acceptable or did not know had developed in the first place. But perhaps the most tragic part of this trend nationwide is that two out of five African-American men between the ages of 17 and 27 are now constrained by the criminal justice system in some way; that is, they are either imprisoned, on probation, or under post-release parole supervision (Mauer, 1990, 1992). But rather than recognizing that this reality is produced by an almost exclusive focus on street crime and the war on drugs, by race- and class-based economic arrangements, and by race-based decision-making patterns within the criminal justice system, a different explanation is offered by a large segment of the population. But it is an explanation that only rarely surfaces in public, namely that many people consciously or subconsciously believe that African Americans, and "people of color" generally, are morally inferior, not-fully-human beings.

But the criminal justice violence or punishment violence we are talking about is prevalent not only in the United States but in many countries, and especially countries that have been ravaged by genocide and human rights violations. Those of us interested in restorative justice have had to grapple with such violence. When we look at the criminal justice system in Rwanda, for example, especially after the 1994 genocide in which more than 800,000 Rwandans were massacred, we see criminal justice violence continuing in gruesome ways. In seeking to deal with the doers of the violence and its aftermath in a prosecutorial/adversarial manner, the Rwandan government had by early 1995 over 100,000 detainees on its hands. When Rwandan newspaper editor André Sibomana (1997:108-109) visited Gitarama Prison, he said what he saw defied human imagination:

There were three layers of prisoners: at the bottom, lying on the ground, there were the dead, rotting on the muddy floor of the prison. Just above them, crouched down, there were the sick, the wounded, those whose strength had drained away. They were waiting to die. Their bodies had begun to rot and their hope of survival was reduced to a matter of days or even hours. Finally, at the top, standing up, there were those who were still healthy. They were standing straight or moving from one foot to the other, half asleep... When a man fell over, it was a gift to the survivors: a few extra centimeters of space. I remember a man who was standing on his shins: his feet had rotted away.

Within nine months, almost 1,000 of that prison's 7,000 detainees had died as a result of ill treatment, which Sibomana had described as deliberate (Cobban, 2002; see also Peterson, 2000; Gourevitch, 1998). Because of his commitment to justice, within a year Sibomana was murdered.

As we run through these disheartening dimensions of criminal injustice, we need to keep in mind the valuable lessons that the French psychiatrist, Michel Foucault, taught us about the relationship between the punishing practices of a society and the kinds of disciplinizing, controlling behavior that prevail in its primary social institutions. Foucault said the methods of punishment a society uses to respond to the harms done by those convicted of crime are already manifest in its primary social institutions in the form of surveillance and disabling discipline, that is, a discipline that destroys an individual's sense of personhood (Maag, 2001). The one goes with the other; they are inseparable. Therefore, just as we keep prisoners separated from each other (from a human reality) for 23 of 24 hours a day, we create family conditions in which children and adults spend less time together than ever before. In 70% or more of those families with young children, either both parents (or the single parent) work outside the home, with the result that children are becoming increasingly institutionalized in day care, preschool, school, and after-school programs. When all the members of a family do happen to be at home, they only rarely eat together and their brief conversations are practically non-existent as the children watch their television sets in their rooms and the parents theirs in another.

And when it comes to real participation in the family's affairs, especially with respect to decision making, more frequently than not the children are excluded. It is part of the gulag ethic. Increasingly disconnected from familial traditions in which the young (and old) are cherished for their wisdom, these children and their peers have come to be identified as a national problem (Tifft et al., 1997) which we pretend to solve by installing 24-hour cameras in our schools to watch their every move. In some states, we allow school authorities to legally search students, their belongings, and lockers as if the young had only the rights of slaves. In some schools, we send in dogs to sniff out student belongings for drugs and other cultural annoyances, turning their home away from home into an asylum, into a disciplinizing, docilizing total institution (Goodwin, 2000; Goffman, 1961). We speak about the necessity of such social control with glib justifications but rarely question whatever happened to those precious young angels we saw in kindergarten or first grade, who now in the eighth and ninth grades and above, require surveillance like convicts on a tier.

Movement toward Restorative Justice

Yet as we intimated earlier, amid such conceptual and structural violence, all is not bleak. As we witness the continuing growth of the U.S. punishment industry at home and abroad, and people's increasingly greater reliance on the government to manage their lives and to create safety in their communities, we are also witnessing considerable interest in processes of justice that counter these trends. There is an increasing interest in pursuing reconciliation, healing and restoration when relationships in families, schools, places of work, and communities at large become ruptured even in the most devastating of ways (Cuneen, 2001; Umbreit et al., 2003). For example, in the past several years we have see a growing and persistent interest in the processes of apology and forgiveness as ways to "make things right" after someone has harmed another (Enright and North, 1998; Kushner, 1996; Müller-Fahrenholz, 1997). Those writing about apology and forgiveness, as well as those directing and participating in restorative programs in which apology and forgiveness are central components, offer convincing evidence of the healing properties of these approaches, regardless of the seriousness and expanse of the harm in question (Alter, 1999; Govier; 2002; Levi, 1997; Minow, 1998; Taft, 2000). This includes individuals and groups within countries that have been traumatized by genocide and gross human rights violations, countries that are searching for some kind of "transitional justice" to help them heal the wounds of victimhood (Kritz, 1995). To better understand the healing power of acknowledgment, apology, and forgiveness, we see workshops and indeed entire conferences dedicated to understanding these processes as part of a narrative that enables those who have been harmed to move on with their lives (Schneider, 2000; Peacemakers Trust, 2003). At the University of Wisconsin, an International Forgiveness Institute has been established to look at the healing and restorative properties of apology and forgiveness, specifically their relation to reconciliation and rebuilding severed relationships (Enright, 2001). But, of course, scholars and practitioners continue to question the extent to which apology and forgiveness can be incorporated into a zero-sum, winner-take-all criminal justice system where the first rule of adversarial law is "never apologize" (Morris, 2003; Alter, 1999).

But such a perverse rule has not deterred advocates of personal and social restoration from continuing on their course; there is too much human pain and suffering that requires ameliorative attention. Hence, we have seen a growing movement toward restorative justice and restorative practices on a global level. This is especially evident in the creation of nearly two dozen truth commissions since 1974 (Hayner, 2001). Earlier we mentioned the most well-known of these commissions, the Truth and Reconciliation Commission (TRC) in South Africa that was established in 1996 to respond to gross human rights violations during apartheid. If in the "testimony" of many of the persons who appeared before the commission, we did not see the level of apology or forgiveness that we would have liked or wished for, we did see many who were responsible for heinous crimes publicly acknowledge what they had done. The award-winning TRC Special Report, broadcast every Sunday evening in primetime with a summary of the events that had taken place in the TRC the previous week, had the largest audience of any televised current affairs program in South Africa's history. While those who championed the TRC were well aware of the limitations of such a process of transitional justice, they also saw its potential for easing the pain of South Africa's violent past (Villa-Vicencio, 1999; Leebaw, 2001; Skelton, 2002; Boraine, 2001). South Africans became witnesses "to what had happened and heard the stories directly from the mouths of the persons concerned. Those who spoke were not complainants in a court denouncing accused persons in the dock. Nor were they litigants demanding damages for themselves, so that the greater the loss, the greater the sum they would receive. Neither punishment nor compensation were at issue, only the opportunity to speak the truth and have their pain acknowledged" (Sachs, 1998).

Similarly in Northern Ireland, we have seen restorative justice programs established as alternatives to the punishment violence practiced by IRA and Loyalist paramilitary groups as well as the government of Northern Ireland (McEvoy and Mika, 2001, 2002; Criminal Justice Review, 2000). These programs have demonstrated that community-based restorative justice projects can become a far more effective venue for responding to harms than comparable projects administered by the state (O'Mahoney et al., 2002; Mika, 2002). Such restorative measures can also prevent punishment violence by reconstituting community links that had dissolved when communities relied on punishment as an expedient to solve problems that required much greater attention and participation. One extremely positive result has been that former paramilitary activists and members of different communities who once embraced "violent punishments against anti-social offenders [are] now making use of restorative projects and accepting back into the community those who were previously banished or severely punished" (McEvoy and Mika, 2002:553).

Earlier we alluded to the trauma and desperation that the 1994 Rwandan genocide caused in the lives of people throughout Rwanda, not only through the original killing but also in its aftermath, the thousands of Rwandans rotting in jails and prisons awaiting trial (de Jonge, 2001; Cobban, 2002, 2004; Vandeginste, 2001). To help the country heal from such widespread and continuing devastation, Rwandans have chosen to introduce an indigenous, restorative practice called *gacaca*, a community-based measure they had practiced before the Belgians took over the country three centuries ago. The *gacaca* process serves as a clearly-defined alternative to the International Criminal Tribunal for Rwanda (ICTR) that the U.N. Security Council established in late 1994 and that has left thousands upon thousands literally rotting in jail. The main objective of the *gacaca* courts is "not to determine guilt or to apply state law...but to restore harmony and social order in a given society, and to re-include the person who was the source of the disorder" (De Jonge, 2001:8-9). As the *gacaca* courts prepare to hear their first cases in late-2004/early 2005, the world is watching with eagerness to see whether this restorative practice can achieve the same level of healing that the TRC did in South Africa.

The gracious effects of these kinds of restorative measures have found their way into popular culture. At the outset we mentioned filmmaker Tim Robbins's *Dead Man Walking*. Here we see the life of Sister Helen Prejean "working" with prisoners on death row in Louisiana and deeply involved in the lives of those devastated by murder who are unable to get beyond feelings of vengeance. The film and book version of her response to people in need show that we as a community have the capacity not only to comfort those responsible for such serious harm, but also to foster in them a desire to acknowledge the horrific nature of their acts, that is, to show remorse to those they've harmed. The restorative nature of Sister Helen's work has transformed the attitudes and behavior of multitudes of people who were previously driven to choose retributive, non-restorative, means to respond to harms: even those harms that are most gruesome. Many people have come to see that when the state – we, the public – engages in retributive violence, it is difficult to tell who is and who is not the victim; who is and who is not the murderer.

As we catalogue some of the efforts away from a retributive response to harm and toward restorative justice in the past decade, we cannot fail to mention the bold and courageous decision of Illinois Governor George Ryan to declare a moratorium on executions in that state on January 31, 2000. In May of that year Ryan also established a 14-member Commission on Capital Punishment to study the death penalty in Illinois. That commission returned two years later with a report proposing 85 substantial reforms that have influenced how other states have come to view issues of justice regarding the execution of persons (Vock, 2002). Ryan's efforts and the reasoning behind them did not go unnoticed. In May 2002, Maryland followed suit when Governor Parris Glendening declared a moratorium on the death penalty, inspiring nearly a dozen other states to seriously examine the feasibility of such a moratorium. These efforts were supported by a growing number of editorials in newspapers across the United States calling for moratoria, and by the public declarations for moratoria in at least 100 local jurisdictions around the U.S. This included large cities such as Atlanta, Baltimore, New York, and San Francisco. Other states and international bodies continue to follow this path. In March 2004, the Pennsylvania Supreme Court Committee on Racial and Gender Bias engaged this issue by calling for a moratorium in that state until the courts could ensure that the death penalty could be administered fairly. The following month the

United Nations Commission on Human Rights called upon all nations to implement a moratorium on executions: upon those that have the death penalty, to remove it from their laws; and upon those that carry out death sentences, to limit the types of crimes punishable by death (Death Penalty Moratorium Implementation Project, 2004).

Personal Witness and Restoration

Perhaps most challenging to the retributive ethic of an "eye for an eye," and most inspiring to those interested in working toward restorative responses to harm, are the examples of some individuals and families whose lives have been shattered by murder. We are thinking specifically of members of Murder Victims Families for Reconciliation (MVFR), people who have lost a family member to murder but who remain steadfast against the employment of the death penalty as a way to make things right (Cushing and Welch, 1999). Through the telling of their traumatic stories many members of MVFR have demonstrated that it is humanly possible to face feelings of rage and devastating loss and, while nearly drowning in the vortex of feelings associated with revenge, to come out the other side, still in pain, but freed of vengeance and a life of disabling victimhood (Rimer, 2001; Hartwell, 2000).

In many instances, therefore, members of MVFR have afforded us a new standard, if you will, of how individuals, groups, and countries might respond to harm situations not only by transcending their own revenge-laden grief, but also by becoming healing agents themselves. The life of Oklahoma City gas station owner Bud Welch after April 19, 1995 serves as one of the best examples we have. Welch became a member of Murder Victims' Families for Reconciliation after his 23-year old daughter Julie Marie was killed on that date when Timothy McVeigh parked a truck filled with explosives in front of the Alfred P. Murrah Federal Building in Oklahoma City. When the truck exploded, 168 people were killed and 700 injured, many of whom were children at the day-care center that was housed in the building. This event is commonly referred to as the Oklahoma City bombing.

So close were Welch and his daughter that the loss brought this grieving father to a near, if not actual, mental breakdown. In the story he tells about his life after that day, he says his immediate response, governed by feelings of revenge and destruction, was: "Fry the Bastards. We didn't need a trial; a trial was simply a delay" (Cushing and Welch, 1999). And like many of us who develop vigilante-like feelings after someone has caused us great harm, Welch said, "Had I thought that there was any opportunity to kill them, I would have done so. I didn't come up with a plan to do it, knew that there was no way I would be able to do it. I wouldn't have cared if they had killed me, if I could have been successful in killing them. So suicide meant nothing to me either during that insanity period" (Cushing and Welch, 1999). In talks and television interviews that Welch gave while the state was preparing to execute Timothy McVeigh, he said, "You've heard people speak of temporary insanity, and you've heard people trying to use it, lawyers try to use it in court. Temporary insanity is real, it exists, I can assure you. I've lived it – I lived about 5 weeks of it" (Cushing and Welch, 1999).

As Welch struggled to regain his emotional balance, one day he saw a television news report that featured Bill McVeigh, Timothy McVeigh's father. A crew had come to the McVeigh home in a rural New York town outside Buffalo and caught Bill McVeigh while he was working in a flowerbed in his garden. Welch said he was stunned when he saw McVeigh look into the camera to respond to a reporter's question. He says, "I saw him look into the television camera for a short 2 or 3 seconds, and I saw a deep pain in a father's eye that probably none of you could have recognized. I could because I was living that pain. And I knew that some day I had to go tell that man that I truly cared about how he felt, I did not blame him or his family for what his son had done" (Cushing and Welch, 1999). Welch had come to the realization that he and Bill McVeigh were in the same boat; he had lost a child and McVeigh was about to lose one of his. Welch was no longer interested in what or who was responsible for the killing; he was interested in meeting with the man whose son was about to die and with whose family he was now connected by extraordinary circumstances.

Through friends, Welch made arrangements to visit Bill McVeigh and his daughter, Jennifer, at their home. The three of them spent an hour and a half sitting around the kitchen table talking. Welch says that he "noticed a photograph – there were some family photos on the kitchen wall up above the table. And I noticed this photo of Tim. I kept looking at it as we were sitting at the table, with Bill sitting off to my left. I knew that I had to comment on it at some point, so finally I looked at it and I said, "God, what a good looking kid." And Bill says to me, "That's Tim's high school graduation picture."

During their conversation, Welch says that Tim's guilt or innocence never came up; that had never been his purpose in going there. He says, "I didn't have to have Bill McVeigh look me in the eye and say, 'I'm sorry my son killed your daughter.' I didn't have to hear that. But I was able to tell him that I truly understood the pain that he was going through, and that he – as I – was a victim of what happened in Oklahoma City." Before he left, Welch promised the McVeighs that he would work as hard as possible to stop the state from killing Tim. Those who watched morning and evening news programs on television before Timothy McVeigh was executed saw Bud Welch as practically the only person who had lost someone in the Oklahoma City bombing arguing against executing the man who was responsible for these deaths. For such a stance he was vilified publicly, openly questioned as to whether he ever really loved his child.

This meeting was an integral part of Welch's continuing personal transformation. While driving back to Buffalo to catch his plane, Welch says, "I couldn't see through my glasses because I was still sobbing. I'm driving practically 80, 85 miles per hour – probably another short time of temporary insanity again. I've thought about it since, I think it was. When I got back to Hope House I sat in the living room and sobbed, and sobbed, and made a total ass out of myself for an hour. I honestly did...[but] once I was through that sobbing, because I felt like there was this load taken completely off my shoulders. I wish I could explain it to you; I wish I could make you understand the way it felt to me" (Cushing and Welch, 1999). Welch says that shortly after his visit to the McVeigh home, he heard from his friend who had set up the meeting that Bill McVeigh's next door neighbor said she had not heard such a spirit in Bill McVeigh's voice since the bombing. Welch's friend said, "I want you to understand that this is the greatest thing you ever could have done for him." But Welch said, "I wasn't doing it for Bill McVeigh, I was doing it for myself" (Cushing and Welch, 1999),

There are other equally gripping stories of personal transformation from members of MVFR and elsewhere that bring the restorative justice movement down to the most personal of levels and which expand the range of nonviolent, personal responses to those who caused devastating loss to others. It is within this growing tradition that in the fall of 2004 the Roman Catholic Diocese of Albany decided upon a program of restorative justice to help victims of clergy sexual abuse, both those indirectly affected by the abuse and those responsible for these harms, to heal and hopefully move on with their lives (Bolton, 2004).

The Victim's Rights Movement: Compensation, Restitution, and Restoration

Proponents of restorative justice, emerging from a variety of walks of life and disparate parts of the globe, have shown us such a wide array of possibilities for responding to harm in a nonviolent manner that some people now speak of restorative justice in terms of a social movement (Daly and Immarigeon, 1998). Whether anyone agrees that restorative justice warrants such a status, it is important to keep in mind that the current diverse and widespread practices of restorative justice – which we will describe in greater detail in subsequent chapters – have not grown out of thin air. On a grand scale, their roots can be traced to the civil rights, women's, and indigenous people's movements in the United States and elsewhere. This is especially true in New Zealand and Australia, where a practice known as family group conferencing developed out of indigenous practices of justice and has become the accepted legal procedure for responding to harms committed by young people in those countries (Love, 2000; Cunneen, 1998; Daly and Hayes, 2001). In the United States, the roots of restorative justice can also be traced to the deinstitutionalization, mental health, and prisoner rights movements of the 1970s, during which activists identified the needless and inhumane over-institutionalization of offenders and the underappreciation of victims' experiences and needs (Knopp, 1996). These movements exposed the larger community's involvement in creating and maintaining social relations that neglect some people's essential needs among whom are included "victims" and "offenders," when communities collectively respond to harms through their criminal justice systems (Englebrecht, 2004; Gil, 1989).

When we examine criminal justice practices more closely, we see that the roots of restorative justice can be traced to the restitution movement of the 1960s (Schafer, 1960; 1965; Wolfgang, 1965; Schultz, 1965; Laster, 1970; Childres, 1965) and the "victim's rights" movement of the 1970s (Wright, 1991). These movements grew out of a concern on the part of many people that, when the criminal justice system responded to a harm situation, "the unfortunate victim of criminality [is] habitually ignored" (Tallack, 1900, pp.10-11; see also, Elias, 1986). This mantra, which is still chanted by many "victim's rights" advocates today (see Amstutz, 2004; Achilles and Amstutz, 2003; Mika et al., 2002), says that criminal justice officials define their work almost exclusively in terms of offenders, exhibiting little concern for the needs of those they harmed (Abel and Marsh, 1984; Roberts, 1990). To rectify this imbalance, victims' advocates have argued for a more active role in the justice process for those harmed (Englebrecht, 2004).

One of the most visible achievements of their efforts has been the development of the "victim impact statement," a part of the sentencing process when victims can tell those responsible for their pain and suffering, the sentencing judge, and the community at large how their lives have been affected by the harm in question. But the question that arises most frequently with respect to the value of these statements is whether the kind of participation they offer fosters healing (Sumner, 1987). In making their statements, victims often engage in a venomous venting of feelings conveyed in a raised voice while the offender looks on. What then, after the victim has emptied him- or herself of feelings of pain and loss and grief and despair? The person might have received a sympathetic ear from the judge, and on occasion from the offender, but does the process help the harmed person heal especially in bringing about that much-debated state of closure (Arrigo and Williams, 2003)?

To be sure, through a process such as the victim impact statement, the victim's rights movement has been successful in giving new meaning to terms such as "victim participation" and "offender accountability," but its lexicon contains few entries concerning the true needs of those harmed, much less of those responsible for a harm (Davis and Smith, 1994; Tobolowsky, 1999). Indeed the legal script is written in such a way that it is believed possible for members of a family, school, workplace, or community who have been harmed to move on with their lives without facilitating healing among those responsible for those harms, "the offender" (Toews and Katounas, 2004).

As we will see in greater detail, concern for the true needs of the victim, and those of the person responsible for a harm, remains missing from the landscape of justice in large part because criminologists and justice practitioners of nearly every ilk have viewed a needs-based approach to justice as an administrative and philosophical impossibility (Wolfgang, 1965). The result is that participation in the justice process for victims continues to be defined through processes such as the victim impact statement, through accusatory testimony, venting, and berating, rather than in terms of narrative, of getting the story, of acknowledgment, apology, and forgiveness. And with respect to reparation, participation is defined almost exclusively in terms of the victim securing restitution or compensation. In the case of the latter, it is believed that justice is served and the needs of victims best met when the state compensates those who have been harmed (Elias, 1986), or when those responsible for the harm pay back what they took from the person harmed (Jacob, 1970; Galaway et al., 1980), or when offenders make amends to both victim and community through some form of public community service (Nutter et al., 1989; Williams et al., 1959).

Our concern here as elsewhere is always one of accountability so we understand that the issue of who makes up for a particular loss is a matter of no small consequence for the person who has been robbed or had his or her face smashed or whose personhood has been willfully violated by a boss at work (Achilles, 2004). Being compensated for one's losses can help relieve the anxiety any one of us experiences after we've suffered a loss due to harm (Hatamiya, 1993). We are less likely to become overwhelmed with worry about not having enough to pay the rent or meet medical bills thrust upon us because we were beaten, robbed, or maltreated. But what many of us fail to recognize, in part because emotional reparation is so often played down, is that money cannot heal our dignity or the lost sense of trust we feel when our life has been upended by a crime.

The sad part of this scenario is that many who administer compensation-type programs encourage those who have been harmed to concentrate their energies almost exclusively on gaining compensation, and thereby become an impediment to healing. Too often this strategy, however unwittingly executed, helps create an unrealistic view of healing and closure (Herman, 1992; Tait and Silver, 1989; Silver, 1982) because the person receiving compensation believes "she can get rid of the terror, shame, and pain of the trauma by retaliating against the perpetrator" through the collection of a monetary award

(Herman, 1992:189). Then in some instances there is the "re-victimization" factor, a situation that occurs when compensation and restitution boards – established to respond to the needs of those who have suffered loss – subject "applicants" to humiliating and degrading procedures. They look upon these applicants with suspicion, treating them as if they were trying to extort money from the government or others under false pretenses. Applicants, even in the most obvious cases of need, have reported that they were required to prove that they were harmed/or injured and in need of assistance, and therefore felt as if *they* were responsible for committing the harm in question or had brought the harm upon themselves (Kerstenberg, 1980).

Such disregard for the world of victims-in-need is aggravated when government officials will pursue compensation for them in, say, "willful negligence" cases, but refuse to meet the demands of victims/survivors for criminal prosecution so as to hold accountable those responsible for the loss in question. And to be fair to the victims/survivors in such cases, most times their desire is not to destroy or punish those responsible for the harm but to create a forum in which the latter will have to publicly acknowledge their wrongdoing. Dramatic examples of such cases abound, especially those involving the Occupational Safety and Health Administration (OSHA). For example, in June 2004, a 22-year-old plumber's apprentice, Patrick Walters, died as a result of having been buried alive while working in a 10-foot-tall, mud-soaked trench because the owners of Moeves Plumbing, the company he worked for, had failed to install a protective trench as required by OSHA standards (Barstow, 2003). Not only had this company been warned the previous week about such an infraction, but it had been cited on several other occasions, indeed heavily fined after another of its workers had been buried alive under similar circumstances. For these "infractions" only money changed hands (ibid.).

In the case of the Walters family, their grief and suffering was aggravated when friends and neighbors spoke of Patrick's death in terms of an "act of God," an "accident," or "fate," reflecting the community's failure to acknowledge the reality of what had occurred. But Jeff Walters, Patrick's father, kept responding to such language by saying, "My son got killed is the way I put it," and continued to seek a criminal charge of "willful violation" against the owner of the plumbing company. He wanted her to acknowledge her failure to prevent Patrick's death by willfully disregarding federal regulations designed to protect life. But, in this case, as they had done previously, OSHA officials – even after they had put together an excellent case for criminal prosecution (for public acknowledgment) – settled with Moeves Plumbing for a fine (ibid.). For the Walters family, their need for an acknowledgment of responsibility was further aggravated when the government not only cut a deal with Moeves Plumbing to reduce the fines in question by 40%, but also allowed Linda Moeves to pay in annual installments, the first of which was not due until the following year (ibid.). The settlement did not require the owner of the company to admit any wrongdoing.

In this case, the government sought and received compensation for the survivors' loss, but created a forum of justice where the healing of those who had suffered that loss was excluded from the equation. Those in charge of the case required no acknowledgment of "intentional disregard" or "plain indifference" for the life of Patrick Walters or for his family, friends, and co-workers. In short, there was no acknowledgment, no apology, no remorse, no forgiveness, only embittered feelings for the Walters family, and the postponement of healing.

In cases such as these, and in cases where seeking restitution or compensation becomes the sole or even major goal of those harmed (or of government officials), we can see why reparation and compensation programs often fall far short of what is required for restorative justice. Indeed, many who administer such programs say it is not their responsibility to help those harmed to address their restorative need for acknowledgment and apology, and that it is not their business to address the corrosive vengeance that distorts people's vision much less to help victims/survivors clarify what they really need to move on with their lives. Hence they fail to gather people together in a caring spirit, following the directives of ongoing research that suggests there is great healing potential for those in pain and suffering when family and friends pay loving attention to meeting their needs – physical, mental, spiritual, emotional, and financial needs. In hospitals, at one time family members and friends were restricted from visiting patients because they were thought to interfere with the healing process, but today family and friends are welcome because we now know that patients who receive emotional support from a variety on fronts heal faster (Kaplan et al., 1997; Cohen and Smyme, 1985). Through such attention we recover or heal more completely, we experience a genuine boost in well-being, the quality of our lives increases markedly (Dakof and Taylor, 1990).

But again this is not what government-sponsored victim compensation programs are about and so they fail to get to the core issue of helping people who have been harmed to heal and move on (Achilles, 2004). Much less do they help us understand our response to those responsible for harms so that they too might move on with their lives and perhaps create a life for themselves for the very first time. Indeed, we have come to see many justice programs stamped with the seal of compensation or restitution or victim's rights which – notwithstanding a rhetoric of wanting to make things right – demonstrate little overt concern for healing, needs-meeting, and reconciliation. In some cases, these programs are just alternative ways to "drop the hammer" on an offender, though in a more palatable manner because some ersatz attention is being paid to the "victim." In fact, in some instances the victim is treated as little more than a lever to advance prosecutorial action. When her husband was killed in the 1998 bombings of the U.S. embassy in Dar es Salaam, Tanzania, Susan Hirsch (2002) says the government was so locked into vengeance and securing a conviction that her needs and the needs of other family survivors were fully discounted. She says that she and they were not only tricked but also re-victimized.

Unfortunately, within the restorative justice movement, we now see an increasing number of experts funded by the government or private agencies who travel around the country directing seminars or giving talks on restorative justice, but who ironically seem to have little interest in the full range of restorative justice issues or who seem to have little sense of what restorative forms of justice require structurally. They do not help matters because they show little interest in thinking about ways to create restoratively just communities in which people who are in pain and suffering can heal with dignity. In this sense, their efforts are insidious for, on one level, they promote themselves as healers when in fact they are official "correctionalists" or "criminal justice system mechanics" whose focus, activities, and interests are undergirded by a philosophy of retribution and by an acceptance of our prevailing political economy and its needs-denying arrangements. Ironically, many of these consultants are paid more in a day than a harmed person might receive as compensation by the government for hospital coverage (see Chapter Three). And the programs that derive from such a perspective are as retributive as any program whose administrators justify the use of punishment outright, for they show little or no concern for the needs of those who were the source of the harm, writing them off as animals or non-persons (Didion, 1992).

One exceedingly worrisome result of this perspective on healing and justice is that far too many scholars and practitioners continue to define the participation of victims/survivors in the justice process in such a narrow, politically-defined framework. However, in the past few years those interested in restorative justice have been forced anew to specify what they mean by a participation that heals, what the participatory requirements of restorative and healing processes are, and what kind of participation is required for people to transcend a harm experience and create a new life for themselves, to achieve closure (Zehr and Mika, 1998; Mika, 2002). What kind of participation is necessary if acknowledgment, remorse, apology, forgiveness, reconciliation, restoration and reintegration – however we wish to describe a healing response to harm – are to occur for those responsible for a harm-done as well as for those harmed (McCold, 2000; Walgrave, 2000; Braithwaite, 2000; Boyes-Watson, 2000; Sullivan and Tifft, 2004)?

From our continuing work over the years, we have seen that a restorative response would require us, at the very least, to offer an opportunity to the person harmed to meet the person responsible for the harm – if such a meeting is physically and emotionally possible and desired. Through such meetings, those whose lives have been shaken by violence can tell their story, can describe how the violence affected them and the lives of those close to them. Here they can raise their lingering questions and concerns about an event that has radically changed their lives; they can inquire about the motives and justifications, the life circumstances, of the person who harmed them; they can bring up anything that might ease their pain or put their minds and fears of future victimization at rest. Here the chances of being restored to a more whole sense of self through the receipt of an apology are increased a hundredfold (Baumeister et al., 1990).

But such meetings would require us to offer to the person who committed the harm a chance to describe his/her life situation and motivation for the harm, to accept responsibility for the harm, apologize for the harmful effects of his/her actions on everyone, including their own families and friends. This might include taking responsibility for identifying their own needs and having them met without harming others in the future. The restorative response we are talking about would also require creating a loving, need-meeting community in which the harmed person might find an exit from the imprisonment of hate and vengeance and embark on a life made better for having moved on from these barriers to health. We would thus begin to create communities of human concern in which needs-meeting relationships were created in our most primary social institutions, for example, the family, the school, and our places of work.

But this puts us ahead of ourselves. We now need to delve more deeply into what is meant by restorative justice, what the requirements of such a justice are, and what basic restorative justice programs look like. But, whatever definition we come up with and whatever conclusions we draw, we will discover that how we define and ultimately practice restorative justice will be derived primarily from how we view and define our relationships with each other in our daily lives, that is, by the political economy of relationship we live by. This includes the impulses that shape our sense of loss and gain as well as the steps we take to avoid and embrace each other in the worst as well as in the best of times.

CHAPTER TWO.
The Core Components of
Restorative Justice

Shortly after 3 a.m. on August 13, 1981, four young men entered the Best Western Inn in Albany, New York and told the night clerk, Gary Geiger, that they were looking for a room. Then, suddenly, they commanded Geiger to give them the cashbox key and get face down on the floor. When Geiger hesitated, one of the four hit him across the face with the butt of the gun. As Geiger fell to the floor, one of the men jumped over the counter and took the $150 sitting in the cash box and left. As Geiger got up to call the police, one of the four re-entered the motel, extended his arm over the counter, shot Geiger once in the right side of the abdomen, and slid out the door into the night. With the entire incident captured on the motel's surveillance camera, not long afterward, the four men were arrested. A 21-year old unemployed man, Wayne Blanchard, was later identified by Geiger as the man who had shot him. Blanchard was later convicted and sentenced to 12-25 years in a New York State prison.

During the days, weeks, and months following the shooting, Gary Geiger did not fare well, either physically or emotionally. He had taken the night job so that he could have his days free to train for competitive track and field events that he had excelled in since high school. Now, his life had been turned completely upside down. As he recounted later in an HBO special, *Confronting Evil* (Monet, 1997):

> For a long period of time, I'd go to sleep and I'd just see
> the incident over and over again. I'd wake up in the

middle of the night drenched in sweat. I'd start shaking.
I'd walk out onto the floor [sic]. I'd be shaking from head
to toe and I didn't know what was wrong with me.

In an effort to relieve himself of what he called his personal
"nightmare," Geiger thought that a meeting with Blanchard
might lift the cloud hovering over his shattered psyche. Six
years after the event he tried to meet with Blanchard to talk
about the night Blanchard had robbed and shot him, but
Geiger could not bring himself to do so. Finally, five years later,
11 years after the incident, with the assistance of Tom
Christian, a skilled mediator with the New York State
Community Dispute Resolution Centers Program, Geiger went
to Ellenville Prison to meet with Blanchard, who was then 32.

Facing the man who shot him from the other side of a
narrow table, Geiger questioned Blanchard about why he came
back into the motel to shoot him after he and his three
accomplices had gotten what they came for. He wanted to know
whether Blanchard intended to kill him and whether
Blanchard had any sense of the extent of the pain and suffering
Geiger and his family had gone through because of the event.
With the bullet from Blanchard's gun still lodged in his lower
back, Geiger told Blanchard how this event had haunted him
all those years and still blocked him from moving on with his
life.

Blanchard was not unsympathetic. Looking into his
confronter's eyes, a teary-eyed Blanchard listened attentively
to what Geiger told him and then, without hesitation, offered
an apology for what he had done at what seemed like lifetimes
earlier. With apparent earnest Blanchard began (Monet, 1997):

I'm really truly sorry for what happened in that motel
that night. I'm not only sorry for the pain that you feel
but what your family had to go through and, you know,
what has led your life to what it is now... As far as the
bullet being inside of you, there is nothing I can do about
that. I can only say that I'm sorry and I really am... The

only reason I accepted to have this confrontation with you was that, if there was something that I could say or something that I could do that I could help you pull through this and put it behind you, I would, you know, gladly do it. And that's why I'm here today. And again, I'm truly sorry for what happened that night.

A worn and wide-eyed Geiger looked relieved. He thanked Blanchard for his honesty, telling him that he had waited all these years to hear those words. Blanchard thanked Geiger for showing the courage to come and face him after what he had gone through. Geiger then said, "The last time that you and I met, you had your hand extended toward me in anger. Now I'd like to extend my hand to you as a sign of healing." The two shook hands and after a few moments of silence, Tom Christian asked both men if they had anything more to say. Each nodded no, and the meeting ended.

As guards led Wayne Blanchard back to his tier, Gary Geiger, about to walk out of the prison in some way a more whole person, wiped the sweat from his hands. Ironically, the man who had been the source of his grief was now responsible for helping his "victim" wade through a mire of disabling feelings. Through his apology, Blanchard demonstrated that he too had become more whole. And, although it might seem unbelievable to some, when Wayne Blanchard came up for parole in May 1994, Gary Geiger appeared before the parole board and spoke in his behalf. Indeed, years after Blanchard's release from prison, when he was struggling to stay afloat in the community, Geiger came forth and spoke in his behalf once again.

What Constitutes Restoration?

For many people, the "victim-offender mediation" session that Gary Geiger and Wayne Blanchard participated in to complete a piece of unfinished business lies at the heart of restorative justice. But the format, for all its positive aspects, raises as many questions as it answers about what the core components of restorative justice are. For example, while Wayne Blanchard did apologize for his actions, Gary Geiger never directly told Blanchard that he forgave him, though clearly his later actions demonstrated this. Perhaps the extended hand and just being there indicated forgiveness and perhaps being forgiven was not one of Blanchard's needs at the time of the mediation, but its omission raises the question whether his needs were any less important because he was a prisoner and responsible for the harm that was the basis for the mediation. It also raises the question whether victim-offender mediation as a restorative justice process is designed primarily or exclusively to meet the needs of the harm survivor. We are led to believe it is from a CBS television *48 Hours* special called "My Daughter's Killer" (broadcast on February 4, 1999), which focused on a mother who asked to meet with the man who had stabbed her daughter to death. After meeting with the prisoner for nearly six hours, she told the man, as she looked into his tearful eyes, that she forgave him, but shortly after the session, when telling a reporter that the meeting had changed how she saw the person who had radically altered her life, she added that she still believed he should be executed by the state. And he was.

Was this encounter between the mother and the man who murdered her daughter restorative? If so, what was restored? What kind of meaning can we assign restoration when it is coupled with a request for retribution, for counterviolence, for killing? What is the meaning of forgiveness if, after a form of reconciliation has unilaterally been achieved, one person seeks to have another executed? Some might interject, well, how much can we expect of each other when we have been hurt so severely? How good can we expect each other to be (Kushner, 1996)? Members of Murder Victims Families for Reconciliation, for example, oppose the death penalty for those responsible for killing a family member on the grounds that an execution would prevent family members from meeting with the person convicted of the killing and from reaching a greater degree of closure and healing (Cushing and Welch, 1999; Rimer, 2001). Was what occurred in the *48 Hours* program a distorted version of this: that once the mother experienced closure and a sense of healing, she could advocate death-dealing? While Murder Victims Families for Reconciliation does not advocate the death penalty, some members do actively support life in prison without parole for those convicted of murder. They say they cannot shake the demands of retribution or punishment. They say they can go only so far. If forsaking retribution is sometimes not possible, so too is forgiveness not possible.

When it comes to the possibility of responding restoratively to the harms that we do to each other, one psychotherapist – who says she still has not forgiven her father for how he treated her family when she was growing up – would tend to agree. She (Safer, 1999:169-70) says that, "Not everything can be repaired, even with the best will in the world; it is not just a matter of trying harder or having a positive attitude or finding the right affirmation. Limitations, born of history and character, made us who we are. To know that some damage can only be contained, never undone, is both tragic and true – as well as strangely comforting." Another psychotherapist (Herman, 1992:190) says that for many who have been hurt, "The fantasy of forgiveness often becomes a cruel torture, because it remains out of reach for most ordinary human beings. Folk wisdom recognizes that to forgive is divine. And even true forgiveness in most religious systems is not unconditional. True forgiveness cannot be granted until the perpetrator has sought and earned it through confession, repentance, and restitution." What are we to conclude about the role of apology and *earned* forgiveness in restorative justice processes?

But as we pose these kinds of questions about what is possible, we must have a clear understanding of what it means to be human in everyday life situations in the first place. We can inquire about our response-ability as human beings in situations in which we and those we care for have been harmed, but what is the answer when we live in a political-economy in which violence, retribution, and vengeance are essential parts of the prevailing social ethic? In other words, can we expect our response to harms to be any different from how we live with and respond to others in everyday situations? The answers to these questions are not easily forthcoming because, as soon as we apply ourselves to discover them, we find ourselves up against the kind of ironies we have been talking about. And turning to the restorative justice movement for clarity can be disheartening because we discover that there exist nearly as many definitions of restorative justice as there are people offering them. While we might not expect to see uniformity in opinion about the direction a social movement should take, what is perplexing is that some definitions of restorative justice have been stretched and distorted to a point beyond ironic, to the absurd. For example, recently, a correctional official who was being interviewed for a high-level position in the State of Florida's Department of Corrections was heard to say that Special Housing Units in prisons, where prisoners are locked up 23 of 24 hours a day, are restorative. In the eyes of some, that such an opinion might be offered with a straight face is not a strange turn of events. They argued all along that as soon as the state adopted the practices and rhetoric of restorative justice, its basic principles would be modified to fit the state's specifications for a punishment-based, retributive paradigm of justice (Harris, 1998).

Differing Definitions of Restorative Justice

To a greater or lesser degree, therefore, we are faced with a definitional problem with respect to what is and what it is not restorative (Johnstone, 2004). Hence, a goal for many who are deeply concerned about furthering restorative justice practices as a response to social harm is to set forth the requirements of restorative justice so that we can say that one particular effort is restorative and another not (Zehr and Mika, 1998). We should mention that some of those with an interest in the development of restorative justice have responded to this question, in part, by avoiding it. They have argued that the problem is not the definition of restorative justice, but that the term itself is too restrictive of the multiple dimensions of the restorative justice movement. In its stead, therefore, some have proposed a "relational justice" to emphasize the personal dimensions of restorative justice (Burnside and Baker, 1994), while others speak of a "restorative justice community" to emphasize the community's central place in restorative justice processes (Young, 1995). Still others speak of a "transformative justice" (Morris, 1994; Sullivan and Tifft, 2000b) to call attention to the social-structural dimensions that restorative justice must attend to if people are to find themselves in a community which is supportive of them following their "victimization" or their "offending." Restorative responses that are supportive of needs-meeting help to develop a new consciousness that social-structural changes must occur if there is to be any significant reduction in the prevalence of harm, and correspondingly, any significant increase in the degrees of freedom, safety, autonomy, opportunity, and quality of life in our communities. Restorative justice in this sense is transformative of the processes we initiate to respond to "offending" – rejecting disempowering, non-participatory, power-based processes – and creating and supporting participatory, democratizing processes (Braithwaite and Strang, 2001). Restorative justice is, as well, transformative of the values that undergrid our responses, rejecting vengence and vindictiveness and supporting healing, reconciliation, and needs-meeting (Braithwaite and Strang, 2001). Furthermore, restorative justice is transformative because it involves committing ourselves to the creation of patterns of interaction that foster human dignity, mutual respect, and equal well-being (Sullivan and Tifft, 2004). Restorative justice is, as John Braithwaite has stated, "not simply a way of reforming the criminal justice system, it is a way of transforming the entire legal system, our family lives, our conduct in the workplace, our practice of politics. Its vision is of a holistic change in the way we do justice in the world" (Braithwaite, 2003:1).

Whatever particular dimension of restorative justice one might wish to give emphasis to in hopes of ensuring its integrity (McCold, 2000), at the most elemental level a restorative response to a harm grows out of a needs-based conception of justice (Sullivan and Tifft, 1998). Such a conception of justice says that, in any social situation, the present needs of all involved must be taken into account. Needs take precedence. Of course, and as we will discuss later (see Chapters Five through Nine), such a political-economy of relationship applies not simply to social situations in which someone has been harmed, but as well to the way we organize and relate to each other in our everyday relationships, in our families, our schools, and our workplaces. By living according to an ethic in which we seek to meet the needs of all in our everyday lives, we are not only making it possible to respond restoratively to harm situations, but also engaging in the prevention of harm, which no degree of intervention, no matter how refined or intense, can achieve (Gil, 1998; Sullivan and Tifft, 2004). Some have made this case in a convincing way even for preventing violence in our most intimate relationships (Tifft, 1993).

When proponents of restorative justice work from within needs-based conceptions of justice, they begin with the premise that violent acts, whether defined by the state as crimes or not, must be viewed first and foremost in personal terms: that is, in terms of the suffering and misery they create for those affected by the violence (Zehr, 1990; Zehr and Mika, 1998). Clearly, such a response counteracts the power-based, retributive logic of those who harm others and of those who see the state as having a principal and perhaps the only claim in responding to harm. A person who harms another is, in effect, showing a blatant disregard for the needs of that person by defining the nature of their interaction unilaterally. A person who harms another is essentially denying the person he disregards, or is unresponsive to, his or her voice and an opportunity to participate in the relationship at any given moment. Such a harm is relational violence. When a person or the state treats others in this way, they are, in effect, defining them *"in a way that is ... disrespectful of their individual worth"* (Hampton, 1988:52-53), disrespectful of their human dignity.

Those of us who seek to respond to harm situations restoratively, therefore, refuse to respond in kind by acting as if those responsible for the harm had little personal worth and, as if pain and suffering were of no consequence for them. Rather, our aim is to respond in terms of needs. Despite what some fear, such a response neither diminishes our attention to, nor denies the feelings of the person harmed – which might be a mixture of feelings of hatred (of self as well as others), resentment, loss, despair, and guilt, all the feelings that arise under such circumstances. Rather, it offers a forum in which these emotions might be expressed and everyone's needs specified and addressed in a straightforward and honest way so we might allow all involved to move on with their lives.

Historically, at least in the past several centuries, a restorative response to harms has been difficult to achieve because we have created and live by a social ethic whereby we turn over to the state our responsibility for handling such matters, thereby extracting ourselves from life processes that can radically alter our lives for the better (Christie, 1977). By living according to such an ethic, we rob ourselves of the means to not only work our way out of deficit situations in a way that heals, but also, and paradoxically, to develop a new and heightened appreciation for life (Janoff-Bulman and Berger, 2000; Collins et al., 1990). We leave ourselves standing in an emotional vacuum because we are not dealing honestly and step-by-step with all of our emotions and all the decisions we need to make if we are to be an active part of the healing process (Penner et al., 2000). By limiting our participation to observing the state's response, we wind up watching our lives being handled for us, at a distance, as if projected onto a movie screen (Updegraff and Taylor, 2000; Brown, 1966). Even for those who have been tortured, "ownership" of the suffering is a critical aspect of their healing, so much so that when the state tries to disallow their participation in the healing process, they feel twice harmed (Weschler, 1995). But because of its *de facto* retributive nature, the state must own the harm situation, defining itself as the victim, and objectify those involved, treating them as *cases* to be processed – offenders to be sentenced, victims to be cooled out and largely dismissed (Hirsch, 2002). For the state, responding to the present and sometimes urgent needs of those affected by a harm is always less a consideration than meeting standards of punitiveness (Kerstenberg, 1980) and preserving the rightness of the social arrangements sanctified by law. Although the state has a welfare component, it is by nature a war machine, most especially when the rights, stratification arrangements, and inequalities it is protecting and preserving are themselves structurally violent and generative of violent crimes. The state, the law, preserves the rights of those who hold specific social positions that have rights attached to them; it preserves the earned privileges of those who possess positions of legal institutional and distributive privilege.

Making Things Right

In order to make things right, that is, to help those whose lives have been affected by a harm in some way, those who favor a restorative approach to justice seek, first of all, to encourage all those directly involved in the life of a survivor of violence to acknowledge the hurt suffered by that person and to examine how it has transformed the lives of all involved, especially the direct recipient of the harmful act(s). An essential part of the healing process is a public acknowledgment of what has taken place by the community at large, an acknowledgment that something has been ruptured and is in need of repair. If this process of repair is to have any meaning for those directly involved, at the very least it will require that we encourage those who have been harmed to tell us about their pain and suffering in their own terms. That is, they must be able to share with us how their lives have been affected by the harm, how they continue to be affected, and what their expanded needs are. In some instances, this process will begin only after a long period of denial and silence, in part because the person suffering may see no forum in which to safely share what occurred or may feel that no one could or desires to understand the trauma they are experiencing (Becker et al., 1995). Within a community committed to restorative principles, those who have been harmed can begin to feel safe; they are less likely then to deny, minimize, or overstate matters related to the harm and the implications of the harm for their lives and the lives of others affected by it.

But encouraging those who have been harmed to tell their stories is easier said than done. They must be convinced that when they tell their stories that these stories are heard and that we will be responsive to their needs as they define them and meet these needs on their time schedule (Achilles, 2004). They must feel that the setting for telling their stories is not going to re-victimize them and that their participation in a restorative conference or encounter – through the telling of their stories – will not lead to their victimization following this conference or encounter. Quite the contrary, they must feel secure that we will support them in their recovery and take action to prevent others from being similary victimized. However, currently, more than a few professionals who are traditionally assigned to listen to such stories are working in agencies that do not afford them the time or reward structure to become personally interested and involved in the lives of those suffering. In these settings, those who need to be listened to, commiserated with, and supported are far too often seen as agency *"cases" or "clients"* to be processed – in other words, they are given an agency identity. In some instances, agency professionals act in a self-protective manner by not getting too deeply involved, for the degree of support they can offer is not commensurate with the needs they feel should be addressed or the degree of support that should be given to those whose stories they hear; their hands and hearts are tied by bureaucratic rigor. They are tied, as well, by work standards that require them to listen and respond to far too many persons without relief and support being given to them, for listening and responding to suffering greatly pains the listener. In other instances, the stories they hear are so grim and disturbing that few wish to hear them, much less be exposed to details which can become numbing (Krystal and Niederland, 1968). Many, for example, who have heard members of Murder Victims Families for Reconciliation speak of the events that changed their lives when a son, parent, or spouse was murdered are shocked and disturbed by the level of detail they provide in the telling of their stories. Yet, while such stories are very disturbing, they often contain no more detail than a story someone might tell about a family wedding or vacation, or an event that happened at work. But because of the painful nature of the harm, its emotional impact is magnified considerably. Often enough, we ourselves intimate that we would prefer to hear only highlights of the story, or that the story not be told so frequently so we are spared a great share in such personal pain (Hocking, 1965). However, the American psychotherapist Carl Rogers (1961) once posed the question: How long will a person in pain continue to talk about things that are the source of pain? His answer was simple: They will do so until they no longer need to, when the residue of the trauma has diminished to the point where they find telling their story boring.

In our efforts to assuage the pain of those who have been harmed and to help them move along in life, many of us have a tendency, for convenience sake or otherwise, to assign our own meanings to what took place and thereby fail to hear the meanings given to the situation by those harmed. We think we are being helpful when we say that life will soon be what it once was, when in fact we know that such a life no longer exists. We cannot, therefore, mandate that they get back to normal "both in terms of (re)adapting to 'normal society' or returning to pre-victimization ways of being and functioning, as if one could resurrect one's previous (destroyed) fabric of life"

(Danieli, 1992:575; see also Danieli, 1981). Indeed, for many there is no longer a "normal" world or self to get back to and part of their dilemma – and that of those who are supposedly helping them – is trying to return to something that no longer exists. As Müller-Fahrenholz (1997:29) has said: "Acts of restitution need not – and indeed cannot – reestablish the situation as it existed before the evil act was done. The word 'restitution' suggests that it is possible to 'repair' the past. But that is an illusion. In a strict sense it is not possible to restitute the status quo ante."

Part of the process of restoration, then, is also cognitive. The person harmed must be encouraged to see things for what they are. As Danieli (1992:575) points out:

> Having been helpless does not mean that one is a helpless person; having witnessed or experienced evil does not mean that the world as a whole is evil; having been betrayed does not mean that betrayal is an overriding human behavior; having been victimized does not necessarily mean that one has to live one's life in constant readiness for its reenactment; having been treated as dispensable vermin does not mean that one is worthless; and, taking the painful risk of bearing witness does not mean that the world will listen, learn, change, and become a better place.

The Community's Role in Healing

We know from our vast experiences with human rights violations, that individual therapeutic intervention is not sufficient to heal. The truth about the matter will be told and healing begin only when the community acknowledges what took place and is prepared to address the roots of such behavior through social-structural change (Mika, 1992; Dyck, 2000). Within restorative justice circles, therefore, great emphasis is placed on the role of community, but oftentimes what that role is, or even what the nature or identity of the relevant community is, is rarely specified (McCold, 2004). Community members who might be involved in the healing process, directly or indirectly, cannot be assigned the role of the Greek chorus standing in the background critiquing the process or the person responsible for the harm. If we live within a just community, we will acknowledge not only that the community has been ruptured in some way, but also that our course of action cannot remain on merely an intellectual level. The acknowledgment is a commitment to change the social-structural conditions that were generative of the choice to the harm in the first place. This is the kind of restorative process that is part and parcel of the workings of many pre-industrial societies, where community members accept their collective responsibility for, and give their collective attention to, the structural conditions of the issue at hand as well as to personal healing matters (Paliwala, 1982; Pavlich, 2004; Thomson, 2004; Johnstone, 2002; Bush and Folger, 1994; Lemonne, 2003; Tifft, 2002; Sullivan and Tifft, 2004; McCold, 2004).

If a woman is raped, for example, a community can provide a loving environment, therapy, medical assistance, a support group of others who have experienced similar harm experiences, and, as well, meet her other needs as she identifies and expresses them. If there comes a time when she has needs that can only be met through meeting with the person who has raped her, then we should very carefully and very sensitively provide this restorative encounter. But we should respect that this set of needs may not necessarily reside at the top of the priority list of needs that victims and their families desire to have fulfilled (Achilles, 2004). If the person who has been harmed is unable to provide meals for her family because of the mental and/or physical effects of the harm, community members might prepare and serve meals for the family for a time. If the partner, parents, or close friends of the person harmed are having a difficult time responding, and are, as well, suffering and having difficulty relating with the person who has been raped, we must provide support and help them with these relational feelings and problems. A single parent who has suffered this harm might need help with getting a child to school or getting groceries from the market. Beyond help with these tasks, age- and maturity-appropriate help, if it is desired, should be provided to the children to understand their life-changed mother and consequently their changed relationship with her. If we are to talk about community as more than a place, that is, as people involved in a process that is restorative, this process must help the harmed person regain what she has lost, whether it is her sense of trust, her sense of freedom to go wherever she pleases without fear, or her comfortabilty in relating with another intimately or with men in general. Our restorative response must have an impact on how others are enabled to move along day by day and to redefine their lives (McCold and Wachtel, 1998a and 1998b).

But, at the same time, as a community which has been dealt a severe blow through the rape of one of its members, we – if we are to take the structural roots of the assault seriously – must examine, confront, and change the fundamental conceptions of being in which male-female relationships are grounded. This means dealing with power and the roots of power in relationships. It means confronting patriarchy: political-economic interaction patterns that emanate from the view of women as having less worth than men, thus, being defined as and interacted with as inferiors. It means addressing the view that says that women's needs and freedoms ought not to be taken seriously, or certainly not as seriously as those of men. It means confronting the personalization and the institutionalization of dominance and control, of male superiority, and of seeing a particular person as a category representative (women) who is to be treated in a certain way. It means deconstructing gender conceptions and depictions, to relate with an individual and their needs of personhood – who they define themselves to be. It means no longer accepting the idea and the ways of relating that follow from seeing others for their use value, that is, no longer accepting patterns of interaction in the home, at work, or anywhere else, where the premise is that it is acceptable to use another for one's own need-satisfaction to see another as an object. And this applies to work and relations both inside and outside the home. It applies to gender exploitation and battering in the home and rape outside the home. It applies to economic exploitation and structural battering in the workplace, and impoverishment and environmental destruction outside the workplace.

When this kind of structural context is present, healing, if it takes place at all, takes a long time, for in this structural context we tend to lose faith in each other and in any sense of collective solidarity or community. We can perhaps grow cynical to the point of letting behavior that requires our attention pass by (Penner et al., 2000). In Gary Geiger's life circumstance, presented at the beginning of this chapter, after he recovered enough physically and mentally so that he felt he was able to return to work, he approached the management of the Best Western Inn and asked if he might resume work. He was told that there was no longer a job for him. While managerial rhetoric might have finessed what was taking place, Geiger was in effect being held responsible for a blip in Best Western's corporate road – the public relations trouble and the corporate tarnish *he* had created for the motel's owners and for the chain's image. Via the company's withdrawal of employment, they were engaging in "blaming the victim" and punishing Geiger as if he were responsible for being robbed and shot. Rather than his employers and his co-workers gathering around as a community to support Geiger in the most imaginative ways possible--for what had happened to him could have happened to any one working the desk at the motel that night – Geiger was robbed and wounded once again, this time with the company's economic bullet. The "victim" had become the "perpetrator" (Kerstenberg, 1980).

Understandably, this kind of response is a long way off from the type of support and participation congruent with a restorative response. Similarly, it is a long way off from the type of support and participation that some physicians see as essential for the proper healing of patients suffering from illnesses of all kinds, even those that are fatal (Pierce et al., 1997; Penner et al., 2000). The kind of response Gary Geiger received is the kind of response that eats away at the foundations of community because it rejects the knowledge or lessons the suffering person has to offer. For, as Siegel (1989:151) has said, "The people who have chosen to take on those diseases [harms] and live as fully as possible in the face of them give a gift to all those whose lives they touch, whether it is their health care providers or their families. And from them we can learn not just how to fight illness, but how to live, and what healing really means." We learn about the requirements of a just community. In a restorative community our response to persons who have been harmed must be to take each person and his/her needs seriously, to listen to their stories, to support them in their needs-meeting choices, and to help them develop a healthy post-trauma self and life. Again, one of the harmed person's needs might be to meet with the person(s) who harmed them, receive a statement of acknowledgment of responsibility for the harm and its effects, receive an apology, understand that person better as a person, understand the nature of the contexts within which this person chose to commit this harmful act, and learn that neither s/he nor anyone else is likely to be revictimized by this person. In addition, our response should clearly indicate our disapproval of the violation of any person's autonomy, freedom, and dignity. It should also indicate that *direct action is being taken to reduce the risk that this type of harm is going to happen to someone else* in the community and that this action may require *fundamental change in the ways we choose to live*. Our response should connect harms and responsibility, both individual and collective. Our response should connect the personal and the social-structural.

The Hardest Part

Up to this point we have spoken mostly about those persons to whom a harm has been done, but for those who have been responsible for creating a harm, becoming part of a restorative process can also be a life-changing experience (Zehr and Mika, 1998). Initially, when people talked theoretically and pro-grammatically about restorative justice, even its most ardent proponents emphasized the rights and needs of victims, almost as if the rights and needs of the persons responsible for these harms ought not to be an equal concern. People in trouble, people who cause trouble, people who deny that they are in trouble, do not go away and their concerns do not dissipate because we put them in prison or consign them to a probation manager's far too large caseload. Problems diminish or disappear only when we attend to the needs of those involved: in the case of harms-done, to the needs of those responsible for harming someone as well as those harmed. Unfortunately, and most recently, discussions of restorative justice practices and their implementation have almost totally reversed the initial primary focus (Roche, 2003). To a considerable degree, many restorative justice programs have become offender-focused, shuffling the needs of victims aside, or minimizing the victims' needs only to benefits that might be drawn from a restorative conference or reconciliation encounter. In the least restorative and least robust programs, the needs of victims seemingly are irrelevant except as they enhance the effectiveness of restorative process outcomes for the offender, leaving the "victim" and his/her supporters feeling betrayed (Mika et al., 2002).

While being called to account for themselves, no matter how painful the process, those responsible for a harm ought not to imagine or experience being part of a "restorative" process that is involuntary and dehumanizing. Rather, they should experience a process that is supportive of their personal growth and integration into a community of human concern. We need to keep in mind that we do not gather together in such circumstances simply to engage in harm denunciation and to affix responsibility. We are there, as well, to give testimony to the essential worth and gifts of all involved, including the person responsible for the harm (Zehr, 1995). When the justice process is truly restorative, all who participate in the circle or conference or meeting are encouraged to interact with each other in a way that counters the logic and experience of the punitive process, a logic which embodies the idea that harming those who harm you is acceptable (Northey, 1992) – that violence can acceptably be met with violence.

What we seek to avoid at all costs, then, is to turn a potential restorative process into a blaming contest (McCold and Wachtel, 1998a). This is not an easy assignment because quite often those responsible for the harm in question could care less about others or themselves (Baumeister, 1997; Baumeister et al., 1990). They are lost to themselves and often feel that the only way they can make a contribution to the process is to regale us with stories of their personal demise or victimization, stories that demonstrate that they have some sense of the structural context of their lives, but little sense of their true self. Maintaining a steady course in such instances is difficult because such a posture can produce considerable tension. Oftentimes, we see the defensiveness or denial of the parents or friends of an offender rear its head: "Our daughter would never do such a thing!" In other instances, the loved ones of the harmed person or the police involved in the process attempt to use the conference to vent their rage, and heap indignities upon the offender. Or they may even receive an apology and in return forgive, but not give up their feelings or "needs" for vengence, as we have seen: "I forgive you, but the state should still execute you."

But, if we pursue a commitment to a high level of restorative quality for such meetings, those responsible for the harm will be encouraged to acknowledge what they have done, which means examining the full range of implications of their acts for themselves and for the lives of all the others affected by their choices – their siblings, their parents, the "victim," the "victim's" parents and friends, and others in the community. When such a path is taken, any one of us is better able to develop greater empathy for those harmed and accept responsibility for our unwarranted actions and for making personal changes to not repeat such actions. We are more readily moved to apologize to the person we have harmed – and to their friends, and family members who have been adversely affected – and, when possible, to offer reparation for the losses created (Umbreit, 1995a). When we are given a chance to participate in making good on our failures, we want to make things better. And, under the best of circumstances, we realize how we can make things better (Mackey, 1997).

Clearly, we are talking about very painful processes for anyone to go through. However, by being encouraged to fully participate in ways that are appropriate to the situation, those of us who have harmed another can begin to put the offense behind us and start anew, regain or perhaps develop for the first time a modicum of self-esteem and, in the process, feel more self-integrated (Angus et al., 2000; Neimeyer and Levitt, 2000). In the process, we are more likely to be reintegrated into and reunited with others in our families, workplaces, schools, and communities.

In many restorative ceremonies or programs there is frequently talk of reparation, but almost always it is designed to get the person responsible for the harm to provide some kind of financial restitution to those he or she has harmed. But, as we indicated in Chapter One, when most people think of restitution they think solely in terms of money/economics: for example, the "offender" paying for the replacement of windows he broke or returning the cash he stole. But reparation also means restoring dignity, and for those harmed dignity can only be restored when a full genuine disclosure is made of what happened and its effects. This is especially true for those whose family members were taken away or "disappeared." Requesting and requiring that this kind of disclosure is not a form of vengeance, but a very direct means of "promoting the personal and social viability of a new society" (Martin-Baro, 1990:571).

Finally, proponents of restorative justice know that the processes we have been talking about take time, patience, and a loving attitude, especially toward those who have done grave harm and who may continue to deny responsibility for the seriousness and the impact of these acts (Axelrod, 1996; Axelrod and Hall, 1999). For this, among other reasons, many associated with the restorative justice movement feel that restorative justice programs should continue to be administered only by community and/or religious-affiliated groups that have a commitment to "forgiving" justice processes, rather than those operated within the bureaucratic confines of state departments of correction and their municipal counterparts, where the structural commitment runs contrary to forgiveness, personal reconstruction, and the meeting of needs (Stuart, 1992, 1994, 1996). The qualities required for successful restorative programs are least likely to be found in social arrangements that are hierarchical, punitive, and non-needs-based. It is no surprise, therefore, that as the state has begun to adopt the language and practices of restorative justice, it has begun to redefine these practices and to vitiate the original intent of restorative justice, which is to foster forgiveness and reconciliation in the most human way possible for all involved: those harmed, those who have chosen to harm, and all of us as the quality of our lives is affected by these harms and our responses to them.

/

CHAPTER THREE.
Restorative Justice Processes and Practices

When its proponents are called upon to discuss the origins of restorative justice practices, without hesitation many will point to the victim-offender reconciliation project that was initiated in the Kitchener, Ontario Probation Department in 1974. While on one level there is a modicum of truth to this observation, upon hearing it more than a few members of the Navajo Nation will shake their heads in dismay. Hurt, insulted, or at the very least non-plussed, they feel that the *bilagaanaas* (Navajo for "White" people), are, in an imperialistic way, overlooking a peacemaking process that had been part of the North American aboriginal tradition for centuries. From the perspective of the Navajo, processes of restorative justice that involve an admission and acknowledgment of one's wrongs, an apology, forgiveness, and reconciliation, have roots that run deep in pre-industrial political economies (La Barre, 1964; Gibbs, 1963). As James Zion (1998:141), Solicitor of the Navajo Nation Court, says, "Indian nations and the other indigenous nations of the world have practiced restorative justice for centuries. Whether denominated as 'traditional Indian law,' 'native law' 'customary law,' 'peacemaking' or some other name, restorative justice is, in fact, the original, pre-state form of law." As we begin to look at the basic models of restorative justice processes or practices in existence today, then, it might be not only historically accurate and insightful, but also deeply respectful, to begin with the peacemaking practice that is, and that was for centuries, an integral part of Navajo culture.

Navajo Peacemaking

In the Navajo tradition, "peacemaking" is a formal communal response to help people in need, especially when that need arises from a harm done to them. Those in need might have been battered by a marriage partner or become dependent on alcohol for their "well-being." Or perhaps, they might have felt isolated and depressed, or had themselves been agents of violence in harming another. Today, one might also become involved in the peacemaking process because one has been arrested for a crime or has been referred to it by a Navajo welfare agency such as Indian Health Services. In some instances, a person may come to the court of his or her own volition seeking help or because a family member has come to the court and asked that peacemaking take place in his or her behalf.

Through peacemaking, those involved in the process not only seek to respond to the specific and present needs of those who come before the peacemaker, but also, when possible, to get to the basic reason why a person has been harmed or has harmed another. When members of the Navajo community try to explain why people do harm to themselves or others, they say that those responsible for a harm behave that way because they have become disconnected from the world around them, from the people they live and work with. They say that that person "acts as if he has no relatives" (Kaplan and Johnson, 1964:216-217; Yazzie, 1998:126). For the Navajo, this lack of connection and social rootedness, this alienation or disengagement, engenders a lifestyle of self-oriented behavior bolstered by twisted logic and a set of excuses (Zion, 1997), which Robert Yazzie, former Chief Justice of the Navajo Nation Court, refers to as "fuzzy thinking" (1998:125). In a culture where alcohol-related violence, especially within the family, is a severe problem, this thinking might manifest itself in a rationalization such as, "Oh, I'm a hopeless drunk, so it's no big deal if I drink and beat my wife" (Zion and Zion, 1993).

When someone comes before the Peacemaking Court because of this or another kind of "bad behavior," the Navajo, consistent with what they believe about the roots of harmful behavior, try to help the person in trouble reconnect with the people around him or her. For them, peacemaking is a way to facilitate the reordering of consciousness and for the resituation of one's self in the world. They seek to achieve this making peace (*hozhooji naat'aannii*) by "talking things out" (Yazzie, 1997:2).

By talking things out, members of the Navajo community hope to foster and invigorate two values important to that community in order to ensure that those participating in the process find a way to incorporate "should-not-have-been-forgotten" values into their lives. One value is *k'e*, which might be translated as solidarity. This concept includes all the feelings and ways of being that foster solidarity with others, such as compassion, cooperation, friendliness, unselfishness, and peacefulness. The other is *k'ei*, which has to do with a person's kinship, with one's lineal connectedness to others: this comes from being part of a clan system, an extended family that is deeply concerned about each person's needs. From a very early age, Navajo children learn the importance of their clan relationships and speak of them in daily life by introducing themselves to others in terms of clan, parentage, and grand parentage (Bluehouse and Zion, 1993). It is no surprise, therefore, that when problems arise and come to the attention of the Peacemaking Court, that the peacemaking process involves not only the person(s) harmed and the person(s) responsible for the harm, but also members of their clans and families. In situations in which a harmed person cannot speak for herself/himself for some reason, members of that person's family will speak in his or her behalf.

As indicated, the process of peacemaking is a matter of "talking things out in a good way" so that all present can come to know what happened and come to an agreement on a practical solution (Ladd, 1957). At the beginning of the ceremony, the peacemaker will offer a prayer or ask an elder to do so, so that all present can seek guidance from the supernatural. Each person can then enter into the session with a frame of mind in which she or he has transcended his or her petty self. The peacemaker will then listen to the stories of the "disputants" to discover why they are so out of harmony and to determine whether they are prepared to attain *hozho*. *Hozho* is a measure of the extent to which a person is in complete harmony and peace (Bluehouse and Zion, 1993).

The talking process is not a matter of presenting legal evidence but of telling one's story, expressing one's feelings, and placing these expressions in the context of one's relational and personal history. Once the source of the conflict becomes known, the peacemaker then gives a "lecture" or "homily" on how those present have not followed the values of *k'e* and *k'ei*. "Lecture" is, however, not an adequately reflective translation because peacemakers don't give an abstract moral lecture. Rather, they draw on ancient creation narratives (*hajine bahane*) "to show how the same problems arose in the past and how traditional figures dealt with them. The stories reach inside people to revive the things they learned or should have learned as children. During this narrative, a peacemaker will apply the teachings of the problem and show how and why the excuses are false" (Yazzie, 1998:126). Clearly, peacemaking is radically different from mediation, where the mediator maintains a position of facilitative neutrality throughout the process. It is also different in the scope of the discussion, in the depth of concern for the persons involved, and in its sense of collective responsibility.

The Peacemaker (*hozhooji naat'aanii*), sometimes referred to as Peace Planner or Peace and Harmony Way Leader, is a respected member of the Navajo community who has been selected for this delicate work because she or he has "character, wisdom, and the ability to make good plans for community actions" (Austin, 1993:10). Peacemakers may come from any walk of life and do not have to possess professional credentials. They do receive some training in the process, however, to better help those who come together to deal with the nature of the specific issues at hand, as well as to help all participants gain some insight into the root "causes" of the conflict or disassociation. In this way, everyone, participant or not, might achieve greater balance within themselves, and steps might be taken to make appropriate relational and structural changes in the community (Nielsen, 1996).

To illustrate, in one situation a young woman was brought into peacemaking by her family members who were very upset because she suffered from a dependency on alcohol. In discussing this issue among family members, friends, and the peacemaker, the woman acknowledged her dependency, but then shocked everyone present by saying that she thought her inability to deal with life straight-on was due in large part to her having been sexually assaulted by a relative, a situation which none of her family members knew anything about (Yazzie, 1996). While the young woman's revelation was very disturbing for the family, they felt great relief, for now they had a better sense of who she was, what was going on in her life, and what steps they might take to offer her support in her healing. Here we can see the value of peacemaking as opposed to an adjudication-based process for responding to personal life-history and family matters that might remain concealed and unattended to. As Yazzie (1996:123) says: "In adjudication, the woman most likely would not have been punished as an offender. That is, she would not have been dealt with at all, since the vertical system primarily deals with troublemakers only if they commit a statutory offense."

In a situation when there is a statutory offense, part of paying attention to the needs of those who have been harmed might eventually result in some form of restitutive payment, which the Navajo refer to as *nalyeeh*. But, it should be pointed out to those who see monetary restitution as a principal component of restorative justice processes, that *nalyeeh* transcends the familiar definitions of restitution and compensation. It does not, for example, dwell on the concept that attorneys refer to as "just compensation," as we alluded to in Chapter One (Bluehouse and Zion, 1993). In *nayleeh*, those involved in the process examine what is needed to make things right for the person who has suffered a loss. Compensation with money or material goods – that is, payment to a harmed person by the person responsible for the harm or by his or her relatives – might be an agreed upon result of the process, but the process is not undertaken in the spirit of equity, of an eye for an eye, of proportionality. Its principal aim is to help those involved adjust their relationships in *k'e*.

As a formal judicial process, the practice of peacemaking has only recently (1982) been reintroduced into the judicial system of the Navajo by the Navajo Nation Judicial Conference (Zion, 1983). Peacemaking had been officially absent from the Navajo cultural landscape since 1868, when the United States government imposed its own system of adjudication on the Navajo and programmatically removed this central component of conflict resolution from their way of life. As we also mentioned in Chapter One, this is how the Belgian government acted toward the people of Rwanda when it excised the restorative practice of *gacaca* from Rwanda's community-based resources for responding to harms. In the case of the Navajo, there are still older Navajo who can remember a time when peacemaking was initiated after a dispute arose or someone had been harmed. But what they recall is that, rather than there being a designated peacemaker, a family member was called upon for help (Zion, 1999). Today, there are approximately 240 peacemakers located in 104 of the 110 chapters or semi-autonomous communities that make up the Navajo Nation.

Conferencing: The New Zealand Model

Through peacemaking, the Navajo offer us a wonderful demonstration project for how we might respond in a non-violent, needs-meeting, and restorative manner to conflict and harms-done. In a similar fashion, the culture and customs of the Maori in New Zealand have influenced another model of restorative justice, the Family Group Conference (Adler and Wundersitz, 1994). In this mode of restoration, as in Navajo peacemaking, family and community members assume a central role in helping people to heal from the pain and suffering that arise from conflicts and harms.

The array of issues that many of us think about when we discuss family group conferencing grew out of the Children, Young Persons and Their Families Act, which was passed by the New Zealand legislature in 1989. To a considerable extent this act was a direct response of New Zealand's legislators to the Maori political challenge to white New Zealanders and to their welfare and criminal justice systems. It was, as well, a response to concerns voiced by social welfare officials about this justice system's failure to administer justice to all its different aboriginal peoples and minority groups in ways that were culturally respectful and appropriate (New Zealand Department of Social Welfare, 1984). Prior to the enactment of this law, the Maori made up only 12% of New Zealand's population, and yet Maori children comprised almost half of those who found their way into the justice system as "juvenile offenders" (Morris and Maxwell, 1993:74). Moreover, when these young people appeared in court, they found themselves in a legal culture that was foreign to the Maori way of handling disputes and caring for those in need.

In the Maori tradition, the extended family (*whanau*), the clan (*hapu*), and the tribe (*iwi*) all share in "the raising of" children. This sharing, of course, includes providing support for them when they get into trouble. Through the passage of its 1989 Act, New Zealand's legislators sought to incorporate this component of Maori culture into the judicial system's response to harms and thereby involve not only Maori families, but all New Zealand families, in decisions affecting their children when those children found their way into juvenile court. The family group conference has thus become a flexible, accommodating, and culturally sensitive response process (Daly, 2001) through which all who come to juvenile court seek to make things right.

The New Zealand family group conferencing process is based in several important beliefs about what best facilitates the growth of young people both before and when they get into trouble with the law. The first is that children grow up best when they themselves participate in decisions that affect their lives. For some who were involved in establishing the family group conference as the official method for processing youth, this principle was believed to be so important that they sought to have the participation of young people made a fundamental right and incorporated into law.

The second is the belief, influenced by Maori tradition that the family, rather than being dysfunctional or pathological, can through the participation of its members be a major positive force in helping to settle disputes and in responding to social situations when someone harms another. The third is the belief that when indigenous peoples and others are able to work within a framework with which they are culturally familiar, they have access to persons and resources that can help them and other community members make things right in radically different and more deeply influencing ways (Daly, 2001).

And finally, the New Zealand conferencing model is derived from the belief that a restorative response to a situation in which someone has been harmed is far more beneficial for all involved than a response based in retribution, where the focus is almost exclusively on punishing the "offender." With harms viewed more as violations of persons and their relationships within communities than as transgressions against the state and its laws, those who come together in the conference can focus on ways not only to hold the wrongdoer accountable and responsible for the harmful actions, but also to support the wrongdoer as a person. And, part of the conference process includes collaboratively designing ways to meet this person's needs and to help him or her heal. Since being established, the family group conference has come to be viewed by many as the most direct, meaningful, and effective way to restore ties within families and communities after they become severed (Hudson et al., 1996; Hassall, 1996).

These conferences are organized and facilitated by a highly trained youth justice coordinator who works for a welfare or social service organization (Umbreit and Zehr, 1996). Invited to attend, in addition to the person responsible for the harm and the person harmed, are the family members of each, and a representative of the police, who serves as a "prosecutor." Those present are invited to share their accounts of the harmful actions and to discuss the ways in which the harm has affected and continues to affect their lives (Hudson et al., 1996a). At the conference there might also be a youth coordinator, a barrister or solicitor, and anyone else the families believe would act as an advocate for those present and thereby help in the healing process (Stewart, 1996).

Perhaps the single most important feature of the conference format is the inclusion of all present in the decision-making processes for making things right. All who have something to say are encouraged to share their views on how they were affected by the harm and what they hope will come from the meeting. They are made aware that they have gathered together not simply to engage in harm denunciation but, as well, to give testimony to the essential worth and gifts of all involved, including the person responsible for the harm (Zehr, 1995; Braithwaite, 1989). This approach, as mentioned earlier, counters the logic and experience of punitive processes that embody the idea that harming those who harm you is desirable and acceptable (Northey, 1992). Those present, therefore, are expected to come to a consensus on all the outcomes of the conference and not solely, for example, on a restitution agreement; the latter is a commonly accepted, yet highly limited, outcome for many victim-offender mediation or reconciliation programs.

Conferencing: The Wagga (police-run) Model

Impressed with the reported success of family group conferencing in New Zealand, in that the number of "cases" going to adjudication in court and the number of youth being admitted to correctional facilities had been significantly reduced (Morris and Maxwell, 1993; Maxwell and Morris, 1996), those interested in establishing a restorative approach to juvenile justice in Australia developed and implemented a variety of conferencing models. By 2001, six of the eight Australian states and territories had legislated conferencing schemes, and conferencing had become a high-volume activity in three jurisdictions – South Australia, New South Wales, and Western Australia. Conferences were conceptualized as decision-making processes about how to best respond when harms are done, rather than as fixed or uniform programs, interventions or treatments (Daly, 2001:63). Legislated approaches, which incorporated conferencing as one component in a set of responses to youth crime, emerged first in South Australia; since then, all but one of the six statutory schemes have rejected the Wagga (police-run) model in favor of the New Zealand model of non-police-run conferences. The Wagga model of police-run conferences was first developed in Wagga Wagga, New South Wales in 1991, and was later legislated in South Australia (Daly, 2001; Moore and O'Connell, 1994), but today in Australia the Wagga model is used in three jurisdictions, in none of them in large numbers (Daly, 2001). In other parts of the world, however, just the opposite trend has occurred, with many jurisdictions adopting the police-run model (Wundersitz and Hetzel, 1996) mostly, though not exclusively, for "diversion from court" or "caution plus" responses to youth harms (Daly, 2001). The Wagga model of conferencing has been modified and implemented in Canada and the United States (McCold and Stahr, 1996; Graber et al., 1996), in England and Wales (Marsh and Crow, 1996; Dignan and Marsh, 2001), in South Africa, the Philippines, Israel, the Netherlands, Singapore, along the Pacific Rim (Morris et al., 1996; Galaway and Hudson, 1996), and in many other places.

The Wagga model differs from the New Zealand model in that the conference is organized by a police officer, usually in uniform, or by a school official. When a young person admits responsibility for school misconduct or for an action that would place him or her in juvenile court, he or she is given an opportunity to choose a conference in lieu of the school disciplinary or judicial process. This model of conferencing is more directly offender-focused, with an emphasis on changing offender behavior through "reintegrative shaming" (Braithwaite, 1989). Conferences are usually held within weeks of the incident if the person harmed agrees to participate. When she or he does, the conference coordinator then invites the family and friends of both persons to attend.

In the conference meeting itself, the coordinator asks the young person responsible for the harm to tell what s/he did and what s/he was thinking about when acting was carried out. Then, the person harmed and her or his family members and friends are asked to talk about the incident from their perspectives and to describe how it had affected them. The harmed person is also asked to consider what s/he would like the outcome of the conference to be, and following a discussion of this proposal and others (if others are also presented) a written agreement is reached (often by consensus) and signed, usually within 60 to 90 minutes. In contrast to the New Zealand model as practiced in New Zealand, in the Wagga model, and in the New Zealand model as practiced in Australia, there is usually no break for private family decision making. As well, the Wagga model conference is more incident-focused with less time spent in pre-conference preparation (Daly, 2001).

Most proponents of restorative juvenile justice recognize the vast potential of family group conferences or youth conferences (Umbreit and Zehr, 1996). Indeed, they say that the conference model of justice better reflects restorative justice values in process and outcome than the victim-offender mediation formats or the victim-offender reconciliation programs that have developed throughout North America in the past twenty years. Part of their (Umbreit and Stacey, 1986) confidence in the family group conference formats derives from the fact that conference conveners, from the outset, involve more community people in the meeting to discuss the offense, its effects, and ways to remedy the harm to the primary victim. Getting a wider range of participants to express their feelings about the impact of the crime/harm on their lives not only promotes the healing of the person harmed, but also helps the person responsible for the harm become better reintegrated into the community.

But despite the restorative potential of family group conferences, implementing such a model, especially in the Wagga, police-run format, has the potential to produce significant problems if certain precautions are not taken (Umbreit and Zehr, 1996). For example, conferences need to be conducted in the most victim-sensitive manner possible. This means providing those who have been harmed with a choice of when and where to meet, and then, at the conference itself, allowing them to present their story first if they so desire (Amstutz, 2004; Strang, 2004). It also means that, when inviting those harmed to consider participating in the conference process, coordinators should not pressure them; and coordinators need to inform those harmed of the potential risks as well as the potential benefits associated with their participation. Nevertheless, most conferencing is primarily offender-centered, and "the offender's liability remains the event around which meetings are convened and deliberations concentrate" (Roche, 2003:143). In Australia (Daly, 2001:70), "in all legislation to date, the place of victims in the conferencing process is generally secondary to offenders."

Correspondingly, conferences are generally not sufficiently focused on the real needs of victims or their families, which are often more extensive than what can be addressed via conferencing (Achilles, 2004; Mika et al., 2002). And on some occasions, because conferences are oriented to the offender's timelines – the requirements of legal processing – victims are not even invited (Roche, 2003:170). Conferences go on with or without the victim or the victim's family members, or "family of concern." Conferences seem to be organized primarily to stimulate the development of an offender's empathy for the victim, to move the offender to take responsibility for the harm and the victim's suffering, and to give the offender some supportive educational, service, or rehabilitative experiences to aid him/her in abstaining from or reducing his/her reoffending. Other significant problems arise especially when police facilitators promote coerced participation and admissions (Daly, 2001), water down the conference model's restorative potential by adopting an almost exclusive focus on the offender, make the proceedings highly removed from public accountability (Roche, 2003), and extend police disciplinary powers (Young, 2001). Furthermore, problems arise when a conference is facilitated by police in a police venue, as this venue intimidates many young people. Problems also emerge when the availability of advocates and free legal advice is restricted and when there is no available independent review to ensure either conference process and outcome quality or public scrutiny of the protections for essential human rights and public safety concerns (Roche, 2003).

No matter which conferencing model is used, should a mutual decision be reached to have a conference, all the primary participants should be prepared, so that each feels safe enough to engage in genuine dialogue. Personal preparation is essential not only for victims but also for young persons responsible for harms in question. This is especially true when the latter are not well supported through the presence of family members or advocates who can help them meet their needs. Such preparation is especially critical when the young persons involved foresee feeling intimidated by being among so many adults, by being in the presence of authorities with power over them, and/or by being in the presence of persons of an unfamiliar culture. If such preparatory and participatory conditions are met, the focus of the conference is much more likely to reflect its restorative intention: those present are more likely to engage in a genuine exchange that moves the participants toward mutual understanding (Johnstone, 2002) and a set of follow-up agreements that help to meet the needs of those harmed and those in trouble. When such preparatory and participatory conditions are not met, there is likely to be a drift away from the conference's restorative focus, and those present are likely to engage in retributive blaming, non-participation or reluctant participation, and resentful compliance with the set of follow-up agreements. This shift might further manifest itself through the shaming of the person who committed the harm, and/or the revictimization of the "victim/survivor" (McCold and Wachtel, 1998a and 1998b; McCold, 2000).

Conditions for Restoration

Evaluations of early conferencing (Morris and Maxwell, 1993; Wundersitz and Wetzel, 1996), as well as of the most recent models (McCold, 2003; Daly, 2001, 2002, 2003b), suggest that conferencing is very unlikely to have a positive impact if the person responsible for the harm: felt coerced into participating in the conference or "volunteered" out of fear of receiving a more severe response from a court or school hearing; experienced no chance to meet with those who had been victimized; felt shamed or stigmatized as a person – felt that they were just "offenders" – during the conference; felt that the agreement was not really mutually derived as s/he had basically no say or influence on the direction and substance of the dialogue or the content of the agreement (Maxwell, Morris, and Anderson, 1999); and merely went through the motions of apology. In such instances, the conferencing process is unlikely to have a positive effect on the harm-doer's sense of responsibility, future behavior, or restorative feelings toward the victim. Correspondingly, the conference would neither embody restorative values nor effectively produce restorative outcomes if the person who was harmed felt: that he or she had not been understood or listened to; that the apology received was insincere or the resolution unjust or unfair; and/or that the person who harmed him or her was still a threat to them and others in the community and, perhaps, was a radically different type of person – an "offender" (Roberts and Masters, 1998). Nevertheless, most offender conference participants report, as do victim participants, that they perceived the conference processes as fair, were satisfied with the "outcome" agreement (Daly, 2003a; Strang et al., 1999), and felt that this encounter and the agreements reached were more fair than what would have been realized had "their case" gone to court processing.

There is also evidence that reoffending is less likely when offenders feel some remorse for their harms, when they feel empathy for those they had harmed because of what they had heard the victim express, and when they genuinely apologize for these harms and, in turn, receive an acceptance of this apology, or at least some perception of forgiveness (Hayes and Daly, 2003; Maxwell and Morris, 2001). In fact, Morris and Maxwell (1997) reported that "offenders" who met their victim but did not apologize were three times more likely to re-offend than those who did apologize (Strang, 2004). It is clear, then, that simply having a conference that the victim attended is not sufficient to yield positive results for the offender. It is, rather, having a conference that the victim attended and that the offender remembers five years later, one in which s/he was not made to feel that s/he was a bad person, one in which one was fully engaged in the discourse of the encounter, one in which the tasks agreed to in the settlement were completed, and one in which one ended up feeling sorry, apologizing, and feeling that the damage had been repaired (Maxwell and Morris, 2001:261; Maxwell and Morris, 2004).

Data from the RISE (Re-Integrative Shaming Experiments) project in Australia, which assessed the police-facilitated conferences of the Wagga model, similarly indicate that there were significantly lower rates of reoffending among young offenders who had committed violent offenses and had attended a conference as compared to those who had been court processed. However, for three other types of offenses (drunk driving, juvenile personal property theft, and juvenile retail theft) there appeared to be no significant differences in reoffending between conferenced and court-adjudicated youth. This seems to indicate that conferencing as compared with court processing may have a differential impact depending on the type of offending that is the subject of the conference (Maxwell and Morris, 2001:246). Conferencing appears to have a greater impact on rates of reoffending involving serious, rather than minor offenses; personal, rather than property offenses; and offenses with a directly-affected victim (McCold, 2003:104). These indications correspond to the emotionally charged discourse processes in conferencing that can lead to mutual understanding and sometimes apology and forgiveness. Unfortunately, researchers also attest that the full sequence – acknowledgment/genuine apology/forgiveness, which is considered by many to be a primary indicator of whether or not a conference is restorative (albeit, in a limited astructural sense [Mika, 1992]) – does not occur as often as many of us would like (Maxwell and Morris, 1996; McCold and Wachtel, 1998a and 1998b; Daly, 2003a; Daly 2003b:224-5). In her research on non-police mediated conferences in South Australia, Daly found that movement toward full reconciliation occurred fairly infrequently, as only 40% of those who had harmed others apologized spontaneously, a full third never apologized, and less than a third of the participating victims believed that when an apology was extended it was, in fact, genuine. So, while victim-attended conferences offer victims a direct and personal opportunity to participate in a collective response to harms, which is generally denied them in court, and while these conferences may reduce a victim's anger toward and fear of the offender, and while these conferences bring these victims face-to-face with those who have harmed them and require those who offended against them to hear the victim's account of the effects of these harms, it is clear that these encounters are far too infrequently fully restorative (Daly, 2001, 2002). Nevertheless, positive responses were more frequently expressed by those victims who received an apology and perceived that this apology was genuine, and by those who perceived that the conference experience had had a positive impact on the offender. Correspondingly, when those who had been harmed felt that they had not been extended a genuine apology; when the offender's explanation of the offense seemed more like a set of excuses, denials, minimizations, or rationalizations for the harm and its effects; or when the conference deteriorated into face-to-face victim-blaming, rather than an expression of feelings of regret, sorrow, and responsibility; then those harmed felt insulted, re-victimized, and far worse for having participated in the conference (Maxwell and Morris, 1996; Presser, 2003).

Data from the RISE project also indicate that significantly more victims whose harm had been court-processed than those whose harms had been addressed via conference expected to be revictimized by the same offender. This assessment was especially true for victims of violent offenses: more that six times as many court-processed as conference-processed victims believed that the person who had harmed them might repeat the offense against them or others in the community. Further, nearly two-thirds of the victims of violent offenses whose harm was in court were worried about this, compared with one-third of those victims who harm was conference-processed. RISE conference victims were also retrospectively asked about their feelings before and after their conference experience. Thirty-two percent of the victims of violent offenses who went to conferences indicated that they felt afraid of the person who had harmed them before the conference, compared with 8% following the conference experience. About two-thirds said that they felt angry beforehand compared with a quarter afterwards. Fewer than 20% said that they felt sympathetic toward the offender before the conference, while half felt sympathetic following the conference. While nearly two-thirds felt anxious before the conference about the harm happening to them again, this declined significantly after the conference to just over 40% (Strang, 2001:188-190). Furthermore, two-thirds said that the conference had made them feel that they could put the whole thing behind them. And of those who had felt that they had lost their sense of security as a result of the offense, two-thirds felt that it had been restored following their conference experience.

Issues related to the sensitivity, preparation, participation, and revictimization of those who have been harmed, and issues related to the coercion and minimal, insincere participation and intimidation of those who had harmed them, lead us to a cautious hopefulness regarding the restorative nature and effectiveness of conferences. Can we expect a model that is institutionally focused on diverting young people from the official juvenile justice system to seriously enable us to attend to the needs of those who have been harmed and those have harmed them? Can we expect such a format to motivate us to show an interest in and attend to the needs of others in the communities violated? Can conferences that are primarily offender-focused regularly foster truly restorative experiences (Maxwell and Morris, 1999) that address the needs of everyone in the community?

Community Sentencing Circles

In their enthusiasm for developing and implementing a wide variety of restorative justice practices, some communities in Canada have sought to remain sensitive to the issues raised above. Although many of the programs there have been influenced by aboriginal responses to conflict and harms (Pennell and Burford, 1996; Longclaws et al., 1996; Griffiths and Hamilton, 1996), we see in them a great amount of variation between what is potentially restorative and what is not. There are, of course, significant differences in culture among aboriginal peoples across Canada. Circles and decision making by consensus may not be part of a particular group's traditions, and therefore they may well choose a different community response, one more congruent with their own traditional ways (Lilles, 2001). While circles may provide an effective way for some communities to communicate and problem solve, this model may not be appropriate either culturally or functionally for others. And, too, sentencing circles are one mode positioned on a long continuum of restorative and non-restorative responses. The Canadian Native Justice Committees (Nielsen, 1996), for example, are quite limited as a restorative response because they serve more as an advisory body whose mandate is to recommend appropriate punishments for offenders to a judge. In contrast, community sentencing circles are a more fully restorative response, but nonetheless a response that works in cooperation with adjudication-based state responses in that circles are part of and/or replace judicial sentencing. The sentencing circle of the Yukon Territorial Court is premised on three cultural beliefs: first, that a criminal offense is a breach of the relationship between the offender and the victim and, as well, the relationship between the offender and the community; second, that the stability of the community is dependent on the healing of these breaches; and third, that the community is well positioned to address the roots of crime, which are often located in the economic, political, and social arrangements of the community and larger society.

In these circles, participation – like that in Navajo peacemaking, and generally in New Zealand and Australian non-police facilitated conferencing – is extended to a more extensive set of significant persons. According to Lilles (2001:163):

> Chairs are arranged in a circle and the session is chaired by a respected member of the community, sometimes called "the keeper of the circle" or by the judge. Usually between fifteen and fifty persons are in attendance. The participants in the circle introduce themselves, the charges are read and the Crown and defense lawyers make brief opening remarks. The community members then speak... Unlike court-based sentencing, the discussions focus on more than just the offense and the offender and often include the following matters:
>
> - The extent of similar crimes within the community;
> - The underlying cause of such crimes;
> - A retrospective analysis of what life in the community had been before crime became so prevalent;
> - The impact of these sorts of crimes on victims generally, on families, and on community life and the impact of this crime on the victim;
> - What can be done within the community to prevent this type of dysfunctional behavior;
> - What must be done to help heal the offender, the victim and the community;

- What will constitute the sentence plan, who will be responsible for carrying out the plan, and who will support the offender and the victim in ensuring the plan is successfully implemented; and,
- A date to review the sentence and a set of goals to be achieved before review.

Sentencing circles share many similar features to the conferencing models we have presented, including "offender" acknowledgment of the harm and its effects, apology, and reparation. Circles also include advising the victim of the offender's application for a circle sentencing hearing, providing the victim with information about the circle process, assisting the victim in creating a support group, and encouraging victims to attend the hearing with their support group to fully present how they have been affected by the harm, and what their needs are as a result of the harm. They are also encouraged to become full participants in the sentencing creation process. In most instances, circle discussions take between two and eight hours, and are usually spread out over two different sessions (Lilles, 2001). Circle discussions and the involvement of support groups in assisting both the "offender" and the "victim," and in shaping the "offender's" sentence, lead all participants to look beyond the actions of the "offender" to address the roots of crime. And through this process, a deeper sense of community and collective responsibility for healing all who have harmed, or been harmed, emerges. Ultimately, advocates for sentencing circles envision them as highly culturally-accommodative and flexible problem-solving processes for the prevention of harms (Stuart, 1992, 1994, 1996).

Because some restorative justice processes, such as peacemaking, family group conferencing, and community sentencing circles, have been influenced by the traditions of some aboriginal cultures and are either alternatives to or partners in adjudication-based justice, the question that continually arises is: Can, or how can, such restorative processes really be incorporated into formal adjudication-based systems of justice (Yazzie,

1998; Harris, 2003) and still be restorative? Stated differently: Is it possible for processes of justice that are truly restorative and, therefore, needs-based, to be incorporated into a harm-response system and a punitive, hierarchical society that are culturally and structurally at odds with needs-based social organization?

Our response to this question is that these processes probably cannot be adopted to any significant degree without calling the larger set of social arrangements into question. And this seems most clearly illustrated in the sentencing circle mode's concerns with the roots of the harms and injustices in our communities and societies. Consequently, the fully extended restorative processes that question and attempt to address root structural issues of how the society is organized are likely to be co-opted and truncated in their intentions and outcomes so as to protect and legitimate desert-based and rights-based stratification and power arrangements in the society (Harris, 1998; Walgrave, 1995). This does not mean, however, that these challenging restorative justice processes should not be initiated, for, even if they are eventually co-opted, they hold the potential for stimulating positive personal, relational, and social change. They hold the potential for the development of healthier persons, for greater participation and equality in social relations, for creating a more civil society, and for increasing the level of needs-meeting in the society.

Victim-offender Reconciliation Processes

It was a recognition of these needs-meeting potentialities that was responsible for the development of the restorative justice process known as the Victim-Offender Reconciliation Program (VORP), which is perhaps the most widely known restorative justice program in North America. The VORP format – as we mentioned at the outset of this chapter – can be traced to Kitchener, Ontario where, in 1974, Mark Yantzi of the Kitchener Probation Department and Dave Worth of the Mennonite Central Committee initiated a restitution/reconciliation program by what now seems to have been almost by chance. In May of that year, two young men, ages 18 and 19, had gone on a Saturday night drunken spree and did considerable damage to homes and businesses in the town of Elmira. Apprehended by the police, the two men subsequently pled guilty to 22 counts of willful damage.

A member of the Mennonite Church, which had become interested in ways to reconcile offenders and victims, Yantzi added a letter to the presentence report for the two men suggesting to the judge that "there could be some therapeutic value in having these two young men personally face the victims of their numerous offenses (Yantzi and Worth, 1976:4). With the approval of the judge, Yantzi and Worth – as two parents might do with their children who had done wrong to neighbors – accompanied the two young men as they went to the houses and businesses where they had broken windows, slashed tires, and damaged property. The young men knocked on doors, apologized, and offered to pay for the damages.

At sentencing, the judge ordered each man to pay a $200 fine, serve 18 months probation, and pay restitution of $550 each, which was to be divided among the persons harmed. Within three months, the two men had visited all the people to whom they had caused harm and handed each a certified check. Commenting on the value of the experience, one of the men said, "I didn't quit because of my self-respect, and I didn't want to have to look over my shoulder all the time" (Yantzi and Worth, 1976:7).

In the next several decades, a wide variety of reconciliation programs, such as that illustrated in the mediated reconciliation session between Gary Geiger and Wayne Blanchard (Chapter Two), have been formalized. Today, in North America, there are well over 200 jurisdictions that offer victim-offender mediation or victim-offender reconciliation programs (Zehr, 1990; Umbreit and Zehr, 1996). These programs offer a person who has been harmed a chance to meet with the person responsible for the harm. A mediator, often a volunteer from the community, arranges this meeting with the intent to help those involved tell their story, hopefully heal and reconcile and perhaps even bring closure to the events that brought them together (Wright, 1991; Umbreit, 1988; Zehr, 1990). As with other restorative justice formats, the person harmed and the person responsible for the harm are encouraged to talk about the events that brought them to the meeting, events that in many situations altered their lives forever. In most instances, they are then encouraged to shape a resolution that is agreeable to both (Harding, 1989; Chupp, 1989, Zehr, 1989). If, for example, restitution is established as a part of the resolution, a payment schedule that is acceptable to both is established.

As in the family group conference and sentencing circle, those who participate in this type of mediated face-to-face exchange may experience empowerment and a reduced sense of fear without taking advantage of or creating a counter-harm for those responsible for the initial harm (Zehr, 1990). As those who have been harmed may gain a greater sense of inner-healing and closure for their traumatic loss of trust, self-worth, and freedom, those responsible for the harm may more fully understand the personal suffering they have caused and experience genuine remorse for their acts (Galaway and Hudson, 1996). This is a very direct way to re-create a community that has been shaken. Increasingly, evaluations of these face-to-face reconciliation encounters demonstrate a great degree of satisfaction on the part of the participants, perhaps, in part, because these meetings are more genuinely voluntary, are often limited in scope, and are often used as a supplement to adjudication procedures.

Restorative Intentions

In any model or form, the intention in each of the restorative justice processes we have presented and discussed here is always "to finish off people's quarrels and to abolish bad feeling" (Beattie, 1957:194; Gibbs, 1963:9-10). In other words, the objective is to support and help everyone involved meet his or her needs and experience personal healing. It is to foster and embody mutual respect, inclusion, participation, collaboration, empowerment, and personal transformation (Toews and Katounas, 2004). It is to help everyone to move on with their lives, while being resituated or reintegrated into their communities. It is in its most robust process expressions and intentions – for example, in peacemaking, conferencing, and circle sentencing – to respond to the roots of the conflicts or crimes/harms with both personal and social-structural change so that others in our communities can feel safer, exercise their freedoms, and live in a more civil society. It is to lead the conveners and peacemakers of such processes to envision preventive, community organizing, restorative justice processes to build coalitions and mobilize people in communities for economic and social justice (Thompson, 2004), for challenging the structural inequities which are the contexts which harm youth and to which some respond by harming others. It is to foster transformative processes and social arrangements so that both the quality of life and the degree of justice increase (McCold, 2004). The aim of restorative justice is never retribution or any process that separates or alienates a person from his or her "community." And yet, when it comes to reintegrating or resituating both those harmed and those who have harmed another in their communities, the question that continues to rear its most troubling head is: Reintegration into what?

CHAPTER FOUR.
Reintegration Into What?

When we begin to examine the existing vocabularies of re-storative justice, one of the words that regularly appear is *reintegration,* especially in the context of reintegrating those who have harmed someone back into their communities (Braithwaite, 1989, 1994). Some ask, for example, not only whether we can reintegrate those responsible for a harm back into their communities, but whether we can do so "without causing bitterness and resentment" (Gibbs, 1963:9) on the part of those who were directly and indirectly affected by the harm. Through reintegration, some question whether the offender isn't "getting off" lightly. At the same time, others wonder about the possibility of reintegrating those who have been harmed – the "victims/survivors," into their "communities" and "families of care" – because in many instances they find them-selves marginalized and "stigmatized by family, friends, and the public" (Salasin, 1986:3). Far too often, the responses of community members lead them to feel "a sense of shame and rejection, compounding the victim trauma response" (Salasin, 1986:3). And, still others wonder how it is possible to reinte-grate anyone – "offenders" or "victims" – into a "community" when there is no sense of community, no solidarity, among the residents of an area or those who are supposed to care. They ask whether we can expect members of a "community" in which a harm has occurred to listen to the stories of all those involved in the harm situation, to pay attention to the needs of victims – never mind, the offenders – when day to day no one pays attention to their stories, or is concerned about meeting their needs. As we asked earlier, to what extent we can rea-sonably expect the restorative tail to wag its dog?

As we try to understand the issues related to reintegration, advocates of restorative justice who refuse to take into account the social contexts in which disputes, crimes, and social harms occur, do not help matters. We hesitate to characterize their perspective as naïve, but we know that reintegration at any level is possible only in places – in neighborhoods or in families of care – where a strong sense of bonded belonging exits, where relationships based in mutual aid thrive (Braithwaite, 1989; Van Ness and Strong, 1997). So what possibility is there for social reintegration to occur in a community or family when no prior integration existed or exists? In other words, how much can we expect of restorative justice processes or practices, of those seeking to help others to be reintegrated into their neighborhoods, or of those seeking to be reintegrated, when they live in what Norwegian criminologist Nils Christie (1993) refers to as a "killed neighborhood"? Far from possessing rein-tegrative capabilities – that is, the resources to provide sup-port in a variety of ways so as to meet human needs – the peo-ple in these communities or neighborhoods are themselves the objects of economic and social-structural violence. Their own life foundations are torn away from underneath them daily. So, rather than the neighborhood having a healing capability, it is a contributor to the conditions, and more than that, constitutes the conditions, whose effects are being attended to in the re-storative justice process in the first place. Rather than serving as facilitators for personal integration, "killed communities" and their social arrangements contribute the opposite. That is, they contribute to people relating to one another as strangers, as people who are seen as posing a threat to one another, and, in far too many instances, as enemies (Sullivan et al., 1998). "Killed communities" embody the current structural inequali-ties, the distributions (Tifft and Sullivan, 1980:57) that are the root of most interpersonal crime (Lemonne, 2003; Garland, 2001; Gil, 1999).

Fortunately, as scholars and practitioners of restorative justice increasingly concern themselves with issues related to the cooptation of restorative justice language and practices, and to the effects of ideology and organizational structure on what kind of stories can be told and responded to, they have attuned themselves, as well, to the collective social and political-economic conditions that make or break restorative justice. Hence, we see a growing recognition on the part of many advocates of restorative justice "that the problem of neighbour disputes and anti-social behaviour...[is] linked to deeper societal problems such as the fragmentation of communities and the related phenomenon of social exclusion" (Dignan, 2000:11). Believing this nexus to be real and to have real consequences, the Social Exclusion Unit (established in the U.K. in 1999) forged ahead with its mission to help "create prosperous, inclusive and sustainable communities for the 21st century – places where people want to live that promote opportunity and a better quality of life for all" (Social Exclusion Unit, 2004). When members of this unit immersed themselves in neighborhoods to gain a better sense of what produced high levels of conflict – and we can add here, non-restorative practices of justice – they found that such upheaval was more likely to thrive in neighborhoods that suffer from a combination of linked problems such as unemployment, low income, low skill development, poor housing, high crime, bad health, and family breakdown. In its analysis of worst estates (housing projects), one of the unit's reports, *Bringing Britain Back Together: A National Strategy for Neighbourhood Renewal* (Social Exclusion Unit, 1998) makes clear that the problems experienced in disintegrated neighborhoods derive from a decline in traditional forms of employment, enforced unemployment, bad housing allocation policies, and the tendency for government officials to "parachute in" solutions from the outside, rather than to engage local community residents in the solution of their problems. (See Mika [2002] regarding "parachuted in" restorative justice programs and research.) With respect to restorative justice, that is, with respect to communities that seek to be inclusive (reintegrative), the report states that those "communities must be consulted and listened to, and the most effective interventions are often those where communities are actively involved in their design and delivery and where possible in the driving seat" (Social Exclusion Unit, 2001:18). In these "neighborhoods," national policies have abandoned young persons growing up at the bottom of class and "racial"/ethnic hierarchies in their pursuit of full-time, living-wage employment and independent adult lives. Simultaneously, these national policies have decreased the safety and social support nets for these youth (James, 1995; Weitekamp, 2001; Johnstone, 2002). Clearly, the needs of offenders and victims for re-integration are linked to the resources and degrees of integration found in the communities or neighborhoods they come from, and most usually wish, or must, return to (Social Exclusion Unit, 2004). Restorative justice that does not expand its scope to address these repressive structural contexts is destined to be highly truncated and ineffective, not only in meeting "offender" needs, but especially in meeting "victims" needs, and for helping people to live a life that is safe and promotive of individual and collective development and well-being. To reintegrate victims and offenders into these structurally violent conditions is anti-restorative and unjust.

As we have said in many different ways throughout this book, if we wish to help victims and offenders heal from the harms they suffer and create, respectively, we must hear their stories regarding the harm and the needs that emerge from these stories. The same can be said for communities as a whole, as was true for the nation of South Africa after it made the courageous decision to listen to its whole self so it could heal from the brutal effects of apartheid and, through that acknowledgement and healing, determine what its needs and collective life plans were for a meaningful future.

When we look at "killed neighborhoods" in the U.S., rather than finding them consulted and listened to – to hear what is killing them and what'll bring them back to life – we see voices muted, muffled, disregarded, and dismissed as inconsequential, so we rarely get to hear the connection between political-economic violence and the collective and the individual lives of those who live within these communities. One community whose voicelessness and resourcelessness have been called to our attention over the past decade is Mott Haven, a section of the South Bronx in New York City. Here we find an area of the city in which the 1991 median family income was $7,600 and which 10 years later rose to only $10,865 (Lee, 2000). When Jonathan Kozol (1996) became a voice of this community in his inspiring work, *Amazing Grace*, nearly 95% (753 of 800) of the children attending the neighborhood elementary school were eligible for the school lunch program. Physically, Mott Haven has been so battered by economic violence that many of its buildings stand in rubble in much the same way as those found in the bombed-out neighborhoods of Kosovo, Fallujah, Baghdad, and Kabul. They will never make *House Beautiful.*

In Mott Haven, addiction from crack cocaine and the intravenous use of heroin are woven into the fabric of social life. When Kozol first entered the community, nearly every child at St. Ann's Church on St. Ann's Avenue could speak about a relative or neighbor who had died of AIDS. One-quarter of the women who were tested in obstetric wards showed up as HIV-positive. And, there were so many shootings on these streets that the New York Times had referred to the streets around St. Ann's as "the deadliest blocks" situated in "the deadliest precinct" of the city, and maybe even the entire United States. In 1991, 84 people, more than half of whom were 21 or younger, were murdered in this precinct, making violence a community health issue (Prothrow-Stith, 1987; Prothrow-Stith and Weissman, 1991). Mott Haven was and remains a "killed neighborhood," a neighborhood whose economic and political rugs have been pulled out from beneath its feet. How are we to address issues of the reintegration of someone just released from Bellevue Hospital or Riker's Island jail after 90 days into such a neighborhood when there is hardly a semblance of social integration within it? They return to the very social and economic circumstances that fostered their harmful behavior in the first place. Where would their story begin? What forum would there be in which their story might be told? Who would listen to their story? And once it was told and heard, in what way would their needs and the needs of those similarly situated be taken into account and ultimately met?

In *Amazing Grace,* Kozol (1996), as the clarion of the people who live in Mott Haven, gives us an opportunity to see people who live there not as cases, as offenders, or as victims, but as people who have been shaken down by a political-economic system that is organized with less concern for meeting human needs than for providing a second or third car for families in suburbia or a second or third mansion in Newport or Providence, Rhode Island. Among the children in Mott Haven, Kozol tells us that psychological depression is common, as it is for Dave, the young man we discuss in the case study below. Parents and neighbors see many children cry, some a great deal of the time, and many seem to be unable to figure out why. Many of the children are consumed by feelings of fear and anxiety. At night they cannot sleep (Kozol, 1996).

A high percentage of these troubled children suffer as well from asthma, perhaps related to the presence of the garbage dump and waste incinerator that borders their neighborhood. The New York City Department of Health is well aware of this situation because the number of young asthma sufferers who miss school regularly due to asthma attacks is high. On its website, the Health Department calls attention to the fact that: "The impact of asthma in the Bronx is the most severe of any borough – and profoundly affects the school system, healthcare system and community life as well as individual families" (*Mott Haven-Longwood Asthma Resource Manual,* 2005). In its offer to provide information and community resources to deal with this public health problem, the department points out that the Bronx has nearly twice the childhood asthma death rate of New York City as a whole. Its nearly 5,000 annual childhood asthma hospitalizations account for

33% of all city childhood hospitalizations, even though only 20% of all the city's children reside in the Bronx. When we break down the statistics for childhood asthma hospitalization further, we discover that the highest rate is found in the Mott Haven-Longwood area (Mott Haven-Longwood Asthma Resource Manual, 2005). The incinerator situated in that part of the city burns "red bag products" – waste products such as amputated limbs, fetal tissue, bloodied bedding, bandages and syringes – from 14 New York City hospitals, (Kozol, 1996:7). Kozol himself (1996:11) has remarked that during the time he spent in Mott Haven among his new family, many people queried, perhaps more rhetorically than not, "Why do you want to put so many people with small children in a place with so much sickness?"

And whereas employees of the U.S. military receive combat pay for being anywhere in the neighborhood of enemy fire, the teachers who work in the trenches of this battleground receive no similar compensation. In fact, when we look at the median salaries of teachers in the New York metropolitan area, we see that in the schools of Mott Haven (District 7, in particular) that salaries are approximately half those of teachers in the affluent communities of Great Neck and Manhasset. The actual figures, compiled annually by the state, show a median salary of $42,000 for a teacher in Mott Haven in contrast to $82,000 for a teacher in the two Long Island suburbs mentioned. And with respect to resources supplied for the operation of a public school, a third-grade class of 25 children in the schools of Great Neck receives at least $200,000 more per year than does a third-grade class of the same size in Mott Haven. An update of these savage inequalities (Kozol, 2000) indicates that the children in a comparable classroom in Manhasset now receive a quarter-million dollars more (Kozol, 2002). No support, no integration! And yet, in spite of these and many other structurally violent conditions, some children experience ordinary resurrections (Kozol, 2000) and transcend these environments.

... so revelatory about Kozol's depiction of so many of ...e children living in Mott Haven is that they manifest the same symptoms that Gary Geiger (see Chapter Two) said he was plagued with after he was assaulted and shot while working in an Albany motel. He suffered anxiety. He could not sleep. He was depressed. For Geiger there was the mediation program through which he found some relief for his ailments by "confronting" and reconciling with Wayne Blanchard, the person who had harmed him. But where can the Mott Haven children go? Whom can they identify as those responsible for the chronic and life-threatening harms they suffer? How can they hope for personal integration and development when they manifest the same symptoms that clinicians identify in persons suffering from post-traumatic stress disorder (Herman, 1992)? Perhaps Dave's story provides some insight.

Dave: A Case Study

Dave lives in Massachusetts and is one of the teens that psychiatrist Robert Coles (1995) spent time with in his travels across the United States listening to children and exploring the day-to-day lives of six families. Dave ordinarily lives with his mother, stepbrother, biological brother, and his mother's boyfriend, Jack. But, in *Listening to Children* (Coles, 1995), the film version of Cole's experiences, we meet Dave as a young teenager in a group home for juvenile offenders. Dave has lashed out violently, both within his family and in the community, striking the principal at his school, sending one of his brother's friends to the hospital, and hitting two different police officers the day they took him out of his home. According to Dave, he feels good when he gets into fights and strives to hurt the person he is fighting as much as he can. The person Dave fights with most is Jack, who Dave feels does not like him because he gets in trouble. Jack rarely talks with him, and does not take him anywhere or just hang out with him. Dave mostly gets in trouble trying to prevent his mother from drinking or trying to prevent Jack from beating on his mother or himself. While showing Coles his room, complete with fistholes in the walls many of which are covered by posters of rock musicians, Dave explains that his real dad left him before he was born, "probably because he thought I was going to be a bad kid."

According to Coles, Dave is a fragile, vulnerable boy who breaks out of depression when he becomes violent. Through his fits of anger he loses some of his depression and is able to break free, to prevail. His drawings of his mother show her to be disheveled, without color, and with very large hands – "perhaps hands that have clubbed him." His crayon drawings of himself present a reddened face, but otherwise the whole drawing is in black, showing a spacious empty house, even black bushes. Clearly, this is a boy who feels great emptiness; his is a bleak and lonely universe. According to Coles, what Dave has going for him is his awareness of his feelings, a recognition of when he begins to become enraged, and a will to control his violence. But, Dave also recognizes the reality that his mother is not going to stop drinking and that Jack is not going to stop beating on her or him. While shaking Coles's hand, he says, in a self-understanding way, "Nothing's going to change when I go home, except me." Dave receives little support in his challenge to integrate his senses of self, to control his fits of anger and rage, to address the roots of his depression, to survive his "family of care." Can Dave transcend his family life? Should Dave be "re-integrated" into such a physically and structurally violent family circumstance? No one seems to be concerned about or responding to Jack's violence or its roots. No one seems to be responding to Dave's mother's suffering or the roots of her drinking. And no one, but Coles, seems to recognize that Dave is living a life of continuous exposure to violent victimization, to which he ordinarily responds with anger, depression, and by venting through listening to "hard rock," but occasionally, with a violent outburst.

Recent research conducted in the Cobb County (Georgia) Juvenile Court attempted to determine the effects of mediation, as compared to court adjudication, in helping teens reorder their lives so that they no longer enhanced their personal well-being by creating loss for others. These data tell us that, in terms of young persons "once again getting into trouble with the law within a year of their official disposition," it made no difference whether one was part of the mediation project's experiences or went through the traditional juvenile court-adjudication system (Stone et al., 1999). One can, of course, question whether "once again getting into trouble with the law" is a valid measure of a restorative justice program's or court's effectiveness or value. And, one can say that this is but one type of restorative justice program organized in a very specific way. Or, one can say that most studies demonstrate a more positive effect of mediation and the more full-bodied restorative modes such as conferencing (see Chapters Two and Three). Furthermore, we would hope that a county's commitment to restorative justice would go beyond mediated agreement plans that might require an apology, restitution, community service, and educational or rehabilitation program compliance, to foster a deeper reflection on how one conducts one's daily life and relationships with friends and family members, and to open up new vistas beyond the issue of reoffending.

But for those who espouse the importance of young people being actively involved in the processes of interpersonal reconciliation, such a finding as that in Cobb County is a source of considerable discouragement. We would hope to see a much more positive connection between active participation in solving one's "personal" problems restoratively and creating a better future for one's self. And, we must ask whether those who feel discouraged have realistic expectations. Can we expect a meeting of perhaps an hour's duration followed up by activities of unknown meaning (Delens-Ravier, 2003) to counteract or neutralize in any long-lasting way the harmful structural conditions and lack of moral intelligence that most of these young people have been exposed to, perhaps since birth (Lederach, 1997)? As there are far too many youth with similar "personal troubles" as those in Cobb County or in Mott Haven, their "personal troubles" added together constitute a social problem – a public policy issue. And social problems cannot be effectively addressed through individualistic responses. They require change in the social policies and social arrangements that lie at their root. Can we expect many of the Daves of the world, many of the children of Mott Haven, to be transcendent supermen and superwomen, able to withstand the violent onslaught of enemy fire they have had no say in creating? If we wish to significantly change the everyday violence we become involved in, and generally to enhance the quality of our lives, we will have to change more than how we "process" one another once one of us gets in trouble with the law (Dyck, 2000). As Dugan says, the latter is simply "not enough" (1996:13). We must alter the existing non-need meeting conditions of our lives – our life contexts. This, perhaps Robert can help us understand.

Robert: A Case Study

Robert is another of the teens Robert Coles met during his journey into children's moral and everyday lives. Like those who live in Mott Haven, Robert does not like growing up in the dirty neighborhood he describes as, "a junky place that smells funky." In the projects of a New Orleans black ghetto neighborhood, Robert dreams of going to stay someplace else, somewhere where there is love, peace, and respect. But like so many young persons in such environments, Robert must face not only the economic and spiritual violence of his neighborhood but, as well, the death of a family member. His Uncle John (27 years old) was jumped by a group of young men and "shot so many times the coroner stopped counting." Robert was then just 11. Now almost 13 (at the time of the filming), he deeply misses his uncle, who was like a big brother to him and used to take him to the park, play basketball and football with him, take him places, and hang out. "How can someone you love just die on you like that?" Robert asks (Coles, 1995).

In one of the crayon sketches he prepares for Coles, Robert draws his Uncle John in a stark black box – a casket in a graveyard. And, in his self-portrait he himself appears boxed in, constrained, surrounded in browns and blacks by what appears to be a prison. His uncle's death has given him both moral and psychological pause. The world he sees everyday when he goes to school or out to play does not offer much hope or inspiration. Yet, in a different sketch, Robert draws himself not black, not doomed or constrained, but rather, as a person with hope, with bounce, in an open vista, a basketball star – a white basketball star – free like white people!

Robert is supported by his church-family, and especially by his mother, who presents him with a strong moral alternative. While she fears that Robert could get caught up in fast-money street games, she demonstrates a path of ambition, honesty, responsibility, and discipline. And, while Robert desires comfort, wealth, and respect, he also fears he could end up like his uncle, a victim of the streets. Can Robert, harmed by the death of his "big brother," and the physical and spiritual violence that engulfs him, trust the example his mother and others in his church-family offer? Can he integrate the harms he experiences each day and transcend the script before him? In Coles's words, Robert's challenge is the shared struggle we all face, within ourselves and with one another, to affirm our humanity and responsibility as moral citizens. As we go from one neighborhood to the next, and from one community to the next, this is the struggle we should all be thinking about (Coles, 1999).

EXPANDING RESTORATIVE JUSTICE

When we speak of the conditions necessary to make restorative justice a reality, to foster the re-integration of people into their communities, to prevent dis-integration in the first place – to create inclusion – we cannot emphasize enough how important it is for us to take into account the political-economic and social-structural conditions that exist within a community and in its families, schools, places of work, and worship. These conditions are not incidental to the restorative justice project, as many insist. They are primary determinants of how successful we will be in resolving interpersonal conflicts (and international conflicts), in healing harms, and in preventing the kind of structural violence that is carried out by impersonal institutional policies and by the ordinary operation of a power-based political-economy wherein decisions are made in places well-distanced from these neighborhoods and districts (or nations), by those non-tangible "perpetrators" (Steinbeck, 1939, Chapter 5).

What is disheartening for us to see is how many proponents of restorative justice continue to limit their conceptualization of restorative justice solely to its correctional dimensions. They refuse to expand the boundaries, the scope, of restorative justice so that it takes into account the transformative, political-economic, and structural dimensions of justice: that is, the social-structural conditions that constrain our lives and affect the extent to which any one of us can live restoratively (Dyck, 2000; Dugan, 1996; Morris, 1994; Sullivan and Tifft, 1998, 2000b). In other words, many proponents of restorative justice continue to speak about restorative processes within the context of, as an adjunct or alternative to, the criminal justice system, and are unwilling to extend their thinking to recognize that these restorative processes have applicability to all areas of our lives (Messmer and Otto, 1992; Bazemore and Schiff, 2001; Johnstone, 2004; Sullivan and Tifft, 2004; Lofton, 2004), and, most especially, to the social-structural and cultural arrangements of our lives. Restorative justice is a justice that sees the justice process as belonging to the community. The community is harmed by both structural inequalities and interpersonal crimes, and our response must be drawn from the community and ought to build and strengthen the community.

The architects and administrators of restorative justice programming must envision preventive, community-organizing
restorative justice processes that mobilize people in the "community" and build coalitions for economic and social justice
(Thomson, 2004), for challenging the structural inequalities.
The community needs to become internally competent to define
and resolve its own internal conflicts (Johnstone, 2002; Bush
and Folger, 1994). Restorative justice responses should, with
this latter focus, embody process dynamics that enhance opportunities for both the participants and the community as a
whole for empowerment and recognition – for moral development.

Empowerment in this sense occurs when a person
strengthens his or her ability to deal with difficulties of all
sorts by engaging in conscious and deliberate refection, choice,
and action (Bush and Folger, 1994:81). Recognition occurs
when a person strengthens his or her ability for experiencing
and expressing concern and consideration for others (Bush and
Folger, 1994:81). In other words, the airing of conflicts and
harms and their effects should be utilized to transform participants from victimized, vengeful, fearful, defensive, and self-
centered persons into confident, responsive, and caring ones
(Johnstone, 2002). The community's collective response ought
to transform our communities into moral communities, respecting diversity and enhancing understanding and tolerance.
It ought to raise political-economic consciousness and prepare
community members and representatives to challenge the current arrangements that have "killed" the community. On an
individual level, we should no longer measure the success or
effectiveness of restorative justice responses solely with reference to the aims of whether or not they achieve healing, personal change, reintegration and a decrease in reoffending; we
should measure them with reference to whether or not they
reach their potential to help people develop the tools and resources needed to solve problems themselves, to develop a
sense of control over their own lives, and to see those with

whom they are in conflict as real persons with real human needs. And, beyond this individual level, restorative justice responses must be invented to counteract the sense of disempowerment and disengagement that is rampant in modern societies (Johnstone, 2002:150) by empowering community members to rally for political-economic and policy change, to vocally challenge the inequities of the current distributions of life chances, health, freedom, safety, and well-being.

Restorative justice programmers must network with others to collaboratively lobby the public for resources to extend services to help victims recover from trauma and rebuild their lives, and to create an enriched environment that prevents the production of interpersonal harm. Such programming must address essential victim needs, those which are largely unrelated to the offender or anything that the offender can provide. It must acknowledge victims' injuries, assure them that their being harmed was not their fault, and take seriously their needs for safety and security, ventilation and validation, and education and information (Mika et al., 2002; Mika, 2002; Zehr and Mika, 1998:51-53). Further, we need to let them know that we are genuinely doing something to try to prevent not only their revictimization, but the victimization of others (McCold, 2003:96). An emotional dialogue with the person who harmed them is a need for some, but it is not necessarily at the top of the list of needs that victims or their families desire to have fulfilled (Achilles, 2004:70). Any desire to volunteer to meet with an offender must be positioned as a choice option (Achilles, 2004:72) that acknowledges and respects the victim's timeline; that is if they feel the need for this sort of emotional restoration, healing, and forgiveness in the first place (Amstutz, 2004; Strang, 2004). Restorative justice programming must reach out to dialogue with those who provide victim services and serve as victim advocates. Together they need to collaboratively develop crisis hotlines, as well as medical, legal, and counseling services, and to provide assistance with victim compensation and financial recovery service organizations.

Justice for victims must provide the short- and long-term care that they require (Achilles, 2004:70) and include the full availability of these services in all communities. There must be community-coordinated follow-up programs and mobilization strategies so as to greatly reduce the structural harms that constrain or repress community members. There must be social structural and cultural changes that are generated from a grander theoretical and programming conceptualization of restorative justice.

Needs-based Restorative Justice

By suggesting that we need to consider applying restorative justice principles within the larger political-economic and social-structural arrangements, we are not simply recommending that restorative justice practices be introduced into our families, schools, and workplaces. Yes, it's important that we have available non-retributive processes or procedures to call upon when someone hurts another and we seek to bring about healing, reconciliation, and inclusion instead of a cycle of harm, vengeance, repression, and exclusion. Of course, having such processes in place is important for fostering personal restoration and for teaching children how to take the point of view of others, to see others' needs as essential (Flaste, 1977; Allers, 1992). But we are talking more about the creation of social arrangements that are from the outset structurally restorative because they are set up to attend to the needs of all involved. They are constructed in such a way that they do not do violence to anyone or create loss or deficits for anyone by either limiting participation or distributing benefits according to one's position or contribution.

Once we begin to view issues of restorative justice within the larger transformative, social-structural context, we can no longer possibly focus on one particular dimension of restorative justice without taking into account all others (Achilles and Zehr, 2001). That is, we cannot focus on restorative justice as an alternative to the criminal justice system without recognizing its needs-based foundation and the possibilities for creating healthy persons in our families, schools, and workplaces. This is because the principles of restorative justice that apply to situations after harm have been shown to derive from a political-economy that is the governing principle in all areas of our lives. These needs-based principles have applicability to making things right not only after someone has harmed another but also up front and structurally, preventively, when we create social arrangements with each other each day. That is, restorative principles derive from a needs-based political-economy, that is, a political-economy that seeks to take into account the needs of all persons in any given social situation, not the other way around, despite how much we must now rely on the tail to wag the dog.

Hence, it should be clear that it will not be possible to continue with restorative justice processes and practices for long without keeping in mind at every step of the way that the true foundations of restorative justice – that is, restorative processes at all levels of social interaction – derive from a needs-based political-economy, from needs-based relationships. Once we embrace this reality, we will see that we can no longer relegate the practice of restorative justice to the work-a-day world of corrections or to the work any of us does, but must acknowledge that it is applicable to every relationship in our lives. For this reason, it is especially important to understand the foundations of needs-based justice so that restorative justice programs will be able to withstand co-optation attempts by the state's multitudinous departments of retributive correction. Let us look in some detail, then, at what we mean by a needs-based political-economy.

CHAPTER FIVE.
Needs-Based Justice as Restorative

Grasping the value of a restorative, needs-based approach to justice is extraordinarily difficult for many people today because the reward/punishment ideas and "what-is-just" ideas that influence how we relate with one another and live our lives derive their currency from a hierarchical and globalizing political-economy. Moreover, the social arrangements that support this political-economy are not systematically structured to meet people's needs. Therefore, rather than needs-meeting, our relationships and daily lives are organized more along two competing views of what is just, namely, rights versus "deserts." According to rights-based ideas and social arrangements, it is believed that people should have access to resources and receive benefits, privileges, and burdens, solely on the basis of the rights affixed to their ascribed social position. That is, each should receive his/her due according to one's social position – with the rights, entitlements, and obligations that are attached to this position. For example, in a male-dominated or patriarchal ascriptive social order, a first-born male child, in contrast to his younger sister, holds a very different position in the family and society – a position of far greater rights and privileges in accord with his sex and order of birth. The principal concern of justice in such an ascriptive hierarchy is maintaining the continuity of the relations between position holders over time. And its primary object is to preserve the existing order of benefits and burdens as well as distributions of rights, possessions, and privileges so that position holders can continue to receive benefits in accord with their station. Individuals are essentially known as, and develop as, holders of differing positions, and when breaches occur – when individuals act out of place or do not know their place – a response is made to reassert the correctness of the ascriptive order. Protecting position holders from harms and preserving the entitlements of place are the order of the day.

In deserts-based social arrangements or hierarchies, it is believed that one should have access to resources and receive benefits, privileges, and burdens on the basis of merit or desert, that is, in accord with the contribution, effort, and investment one puts forth. Deserts-based arrangements embody the widely-held cultural belief that we should receive benefits on the basis of what we have done, rather than on the basis of holding an ascribed social position (Kleinig, 1971; Lamont, 1994). Each should receive her/his due according to that individual's "deserts," that is, based on one's demonstrated moral virtue, productive efforts, and the qualities he or she has developed. In other words, a person should receive her/his due in accord with his/her actions or contributions. For example, in a deserts-based social order a first-born male child, in contrast to his younger sister, would have privileged access to the resources of the family and society only if his actions, contributions and positive qualities warranted this differential access. While deserts-based thinking is most prevalent in the social arrangements of our current world order, there are some major practical problems with its principles. For example, how do we disentangle one person's contributions from those of others since most tasks are collective efforts? How do we assess whether the value that each creates is due to her/his volitional qualities, talents, and actions? And how do we measure the value of what is produced?

When we look at deserts in relation to rights-based distributions, we see ways in which deserts can modify or challenge rights-based legitimacy, for those persons/position holders who have certain rights and entitlements (and therefore differential access to societal resources) may not be those who deserve to have them according to some criteria of desert. The problem with this, however, is determining what these desert-based criteria are and who decides or determines their content and the relative worth of differing contributions. Ascriptive positions are based on lineage, sex, ethnicity, birth-order, or interpersonal or interfamily connections, and not on one's volitional actions or individually-developed abilities and efforts. Most people in our society today believe that, if a person works hard to develop his or her skills and puts forth a great amount of effort, he or she will be rewarded and live well (Feinberg, 1970). Similarly, when it comes to burdens and punishments, many believe that one should bear burdens and receive punishments based solely on one's actions, not unjustly on the basis of one's position in the social order. Most believe that one should not be burdened – that is, that it is unjust to be burdened – on the basis of heritage, birth-order, or sex or any other ascriptive criterion. Moreover, those who adhere to deserts-based conceptions of justice assert that rights-based principles of distributive justice are unjust because one does not choose to be born female/male, black/white, in a particular birth-order, or to a particular social position of class privilege or deprivation. In response to the injustice and burden of holding an ascribed social position that denies one an opportunity to develop one's talents and make contributions (and therefore to receive benefits and burdens on the basis of one's developed talents and actions), the familiar ameliorative remedies such as "equal opportunity," "equal rights" legislation, "head start," "affirmative action," and "job corps" programs are offered.

And with respect to appropriate responses to harms done or to negative contributions to society in other ways, those who embrace deserts-based ideas of justice assert that justice requires that no one should be punished, incarcerated, or executed if he or she has not committed a harmful act or crime that proportionately justifies such a response. In the retributive, deserts-based idiom of the day, no one should do the time if he or she has not done the crime (Miller, 1999). And, if one has done the crime, certainly one should not be exempt from doing the time because of one's social position.

As a consequence of our constant exposure to deserts-based and rights-based ideas and social arrangements, it is not un-reasonable to expect us to have much competence in thinking about needs-based arrangements with any kind of facility and in implementing restorative process for those who have been involved in a harm situation. Not having embraced needs-based living arrangements and restorative values in our daily lives – in our families, schools, and workplaces – our repertoire of skills for managing the complex of ideas, feelings, and deci-sions that arise when we seek to create and apply restorative values and meet everyone's needs in a harm situation is se-verely limited. Acting in this way is counter-cultural, counter-relational, counter to the rights-based and deserts-based ways of life we are inundated with daily. Indeed for some, acting this way – especially for those who benefit from their ascriptive or achieved positions – is deemed a threat, disruptive. It calls into question their beliefs, their privileges, and the ways they desire social life to be organized. Of course, this is in fact the case be-cause debates about the meanings of justice are really debates about the desirability of certain ways of living – of organizing social life – of how freedom, participation, liberty, life-chances, access to material goods, food, water, health, health care, wealth, and well-being are to be distributed (Miller, 1976:22). So, in the eyes of some, a needs-meeting restorative justice is an idea totally out of sync with reality because it is totally out of step with the ideologies that support ascriptive hierarchy and market meritocracy. In the eyes of others, needs-meeting justice is simply madness, even if they are not sure why they think so, and especially when they lack a clear understanding of how deserts-based and rights-based political-economies work in their lives.

While we take the bold and oftentimes unrelenting critiques of needs-based justice seriously, and listen with care to what people say, we also to some extent have to take what is said with a grain of salt. This is due in large part to the fact that we see, and increasingly so, more and more people who are seem-ingly unreflective, unaware of the principles or assumptions of the political-economy that underlie their sense of themselves, how this self is created, and how it proceeds in its world of relationships with others. This is true even for those who profess a familiarity with religious principles and can tell us how they apply these principles in their everyday dealings with others. The problem there is that, in far too many instances, many of us who embrace such principles treat matters of justice as if feelings, bodily needs, and ideas were not grounded in relationships or in social-structural contexts and vice versa. Regardless, one of the primary reasons that any of us puts off making such an examination of self, our relationships, and what kind of justice prevails in these relationships is that this is a very painful process. By taking on such a task in earnest, we are making a commitment to examine the foundations of the social ethic by which we live, interact with, and "treat" others, which, in turn, requires us to scrutinize our desires and our self-needs-satisfaction motives. What we find might contradict how we perceive ourselves, how we project ourselves into the world, and what kinds of actions we believe we are responsible for (Klein, 1964).

At the most basic level, the political-economy of relationship that each of us develops is a measure of the relative value or worth we assign to ourselves and to others. When we develop a rights-based or deserts-based political-economy, we create hierarchical classification or ranking systems whereby we situate some people as more worthy and others as less worthy; some people of more, and others of less, value. And personal worth here is defined in terms of the degree to which a person is considered worthy of our attention: that is, of having his or her needs listened to, taken seriously, and met in everyday situations, especially in times of crisis (Herman and Chomsky, 1988). These political-economies of relationship reflect the reasons or justifications we proffer to legitimate our hierarchies, our classification systems, and our definitions of superior/inferior. And they, as well, specify, in our current market political-economy, the most cost-effective actions we should take to produce the best payoff for ourselves in the competitive struggle in support of these conceptual and social arrangements. Once our personal political-economy is set in motion, we develop a working sense of what we expect of others, what we believe they expect of us, and how much we think we should charge them for our efforts and talents relative to what they mean to us or to what they have done for us. Of course, such decisions may be influenced by our feelings about what these others have charged us in the past. So an important maxim when harms and felt injustices occur might be: "You made me suffer a loss (of this degree of seriousness) and now, to you, I will do likewise," because you have by your actions come to deserve this loss and because such a responsive action is necessary to preserve (in this example) the deserts-basis of our relative competitive positions in the hierarchy.

Deserts-based Justice

In accord with the principles of a deserts-based perspective, many people believe that personal and collective well-being are best served when personal ambition and personal gain are fostered. When it comes to income, for example, it is believed that whatever people earn through their actions, developed talents, and effort, they deserve to keep. Justice is done when a person's income reflects her or his contributions and efforts. This also means, however, that when someone fails to contribute, contributes very little, or fails to achieve in an endeavor, as we indicated at the outset, he or she deserves whatever pain, loss, burden, or punishment that derives from his or her ineffective, misguided, or harmful actions and efforts. Justice is done when available benefits and burdens are distributed in proportion to what someone has done to merit them (Lane, 1986; Miller, 1976).

When it comes to issues of power and control in personal relationships, a deserts-based political-economy of life translates into the belief that the person who has obtained a higher social position because of his or her achievements deserves to participate in daily affairs in proportion to that position's earned privileges. Let us imagine that we have a family composed of two parents and two young children, and that this family operates according to a deserts-based social ethic. Let us also assert that the mother makes $60,000 a year and the father $40,000, and that neither child contributes financial resources to the family's collective wealth. Deserts-based thinking (simplified for illustration purposes) would have it that each person deserves to participate in decisions about the family's use of its resources and in other matters affecting the family according to the level of each person's earnings and financial contribution. Personal worth, participation in family decision-making processes, and ultimately one's power would be commensurate with each person's contribution.

In this illustration, since the children make no financial contribution to the family, they are not expected to, or allowed to, participate in the family's economic decision-making processes. They learn not to expect to participate, not to have voice, and are accorded little or no access to the family's wealth except at that level of access determined by the family's contribution-deserving superiors. In principle, the person who owns or contributes the most money or other prevailing currency is expected to have and is likely to have the greatest say in how the family is organized and run, how needs will be defined, whose needs are defined as legitimate and satisfied, in what order, and with how much of the family's resources. In the family's collective narrative, the "deserving" power-holder's story will count most, her or his account of life will prevail, and he/she will make the rules for the subordinates/inferiors to follow. With the degree of allowable participation of some being defined by others, participation by those over whom power is exercised – those believed deserving of being subjected to power – will be limited to that of an observer, a spectator or voyeur of one's life. Those family members whose lives are lived through the experiences of those who exercise power over them, experience "mental alienation; a permanent reduction of the self to a condition of tutelage, as in minors or madmen" (Brown,

1966:117). With one's voice constantly muted, a sense of one's true self is negated, and gradually a person begins to believe that she or he is not merely a deserved subordinate, but, in fact, a deserved inferior who has limited needs or needs that are not worthy of serious consideration by others. Of course, in our illustrative family, in our current societal context, the power of the highest financial contributor, the holder of this deserved, achieved position, the mother, is likely to be challenged if she or her partner, or both, also believe in ascriptive rights-based ideas of justice that might here manifest themselves in male superiority and patriarchy.

In such a mixed deserts-based and rights-based political-economy, in the family, the school, the workplace, and in the society generally, those with the greater contributions of wealth and resources or ascriptive authority in effect whittle down the human dimensions of others to a size that fits within their organization's profit or ideological margins. Some of us, therefore, are forced to pay a price in our daily lives because of our lesser, imposed, deserts-based status or rights-based position, as we are passively expected to and forced to pick up the bill for others. After all, this is our deserved obligation or our ascriptive fate. It is easy to say that those who hold positions of power, those successful in the exercise of power, deserve to be rewarded for what they do for others or to others, but most of us pay this price out of fear that our well-being will be lessened further or, when we clamor for an equal voice, of having that voice or life taken away altogether (Chomsky, 2000).

When it comes to responding to a harm situation within this kind of economy, the intention of those who live according to such arrangements and values is to impose a counter-loss upon the person responsible for the harm because this person *deserves* that loss. His or her actions threaten existing deserts arrangements. Since deserts-based justice has to do with equalizing unequal situations, it is believed that this equalization can be best achieved through the equalization of loss, through the creation of equal ill-being. Only through the imposition of a counter-debt can the original debt be paid. Paradoxically, only through the imposition of a counter-debt will the "believed to be just" pattern of interaction that has been violated, be restored.

When a child takes money from his or her mother's purse without her permission and that the child does not deserve to take, a counter-debt is extracted to restore the mother's rights to deny access to her purse and the resources within it – her personal private property rights. The counter-debt lets the child know that property rights and distributions are to be upheld even if they prevent the child's needs from being met. The mother has a right to this money and to deny access because of her ascribed position of mother (rights-based), or she has an expectation that this money will not be taken as she has acted to deserve this money and therefore to deny others access to it (deserts-based).

When a child hits a sibling, a counter-debt is believed to be required or deserved (perhaps in kind as most U.S. parents claim) to restore the right of the person hit to deny others access to his or her physical person, his or her autonomy. And even if the in-kind hitting perpetuates the cycle of hitting, harm, or violence, it serves notice as to the legitimacy of a parent's right or deserved privilege to exercise a pattern of parental power and control – parental hierarchy. Whether or not the hit affects either child's behavior, it serves to let each child know who is "in power" and who has the right to hit others whether they deserve it (deserts-based) or not (rights-based). It tells the children that power-based relationships are acceptable and that violence or hitting is acceptable, but only by those who can successfully claim a right to hit. And it tells the children that these power arrangements are to be reestablished if and when parental rules are violated. One should note in this scenario that the conflict between the children is neither responded to nor inquired about. What lies at the root of this child hitting her/his sibling? Why is there no attempt to respond to the needs of each child? Here one could claim that neither the needs of either child, nor the roots of the conflict that led one of the siblings to hit the other, are the real issues as perceived and acted upon by the parent. The real issue appears to be reestablishing the family's hierarchical power arrangements, rather than attending to the roots of the harm or the needs of either of the children.

We should note here, as well, that in our view no child deserves to be hit by a sibling or parent, nor does anyone ever deserve to be hit. One should also note, following deserts-based logic, that the hurt sibling's needs are interjected by the parent, rather than being voiced by the child and thereby known to the parent. And because the hurt child has not acted so as to deserve the parent's attention, no attention was paid. Only the person who has harmed has acted so as to deserve a response from the parent. We can see why, then, that those who undertake retributive justice processes pay little attention to the *victim* and her/his needs and have focused almost exclusively on the acting, and therefore, deserving, *offender*. Acting to meet the needs of the *victim* is not a worthy enterprise, for this person has not acted to deserve our attention. Moreover, attending to this person's needs does not necessarily preserve or restore the arrangements, deserved privileges, or rights that were violated by the harm. This understanding gives us solid insight as to why the needs of victims are largely ignored, especially in court-adjudicated processes, and why the real needs of the offender are not of great concern either. The core response in retributive justice processes is focused on reasserting the rightness or correctness of the social arrangements in the society – the distributions – and their idea base.

When we examine the ramifications of this kind of political-economy, it is not surprising that the possibility of achieving a justice that fosters personal healing and need-meeting is almost always thwarted because deserts-based and rights-based retributive actions destroy human presence. They shut people down. They are personally deconstructive (Denzin, 1984; Scarry, 1985; Tifft, 1993), and produce a kind of non-presence. Those subjected to the violence of power are forced to sacrifice their true self, voice, energies, and talents to pay for the satisfaction of the power-wielder and the social arrangements for which the power-wielder acts as a representative. And, again, we have to keep in mind that this power-wielder might be a parent, teacher, physician, employer, or supervisor. As well, this power-wielder may be an agent of the state or a corporate decision maker. Deficit-creating acts can and do occur in all spheres of our lives (Tifft, 1993; Chomsky, 1994a).

As we have seen, sometimes these processes occur in very subtle ways, and even close familiarity with others at home, school, or work does not seem to diminish our ability to prefer our own social standing or interests to those of others, even when these others are suffering considerably. To give an illustration, during the winter of 1997, a woman who worked in an office of a New York State agency had to leave work early one day because she was having great difficulty breathing. When she returned to work the following day, she told her supervisor and co-workers that her chronic asthmatic condition had become quite aggravated because others in the office were wearing to work each day heavy fragrances in the form of colognes and perfumes. Sensitive to her suffering and needs, her supervisor called a meeting of everyone in the office to discuss this issue. During the meeting it was discovered that four or five others had also experienced adverse physical reactions to fragrances, some suffering migraine headaches on a fairly regular basis. To respond to the needs of these suffering persons, the supervisor suggested that maybe the office should be declared "fragrance-free."

Some co-workers were immediately sympathetic to the needs of their colleagues and agreed to declare the office "fragrance-free." They said that the health needs of those who were suffering (needs-based) should take precedence over other individuals' personal preferences for bodily enhancement. There were others at the meeting, however, who said that they did not wish to change the way things were, asserting that each person who worked in the office should have the free choice or the right to wear to work whatever fragrances he or she wanted (rights-based). In contrast to these persons' perspectives, there were still others who insisted that the issue was not a matter of individual freedoms or rights or individual health needs, but rather an issue of deserts. The latter claimed that, while it was unfortunate that some who worked in the office were suffering from others' use of perfume – and they agreed that those who were suffering had done nothing to deserve their headaches and aggravated asthma attacks – that the perfume users had worked in the agency for a long period of time and had put forth a great amount of energy and skill to attain a certain grade level and, therefore, deserved to wear whatever they wanted in the office (deserts-based): that is, they had by their past actions earned this privilege. This set of persons and those who asserted that they had a right to wear whatever they wanted at any time, in essence, believed that their feelings, freedoms, rights, and earned privileges – their political-economies of relationship – should take precedence over those of their co-workers who claimed to be harmed and, therefore, were "in need." After some very intense discussions, and faced with the consciousness that exercising one's earned privileges or one's personal rights would directly lead to significantly harming others with whom one must work and relate each day, everyone in the office eventually agreed to declare their common workplace "fragrance-free." A needs-based, face-to-face political-economy prevailed. We should also note that the supervisor did not, as she might have, exercise the power of her position to declare the workplace "fragrance free." And note, as well, that those who had worn the offending fragrances were not singled out as deserving to be admonished or punished or required to apologize to those who were harmed. The focus of the response moved to developing an understanding of the situation and each other's perspectives, and to a consensual decision making regarding the prevention of harm and suffering.

Even in the service industry, where the needs of the paying customer are said to be paramount, we can experience a similar insensitivity to the needs of those who are suffering. For example, when several of us were returning by train from the annual meeting of the American Society of Criminology in Toronto, we were seated in a "coach class" car designated for passengers traveling to Albany, New York. But, while seated and waiting for the train to depart, we moved to the next car, a "first class" car, because all of us had begun to smell sickening diesel fumes. We felt nauseous. And having told the conductor who was passing through the reason for our move, he said that he too smelled the fumes and that our move was fine with him.

However, shortly after we were situated in our new location, a second conductor came through and asked why we were not sitting in the Albany car. We told her about the fumes and how we had felt sick because of them. In response, she said that such fumes sometimes appear at the beginning of a trip but usually go away, and requested that we return to our designated car. We told her that we still did not feel well, and that we had informed her colleague why we were moving and that he said that that was fine. She said in a somewhat unbelieving manner, that she would ask him whether that was the case, that is, whether or not we had told him. She then made a further effort to get us to return to the Albany car. But we insisted that we were still not feeling well and that under no circumstances were we going to return. She said, "Well, if you are sick...."

What is interesting about this encounter is that, when we look at the possible range of responses available to the conductor to respond to the situation, she never asked how we felt. She never asked if she could do anything for us, to in some way respond to our feeling ill, to our needs. And she never inquired about the well-being of the other passengers who remained in the Albany car. Rather, her concern was how to get us to return to our proper place in accord with the value of the tickets we had purchased. Her concern was how to "reintegrate or resituate us offenders" to the conditions we deserved via our purchases, regardless of how deleterious (harms-producing) our place in the order of the train had become.

Needs-based Justice

From the deserts-based illustrations we have offered, we can see how difficult it is for someone to put a needs-based concept of justice into practice in her or his own life because doing so requires that one abandon the principal currency of our deserts-based and rights-based perspectives, namely, power – whether that power is derived from rights granted by authority of the state, or by the mechanisms of the market. When we examine what is required to embrace a restorative approach to justice, we see a political-economy in which the needs of all are met, but met as they are defined by each person. In needs-based social arrangements, it is believed that one should have access to resources and receive benefits in accord with one's needs, taking into account the resources of the community or collectivity (e.g., family or workgroup). It is the intention in needs-based justice to separate distribution from contribution – *from* each in accord with her/his desire, commitment, effort, and talents, *to* each in accord with her/his needs, taking into account the resources of the community. The principal concern of needs-based justice is encouraging the full development of each individual in accord with each individual's intelligible life plan and to simultaneously meet the needs of others so as to support the equal well-being of everyone at a satisfying level. In contrast to the self as position holder in rights-based societies, and self as atomized, self-interested actor in deserts-based political-economies, the self in a needs-based political-economy develops personhood, that is, a moral self that is welcoming of and inseparable from others. An intelligible life plan is any articulated developmental direction an individual chooses unless one can only satisfy one's needs at the expense of others (Miller, 1976:141). In the latter instance, the life-plan is not intelligible. Beyond needs being articulated by individuals in accord with their life-plans, it is important to attempt to state what might constitute a need. A person may have a need for glasses if she/he will be harmed by the lack of them, and to determine whether or not she/he will be harmed we must refer to her/his intelligible plan of life. If this person lives by reading (e.g., an author or teacher) or painting (e.g., an artist), and her/his eyesight is so impaired that she/he can hardly see the print on the page of a book or the differing colors of paint on a palette or canvas, then she/he has a need for glasses (Miller, 1976:138).

We can see why then a needs-based approach toward justice puts a great premium on the participation of everyone, and on the expression of the voice of each. If the well-being of everyone involved in a given social situation is going to be taken into account, the thoughts, ideas, and feelings of everyone involved must be listened to, taken seriously. In social arrangements structured for the satisfaction of the needs of all, the feelings, thoughts, sentiments, and needs of everyone involved are of paramount concern from the outset, structurally. Everyone feels that his or her present needs are being presented, acknowledged, respected, and met, and, therefore, feels justly "treated" (Kropotkin, 1924). When differences in need exist, for whatever reason, they are not dismissed, or homogenized, or sacrificed in the interest of a standardized format, but rather, are reconciled with one another so that there is a collaboration of all, and all involved feel equally responded to even if differentially responded to. The aim of needs-based, restorative justice is to respond to the unique needs of each person, and thereby achieve a level of "equal well-being" that expands the collective well-being of all (Kropotkin, 1924; Piercy, 1976).

Introducing needs-based justice into family life is sometimes very difficult because many parents (and many children agree) feel that they are not doing justice to each of their children unless they distribute their time, love, attention, and resources equally to each child, even when what is distributed may be less or more than what each child needs. So, if Mary receives $10, so must Quinn and Harry and Erin. If a parent spends an hour with Mary, so must he/she feel obligated to spend an hour of one-on-one-time with Quinn, Harry, and Erin. This is done because each child is perceived as equal in the rights-based sense of each holding the same social position – of being a child of the parents. Through this equal distribution they might have satisfied the rights requirements of equality of position holders, but not an equality of well-being. If the parents' values are vested in deserts-based ideas and arrangements, then they may feel that they are obligated to allocate their time, attention, and resources on the basis of whether or not a child has earned their attention. Mary may have had to wash dishes or take out the garbage to receive her $10 or to receive the hour of one-on-one time with her dad. Each child might earn these benefits in different ways, but nevertheless, if attention, love, material goods, television viewing time, or any other benefit is to be received, it must be earned. We imagine that in some families one can even earn benefits by not causing trouble, by following the rules, and by being good.

For a needs-based contrast, let us consider a situation in a family where there are three children and, for simplicity's sake, that each needs a writing implement for school. One says she needs a good fountain pen, another a laptop computer, and the third, a few pencils. Clearly, there are great differential costs in the items requested and each reflects different life plans in learning at school in accord with their differing ages and development. The fountain pen might cost $30, the computer $600, and a pack of pencils only a few dollars. If each of the children were provided with what she or he said was needed regardless of the cost, each of the children will feel that her or his needs have been met; each will feel that justice has been done, for each will feel a level of well-being that is equal to that of her or his siblings. Here, we see needs-based justice as reaching, not equal distribution, but an equality of well-being. Clearly, within families that operate according to a needs-based economy, parents can respond to, provide for, support, and show love for each of the children in quite different ways, with quite different resources, while still achieving justice and fostering the growth of each child, for each child feels that his or her uniqueness is being cherished.

We are suggesting that by attempting to meet needs and achieve equal well-being, we are not vitiating the requirements of equality, because a needs-based conception of justice "does not demand that each person receive the same physical treatment, rather that each person should be treated in such a way that [she/he] achieves the same level of well-being as every other" (Miller, 1976:149). As we have shown in the illustration of the distribution of writing implements, it means that "physical resources such as food, medicine, and education should not be assigned in equal quantities to each [person], but in different proportions to different people, according to their peculiar…[stated needs]" (Miller, 1976:149).

To further explore needs-based justice processes and arrangements, let us return to our sibling/parent hitting illustration. In a family attempting to live in accord with needs-based justice, the parent would intervene to stop the hitting, separate the children, and ask each of them for their version of what was going on – what led the one child to hit the other. Each child is responded to with dignity and respect, taken seriously, listened to, and asked if they could think of other ways that s/he might have responded to the conflict rather than by hitting – other ways that they might respond if this or a similar conflict arises in the future. Then, each might be asked what the roots of the argument were and what needs were not being met such that they became upset or angry with one another, if that was the situation. And they might be asked what their current needs are and how these might be met. They might also be asked to problem-solve with the parent as a participant, as perhaps a guiding collaborator in the discussion, to find ways to meet everyone's needs, including hers. Please note that there is no reason for the parent to hit the child who has hit her/his sibling; no reason to extract an apology (though one might emerge spontaneously) so that forgiveness is earned; no need to inflict a counter-harm, and no need to assert parental hierarchy, as the children themselves are likely to present creative ways of addressing their differences.

Clearly, such a view of justice and the practices it requires to achieve personal well-being differs radically from those of deserts-based and rights-based justice. In the former, needs are responded to according to the efforts, developed talents, and achievements or failures of the person, and in the latter according to one's social position in the family hierarchy or one's social location as established by state law (Tifft and Sullivan, 2000).

Needs-based Justice and Restorative Justice

When we speak of the intention of justice as achieving equal well-being, then, we see the great potential that restorative justice demonstrates. Proponents of restorative justice know that justice cannot be *done by* someone or *administered to* someone. Rather, as in family group conferencing, circle sentencing, victim-offender reconciliation pro-grams, and other forms of restorative justice at their best, it can be created, developed, or emerge only when all involved in the given situation are participants taking the opportunity to *collaborate* in justice-making processes. This means that each of those involved in the situation be given an opportunity to tell their stories (Baumeister et al., 1990), which might include not only the specifics about the harm in question, but also the structural dimensions that lie at the root of the harm (Dyke, 2000; Mika, 1989). But this will not be possible unless the stories of each person involved in a harm situation are taken seriously and viewed as authentic, which means that efforts are made to meet the needs of all the persons who have told their stories. Only then can all the participants in the process feel that justice has been done.

And, it is important to reiterate that the restorative aspect of justice does not mean simply responding to harms and injustices that have already been done so as to meet the needs of all involved, but, as well, striving to create patterns of interaction among us all that take into account the needs of all from the very outset, structurally. As indicated, by stipulating the essential nature of this structural requirement for justice-done, proponents of restorative justice raise considerable issue not only with how interpersonal harms are responded to – that is, via vengeful, punishing means – but also with power-based social arrangements and hierarchically-ordered relationships that by definition deny the possibility of the satisfaction of the needs of all (Sullivan and Tifft, 1998).

And even when we see the value in and seek ways to implement needs-based, restorative justice when a harm has been done, we find ourselves up against some grave cultural barriers. Within the context of the growing market economy, many seem to have become confused about what a need is and what process a person must engage in to determine what his or her needs are. One result of this is, for example, that we have come to accept as needs whatever professionals of all types have indicated we must have for our well-being, whether that well-being be defined in terms of health, knowledge, salvation, or bodily enjoyment (Sullivan, 1980). Consequently, what we have come to define as a human or personal need "is the individual offprint of a professional pattern; it is a plastic-foam replica of the mold in which professionals cast their staples... The good citizen is one who imputes standardized needs to himself [sic] with such conviction that he [sic] drowns out any desire for alternatives, much less for the renunciation of needs" (Illich, 1977:31).

But this does not mean that we reject needs as the basis for restoring severed relationships and for preventing relationships from becoming severed in the first place. "Need is essential as the basis for human economics, for it is that dimension of self or being that gives a person his or her uniqueness or difference – bodily, emotionally, [spiritually], and intellectually. It is through our needs, their recognition, expression, and satisfaction or denial, that we come to create, to be who we are" (Sullivan, 1980:147). It is through the understanding, expression, and satisfaction of what our true needs are that, "we are most fully a part of the human [species]. Need 'qualifies' us, not [rights], [social position], wealth, or certification ribbons" (ibid.).

When we speak of equality of well-being as a goal or an endpoint for defining justice, we are not suggesting that some state of finality will be achieved, for justice defined according to these terms is a dualistic process. We are always engaged in responding to a continually changing state of unequal well-being (Tifft, 1978). It is a process of presenting and listening to the other, of understanding, respecting and reconciling divergent realities and truths. Hence, justice-done restoratively requires that participants continually remain open to each other's concerns, ideas, needs, feelings, desires, pain and suffering, so that each can see the other, not as a resource to be used or exploited or as an object to be derided or scorned, but as he or she is, similar to oneself, a person engaged in an unending struggle to become human, with dignity (Tifft and Sullivan, 1980; Burnside and Baker, 1994). And just as a person expressing himself or herself does not remain static but is modified by engaging in such a shared venture, so too is the community of listeners simultaneously modified because the concerns at hand are now mutual. When such collaboration takes place, we experience the beginnings of a restorative community, of a political-economy of peace and democracy (Pepinsky, 1995). Some would argue, and we would agree, that such a sense of justice resides at the core of moral development (Coles, 1997; Brazelton, 1982; 1992; Kropotkin, 1968; Tifft et al., 1997), and that this is the quality by which each of us reveals his or her essential being to the world (Pieper, 1966).

But, as we have seen, others assert that we show our essential being to the world and meet our needs best through the accumulation and exercise of power. To the contrary, we suggest that power is a form of violence and that, while it might enhance the well-being of those who rely on it, it does, in fact, destroy the well-being of others and the possibility of their needs being met. It will serve us well, at this point therefore, to examine power as a form of violence and how it vitiates the possibility of doing justice restoratively.

CHAPTER SIX.
The Violence of Power and Restorative Justice

As we explore the requirements for doing justice as equal well-being, a justice that is needs-based and restorative, it becomes readily apparent that a justice concerned with personal healing and reconciliation cannot be achieved in the face of violence. That is, it cannot be achieved when we interact with others and dismiss their personhood while doing so. When we look for a definition of what constitutes violence, we see today that most people are willing to acknowledge that most, if not all, forms of intentional physical injury to another constitute violence and are the kind of violence that is destructive of human well-being. This is the kind of violence we usually associate with what occurs "on the street," one person punching another in the face and taking their wallet, or a person stabbing another at 3 a.m. outside a tavern in a poorly lighted neighborhood. This is the type of violence we see most frequently presented as crime on television news and entertainment programs (Welch, 2003). But the problem with limiting our definition of violence almost exclusively to interpersonal harm of this sort is that we fail to take into account the forms of violence that David Gil has described as "social structural" in nature (Gil, 1996, 1999; Galtung, 1969, 1976). Social-structural violence is a different kind of violence from interpersonal violence and yet it is similar in that it too constitutes an exercise of power over others. Social-structural violence refers to all the violence that derives from the way we organize our primary social relationships, for example: how we organize family life to care for and pass on our culture to our children; how decisions that affect everyone's life in the society are made; how we organize the work that needs to be done; and how we distribute the product of this work. Each of us can think of examples of harms and injuries that derive from any of these specific patterns of interaction that allow some to thrive and benefit at the expense of others. These patterns are given currency in social arrangements in which the well-being of some is defined as less important than that of others, so that their needs are dismissed as unimportant or minimized while others who control the process receive far more than they need (Gil, 1996).

In our current deserts-based, market economy it is not surprising that many, if not most, of us are unaccustomed to viewing the use of power in our relationships with others – interpersonal or structural – as a form of violence, much less an act of injustice. A social ethic prevails in this economy which states that the achievement of human well-being (whether we define it as success or happiness or whatever) is dependent on the constant exercise of power over others. This is manifested in the accumulation and investiture of private wealth as well as in the creation and maintenance of hierarchical relationships that define and reinforce the relative worth of some over that of others. This ethic promotes the needs-satisfaction of some at the expense of others, while enforcing differential conceptions of human value, worth, and well-being through a variety of modes of discipline and punishment. We are talking about a "worth war," a type of culture war.

By including the exercise of power in our typology of violence, we can see how each of us might grow a bit edgy and want to deflect attention away from examining its effects, because within our current social arrangements we all are consigned to share in its use to some degree or other. To acknowledge that power-based acts are a form of violence is tantamount to pointing a finger at ourselves as power-wielders, as a source of violence and harm. Yet, when we continue to hold in high esteem and adopt as the most cost-effective means for securing our needs-satisfaction acts that force others into lesser or deficit status through minimizing their personhood, only with great difficulty can we assert that we ourselves are "beyond incrimination" (Kennedy, 1970). And, we are forced to admit that this kind of violence has a great deal to do with our actions as parents, teachers, hospital administrators, corporate officers, and judges (Pepinsky, 1995). It begins to manifest itself whenever we deny others their voice and active participation in decisions that affect their lives, and ultimately finds itself giving life to the kinds of crime and harm we see committed "in the streets." These harms emanate from our violent economic structures. For example, young men who live in the ghettos or barrios of the U.S. find few legitimate jobs available to them and most of these jobs pay low wages, do not include benefit packages, are sometimes dangerous, and are frequently temporary. They are structurally anxiety-producing because their holders live in constant fear of being laid off. These quasi-legitimate jobs oftentimes affront the job holder's dignity as well because of the violent manner in which the workplace is organized, one in which the worker is rarely permitted to use or develop his or her talents. In contrast, illegitimate economic work is often readily available, pays relatively well, allows one to live large at least momentarily, often carries a low risk of arrest, is only sometimes dangerous, and receives a great amount of peer respect (Gordon, 1973). Facing such structural economic choices, is it any surprise that some young men decide to engage in drug dealing, theft, burglaries, and other "street" economic harms? Were we to face these personal choice circumstances, what would our choices be and what relational structures would buffer us from not choosing illegal economic activities to earn the money we need even to live small?

The revered co-founder of the Catholic Worker Movement, Dorothy Day, was acutely aware of the dilemmas each of us faces daily because our lives are so intertwined with power-based structures and processes designed to deny well-being to others. But while Day might point to our complicity in such violence, she always emphasized that our focus should be less on making judgments about particular individuals than on the structural nature of the violence, on "the *system* under which we live and with which we admit that we ourselves compromise daily in many small ways" (Ellsberg, 1983:295). She was interested in how we might change social-structural conditions so that we might create a society in which, as co-founder of the Catholic Worker Movement, Peter Maurin, used to say, "it is easier for people to be good."

Of course, rather than examine the ways we ourselves make such compromises, rather than engage in what some have described as a power-reflexive process (Pfohl, 1994), our tendency is to focus our eyes "out there," to identify the on-the-street others as the real perpetrators or offenders. We feel that they deserve surveillance, control, criminal justice processing, and punishment. By taking such a stance, we up the ante of violence because we now engage ourselves in the creation of scapegoat populations and clienteles in a deviant-identifying and corralling process that is essentially sadistic in nature (Gil, 1996; Pfohl, 1994; Sklar, 1994). In developing such a scapegoating perspective on harm production and harm correction, at first our ideological eyes focus on a particular individual or group. Then our physical eyes follow, excluding from view or minimizing the acts of those who are involved in the far more prevalent and oftentimes more serious structural harms that threaten our safety, security, health, well-being, and spirit (Reiman, 2003; Frank and Lynch, 1992; Tifft, 1982; Barstow, 2003). Is it not much less painful to cast a condemnatory finger personally, or even through "scientific" conceptions of what is criminal and violent, at a "mugger" who stuffs a sock into his victim's mouth and steals her purse in the night, than it is to examine the destructive effects of a managerial style we might employ or lend support to that frightens our co-workers or those we supervise, or are supposed to assist, into silent submission and, in so doing, robs them of their dignity, voice, and the riches of their talents? Is it not easier to point this finger at a "batterer" who screams in the face of and punches his wife in the mouth, than it is to examine the destructive effects of our everyday economic arrangements that fail to provide many "workers" with a safe workplace, a living wage, and access to affordable housing and healthcare, and that fail to meet the nutritional needs of one in four children in our society? These patterns of structural violence are generally taken for granted, accepted, viewed as necessary, and defended as not violence, though they are the kind of violence that Dorothy Day said, "we must try and wish to withdraw from as much as possible" (Ellsberg, 1983:295).

When we begin to look around and assess the actual and collateral damage of power-based acts and hierarchically-based social arrangements, we gain a vivid picture of the effects of such violence. When we live and force others to live according to the specifications of power-based existence, we fix their identities, giving them a master status or radically different character or human nature than ourselves. They thus become "muggers," "rapists," "murderers," "batterers," "addicts," and "workers" – moral inferiors, people highly different from you and us. As we set boundaries around the kind of persons they are permitted to become, we imprison their self potential. We force them to accept a definition of self, of personhood, of what it means to be human that is – unless they have fully accepted these "other" identities – radically different from how they down deep know themselves to be. Of course, as a user of power, we are unlikely to know the degree to which we are the source of such repression because the ethic we abide by does not require that we listen to the stories of pain and suffering of those subjected to power, except perhaps our own. Their stories (our stories?) of suffering and victimization are classified as not sufficiently valuable to be taken into account.

To aid ourselves in furthering our one-way-needs-satisfaction quest, we often create and maintain a propaganda system (or operate within a market-based ideological framework) that justifies the ordering of worth and accepts the needs of some as superior to those of others. For example, when commenting on why the Washington Post gave very little coverage to 2000 Presidential candidate, Ralph Nader, managing editor, Jackson Diehl, said: "We're not a public utility. We're a newspaper, and we cover things based on what is newsworthy. People who have a half percent or less following among the public are much less newsworthy than people with 40 and 50 percent" (Leon, 2000:16). This is a very telling story, especially when we translate it into needs-based language. The editor's statement implies that human worth, value, and dignity are dependent upon market or political value. The demands of a deserts-based, market economy dictate that certain conceptions of reality take precedence over the stories or points of view of millions of people struggling to deal with the pain and suffering inflicted on them because they are not market-worthy. Those who submit to the dictates of the market (and nation-state) seek to manufacture consent on the part of those subjected to power about the primacy of the needs of the power-wielder and, therefore, the power-wielder's right or legitimacy to use power to achieve his or her goals at their expense (Herman and Chomsky, 1988; Stauber and Rampton, 1995; Tifft and Markham, 1991). Within this consent-manufacturing process, power-wielders boldly define certain needs-denying, violent behaviors as acceptable for themselves, such as physical battering, spanking, creating intolerable or unsafe working conditions, executing people, and waging war. And when such patterned modes of violence no longer appear legitimate or profitable, these power-wielders substitute more benevolent modes of violence such as psychological or emotional battering, imprisonment, economic boycotts, and colonization. In other words, rather than abandon their commitment to structural violence to achieve their ends, those committed to power as a means to satisfy their needs will move their violent acts out of sight (indoors, behind walls, overseas), or transform them into more subtle or refined forms of hierarchic policy (temporary employment agencies) and control (surveillance cameras in schools) so that they might continue to manage the resources, energies, and talents of the less powerful (worthy) for their continuing advantage (Foucault, 1977; Wright, 2000).

So, for example, when the new owners of the Starrett-Lehigh Building in Manhattan turned a worn-out structure into a fashionable piece of real estate that attracted high-end tenants such as Hugo Boss, Ralph Lauren's Club Monaco, and Martha Stewart, the landlord "requested" that the owners of the Starrett Coffee Shop Restaurant, which had conducted business in the building for 40 years, overhaul the restaurant to make it aesthetically consistent with the new level of clientele. The owners of the coffee shop complied; they installed new Formica counters, revised the menu, and made other aesthetic changes in response to the building-owners' requests. But these changes were not deemed up to snuff by the building's owners, who proceeded to set up a coffee cart in the lobby near the restaurant to sell coffee and snacks, even though the coffee shop/restaurant's owners had a "sole-purveyor clause" in their lease. Forced to go to court to challenge the legality of the building owners' actions, the restaurant owners were left in the lurch, questioning whether the scaffolding that girded the front of the building and blocked daylight from entering the coffee shop/restaurant was not erected to harass them. The wife of one of the restaurant owners said that, when her son celebrated his ninth birthday, his birthday-wish was that, "... the landlord would stop harassing my parents" (Gopnik, 2000:68). It is important to keep in mind that, whether power is exercised through harassing actions, the guillotine, a carceral archipelago, "lean and mean" managerial strategies, power-based teaching methods, or authoritarian parenting, the power-wielding individuals who carry out their roles within hierarchical, power-rewarding institutions continually assess the extent to which their disciplining, deconstructing, punishing, and confining acts are profitable to their interests, rather than assessing how such acts affect the well-being of others (Tifft, 1994-95). The rationale for strategies conceptualized and subsequently implemented can be boiled down to a political-economy of rationally-calculated credits and debits, surplus enhancement for "self," scarcity creation for others, more for me, less for you. Clearly, such a rationale and the practices it generates and defends are not restorative in nature; they are personally destructive and humanly deconstructive.

This means then that, as proponents of restorative justice who desire to respond to all harm situations in a needs-meeting way, we are committed to examining all forms of violence and power, all ideologies, perspectives, practices, and social arrangements that in any way force others into positions of lesser being, into deficit status, and that generally disallow others' needs to be taken into account. It also means that we are no longer willing to single out and define as harmful the violent and power-based acts of some, especially the acts of those differently situated or situated lower on the hierarchical scales, but to examine and accept our own complicity in the use of power, interpersonally as well as through the social arrangements we create, help to support, and assent to participate in.

Before moving on we wish to reiterate for emphasis that, by defining power-based acts and needs-denying hierarchical structures as forms of violence, we are not striving for dramatic effect. When power is manifested in the social arrangements we create and assent to be part of, it is every bit as violent as acts of interpersonal or street violence because, by denying the voice and precluding the participation of others, power-exercise destroys human presence. It eats away at the human spirit in the same way that acts of violence on the street do (Sullivan and Tifft, 1998a, 1998c; Gil, 1987; Proudhon, 1888). But, a major difference is that the effects of structural or institutional power exercise are oftentimes ideologically masked, incremental, slow to appear, and indirect, and so are more easily disassociated and unreflectively accommodated. But such effects increasingly manifest themselves in devastating counterviolence as we have seen in the student violence at Columbine and other schools, and in the death of a

12-year old student in Meriden, Connecticut who hanged him-self because his schoolmates bullied him to death while adults did little to intervene (Santora, 2002; Stowe, 2002). Whether power is exercised in the family, the school, places of worship, or the workplace, many people's lives are reduced to submit-ting to power-wielders, to obedience, to carrying out orders, and to completing packaged assignments (Kierkegaard, 1941; Rogers, 1961, 1980). As we will see in the following chapter, such a view has extensive ramifications for how we define crime and social harm and how we respond to these modes of violence.

Power-based Identities

We have already alluded to some of the negative effects of structural violence on personal growth and development, but more needs to be said about how most, if not all of us respond when we become the objects of such violence. To survive eco-nomically, emotionally, and even physically in person-dismissing, person-degrading arrangements, we begin to en-gage in a process of identity-editing and self-falsification. This entails the steady dismantling of what we believe is our au-thentic self and, in its stead, the construction of an alias self, an alien or alienated self, a meta-identity, through which we come to live an abstracted, disembodied existence, someone else's life. We can understand why, under such conditions, so many people hate to go to work or school or spend time at home with their family. The possibility of living a life of au-thenticity, of dignity, and mutual respect in such environments is virtually nonexistent. There is little hope of getting to or keeping in touch with that core part of ourselves where we have a strong and clear sense of who we truly are and through which we are enabled to connect with others in enjoyable ways. And since, under the influence of power, we exist as only very select parts of our true self, and others exist as only very select parts of their true selves, we live out relationships of partial selves. Understandably, trust in and commitment to others under such circumstances becomes most problematic because the only material we have to work with in our relationships are these partial selves, selves that play hide and seek in a continuous contest to outstrip the other, followed by masked retreat. By denying light to those dimensions of ourselves that we see as interfering with market-imposed standards of personhood, true enjoyment of life is vitiated from the outset (Brown, 1959). We consign ourselves to living morbid lives, for we are forever fearful that those dimensions of self that we repressed and keep hidden from view will burst forth and blow our cover, or worse, cause considerable harm to others. That is, we come to believe we are the Hobbesian dog that will eat the dog next door. At the same time, we are perpetually vigilant of those we keep down and fixed through power, for we fear that the dimensions of self they have been forced to hide from view will rear their heads, and like an army in the night, slay the dog next door.

What is most insidious about this dehumanizing self-editing, facade-maintaining process is that we come to believe that, by incrementally taking our life in the interest of having an enriched life, by dismantling our person piece by piece in the interest of one day becoming whole, we will achieve some fulfillment. On the contrary, those of us who "buy into" this process ultimately develop a self that negotiates the world without a voice or with a muted or pre-edited voice. We become dummies worked from behind by ventriloquists of power. We become structure-bound in the way we view ourselves and the world, and how we communicate our experiences to others (Rogers, 1961). Increasingly, we see the world in black and white, show less and less ability to differentiate personal meanings and, when we do, express such differentiations in only the crudest of terms.

As those in power, or in higher positions of power, see these hybridized forms of the human person emerge, they define them as belonging to a whole other category of being, a dangerous category at that (Shibutani, 1970; Asma, 2000). They also afford themselves the justifications needed for the further surveillance, control, and disciplining of their inferiors. As we know from the hierarchies we are a part of at work, in school, in our families, and in other areas of life, this demeaning drama is transferred from level to level so that a person's value or worth progressively diminishes the farther down the scale that she or he is situated. And since access to resources and rewards is allocated in proportion to one's ascribed or earned "scale index," the magnitude of one's power, voice, and worth and the volume of one's psychological and financial resources for those subject to the most intense forms of marginalization are all but eradicated. As they are, those in higher positions of power are reconfirmed in their original suppositions that these lesser beings do, in fact, belong to a whole other category of being, one whose members lack the credentials or capabilities to be deserving of the right to participate as an equal, indeed to participate at all. While ensuring that his or her own needs are met in the least costly ways, each higher-up affords him- or herself the final justification needed to disqualify the next lower-down from sharing in needs-defining, needs-satisfying processes. And should those excluded from participating in decisions that affect their lives begin to raise their voices in protest against those who produce their structurally-ignored needs, they are defined as "ignorant and meddlesome outsiders" who insidiously threaten personal/organizational/national security and, therefore, require additional doses of power-exercise, surveillance, discipline, and punishment (Chomsky, 1994b). As we have indicated in several ways already, power has an infinite number of ways of regenerating strategies and justifications for its continued existence, all to protect the status, prestige, and position of the power-wielder, the ownership and control of the power process, and privileged access to benefits that were and continue to be collectively-produced (Kropotkin, 1968).

Power-wielding Realities

How then are we to assess the difference between violence that produces bodily loss or damage on the street with violence which produces loss or damage to an individual's personhood, dignity, and true-self consciousness in the home, school, or office? This is a rhetorical question, of course, because the most basic elements of a justice that takes into account people's needs, a justice that seeks to foster an equality of well-being – that is, a justice that is restorative – are missing. These core elements of a truly restorative justice include: the opportunity to articulate one's needs; access to the processes that affect the satisfaction of one's needs; and the chance to participate in the evaluation of whether or not one's needs have been met, so that one can feel justly "treated" (Illich, 1977). And, as we have stated from the outset, the dismissal of another's personhood, which forces him or her into a deficit status, occurs not only in crime-related situations on the street but also whenever power is exercised. Moreover, the creation of such loss takes place in "punishment-related" situations as well when an individual, be that person a parent, a teacher, or a decision maker in the criminal justice system, uses punishment-violence as a way to deal with a prior act of harm (Gil, 1999).

We can better understand how punishment-violence is no different from crime-violence if we look at an instance of sexual assault. On an interpersonal level, an act of sexual assault, whether criminalized by law or not, is a good example of a deficit-creating interaction. In such an interaction, the power-wielder defines the beginning and the end of the encounter, as well as determining its content, taking only his needs or his unilaterally-defined agenda into account. The possibility of the other person participating in a way that she might have a say, might achieve an equal level of well-being, is ruled out from the outset. The brutalized "victim/survivor," no matter her mode of resistance, is forced to pay a price for the one-way needs-satisfaction of the power-wielder. The importance of her presence is dismissed, her voice is stifled, she is allowed no share in decisions that affect her well-being, her story is inconsequential.

When we look at intimate relations that are based in power, where one partner dominates and controls the other, we see the same kind of interaction and the same kind of effects. In such situations we might not always see physical violence, but power manifests itself in threat, coercion, and in the micromanagement of one person's life by another (Tifft, 1993). The partner subjected to power is denied an authentic reality, a personhood of her own edited construction. What she has to say is belittled and ridiculed; her needs, if considered at all, are viewed as inconsequential. Decisions are made in her behalf as the dominant partner rations out the family's resources as though managing the needs-meeting of a person with a severe disability. Though the relatively intimate and physical context of this interaction may differ from that of the sexual assault mentioned above, similar harmful conditions and effects are present. The importance of her participation is not acknowledged, indeed dismissed outright; her voice, her story, is silenced; she is allowed no part in decisions that affect who she is or wishes to be.

And, as we mentioned earlier, acts of correction as punishment-violence fit into this same genre of person-deconstructing behavior. The needs of the punishing individual or position holder (e.g., parent, teacher, judge, corrections officer), regardless of the justifications offered for the use of the punishment, take precedence over the well-being of those punished. The needs of the person being corrected are deemed inconsequential: his or her story is deemed unworthy of a hearing; active participation is withheld; voice is muffled; and decision making is preempted. The conditions for healing and restoration are absent. The conclusion we are led to draw is that any time we see the exercise of power, whether it manifests itself in the raw violence of the person who rapes, in the power-based acts of a dominating parent, intimate, or boss, or in the punishing, corrective acts of the state, the intention of the power-wielder is to have someone else pay for their needs-satisfaction or for fulfilling the needs of the elites for whom they act as representatives (Pence, 1983, 1987, 1989).

So we begin and end here with the axiom that the full participation of each person in the life s/he lives (regardless of their status) is essential for both individual development and the collective well-being of the community. It is essential for the development of personhood since we become persons only when we actively participate in the construction of self, a self created in non-power-based relations and structural arrangements. And communities evolve successfully in proportion to the number of persons they contain, people who cherish voice, participation, and needs-meeting (Kropotkin, 1924). Within the context of power, the opposite reality is propagated, reinforced, and rewarded, based on the patently false premise that, when everyone is involved, life becomes chaotic, nothing gets done, and people act like the rabble that elites always thought they were (Chomsky, 1994a). When the threat of power and ensuing economic sanctions pressure us to "buy into" this ideology, we soon accept voicelessness and non-participation as a means to human well-being, or at least the most cost-effective way to accomplish things. And, sooner or later, we come to believe that this way of living is natural, part of human nature, the way it has always been, the way it must be forever. And thus, we consign our personhood to oblivion before it ever begins on its journey. This is an age-old struggle that has very early roots. When we look at the seasonal ceremonies of the earliest civilizations, before there were priests and magicians, before the hierarchy of kingships became a part of the community's structure, we see such ceremonies performed collectively by the community as a whole. Everybody sang and everybody danced. Then, over time "the tendency [grew] to concentrate [collective knowledge and desired qualities] in a single individual who is [then] taken to personify and epitomize the entire group... Consequently all the things which were previously done by the group as a whole in order to ensure and maintain its existence, [soon tended] to be done representatively by the king" (Gaster, 1961:48). And so the king's story – and now in history, the story of the market elite and the state or their representatives – becomes the official story, the story that prevails. As we have discussed throughout this chapter, this move toward the concentration of power, toward the centralization of decision making and the usurpation of voice, has grave implications for the degree of needs-meeting we are capable of and for the restorative ways of life we can now achieve with each other. However, we have also seen that these trends have given rise to the development of new and different and vibrant forms of collective, restorative life.

CHAPTER SEVEN.
Postulates on Responding to Crime and Social Harm

Once we recognize that there is an integral connection between social-structural harms and interpersonal harms, we find ourselves faced with an ethical or moral choice. For us the choice has been in the direction of creating and implementing social distributions, social policies, and social processes that are structurally preventive of crime and social harm, and that are restorative when these crimes and harms occur. That is, we are committed to creating and implementing social arrangements that embody equality and a concern for both individual and collective well-being. This leads us, in turn, to embrace a set of postulates that clarifies for us what a restorative response to crime and social harm is. The first is that we have a collective responsibility for responding to actions that harm others because we have created the social distributions, policies, and conditions within which these persons have been harmed and within which others have chosen to harm them. And the second is that we have a collective responsibility to act restoratively to meet the needs of all the persons involved, those harmed, those responsible for the harm, and all of us collectively. Furthermore, when a pattern of similar harms develops, we have a collective responsibility to create new social distributions, social policies, and social arrangements that better meet both individual and collective needs, thus preventing social situations from arising in which needs are not taken into account (Tifft, 2000). To create some assurance that these response postulates are clearly understood, we have selected several kinds of social harms by way of illustration and to suggest ways that we might respond to each restoratively.

Socially Injurious Economic Relationships

When corporate decision makers decide to produce and distribute a known-to-be-harmful product in the interest of profit and market share (e.g., the Dalkon Shield, Ford Pinto, Bridgestone tires, Vioxx, asbestos), we have a collective responsibility to respond, for these actions have led persons to lose their lives, their children's lives, their procreative potentialities, their positive self-identities, and their full physical and spiritual capacities. We have a responsibility to respond in order to make it clear that these decisions and their effects are clearly unacceptable, were preventable, and must not continue. Furthermore, we have a collective responsibility to see that those harmed directly and indirectly have their needs met. And, if one of these needs is to meet with those who have harmed them, then such a restorative conference should be arranged. Moreover, we have a responsibility to restoratively respond to those who have made these harmful decisions, to help them understand the grave consequences of their decisions, to accept individual and corporate responsibility for their actions and the effects of these actions, and to meet their needs so that they begin to live differently, to make things right, and are far less likely to repeat such harms. Additionally, we have a collective responsibility to change corporate and regulatory arrangements so as to prevent the production and distribution of harmful products. If we do not collectively respond, we are making a strong statement that it is acceptable for those who knowingly produce and distribute harmful products to take the lives and thwart the needs and potentialities of others. And, if we do not take the responsibility to change the arrangements of production/distribution – which are highly non-transparent and undemocratic – to prevent such social harms, we are stating that these arrangements are acceptable, and that the lives, potentialities, talents, health, safety, and freedom of those who have been harmed by the use of these products are not worth protecting or preserving. Moreover, we would be stating that it is acceptable to leave the nexus of these production-of-harms relationships intact with the knowledge that in the future there will be similarly produced grave social harms because we have left these production-of-harms relations unchanged.

A problem for many who teach and study criminology, criminal justice, and even restorative justice is that the kinds of inquiries we are talking about are deemed to be beyond the pale of their disciplines. That is, when these issues are raised, people say, "This is not criminology," or "That has nothing to do with criminal justice," or, "The proper domain of restorative justice has nothing to do with structural issues, only interpersonal harms." This is especially true when the harms in question occur in workplaces that are seen as producing "legitimate" products and even needed services. Some of these production/distribution/management systems in some cases are structurally violent, in others criminal, and in nearly every case non-restorative. In Chapter One we spoke briefly about the management "style" of a plumbing company that resulted in the death of at least two of its employees, but it was behavior that the federal government refused to see as willfully neglectful of workers' needs (their lives) (Barstow, 2003). In a three-part investigative series on the production of death and accidents in the workplace for the New York Times, David Barstow and Lowell Bergman (2003a, 2003b, 2003c) focused on operations in the McWane, Inc. pipe manufacturing plants across the country. In these plants, from 1995 to late 2002 the reporters found that at least nine workers had died from what they determined to be preventable causes. And during that same period, the company's 5,000 workers suffered more than 4,600 injuries. In addition, McWane had been cited for more than 400 federal health and safety violations for that period, more than their six major competitors combined (Barstow and Bergman, 2003a, 2003b, 2003c). How are we to characterize this corporation when in some instances it blamed workers who suffered serious injuries as malingerers while the fault actually lay in the way the workplace was structured?

In the first edition of this book, we pointed to the managerial style of at least one asbestos manufacturing plant in which the company's officials withheld information from workers who had contracted asbestosis, a disease caused by breathing asbestos fibers and which if untreated is frequently fatal (Epstein, 1980; Brodeur, 1974). Far from taking into account the needs of workers to know about real threats to their longevity, the medical officer in one of the company's plants explained that the men who has contracted the disease were not told "for it is felt that as long as the man feels well, is happy at home and at work, and his physical condition remains good, nothing should be said...it is felt that he should not be told of his condition so that he can live and work in peace and the Company can benefit by his many years of experience" (Epstein, 1980:157).

In an effort to ferret out other instances of harm and injury through managerial violence, Wall Street Journal reporter Tony Horwitz (1994) signed on to work in several poultry processing plants in the United States. Once inside he saw that the technology in these plants consigned large numbers of workers to what he described as "a Dickensian time warp, laboring not just for meager wages, but also under dehumanized and often dangerous conditions" (Horwitz, 1994:A3). Automation and automation-appropriate management styles had created for the poultry processing workers not freedom from backbreaking drudgery but "a new and insidious toil...work that is faster than ever before, subject to Orwellian control and electronic surveillance, and reduced to limited tasks that are numbingly repetitive, potentially crippling, and stripped of any meaningful skills or the chance to develop them" (Horwitz, 1994:A3). In some of the plants that were investigated, workers who were new to the job were apprised of the hazardous chemicals they were exposed to only in lip-service fashion, as if their health and future earning capacity for their families did not matter. In one plant, Horwitz discovered the rigorous enforcement of a rule that forbade workers from walking off the line to relieve themselves. Indeed, when they did so, it was considered a voluntary quit. At a Pilgrim's Pride plant, unexcused bathroom trips were punishable by a three-day suspension. One result of such conditions was that some workers had been forced to urinate on themselves because they were unable to locate a foreperson to ask for permission to leave the processing line (Horwitz, 1994).

In this same plant, the processing line had been sped up over the past 15 years from under 60 chickens a minute to the government-allowable rate of 91 per minute. With the line moving at this speed, workers in the cut-up department at a B.C. Rogers plant had to lift five-pound boxes at a rate of 12 boxes or more per minute into larger boxes, which were then lifted onto a conveyor belt. These workers wound up lifting 3,600 pounds an hour during an eight-hour shift. Horwitz (1994:A3) said the work process "was so fast-paced that it took on a zany chaos, with arms and boxes and poultry flying in every direction. At break times I would find fat globulates and blood speckling my glasses, bits of chicken caught in my collar, water and slime soaking my feet and ankles, and nicks covering my wrists."

Oftentimes, organizational climates and managerial styles that fail to take into account worker needs can be found implemented in companies that are recently bought or taken over. In a pet food plant in Topeka, Kansas, built by General Foods, workers had created "the longest-running employee-designed team-based factory in the United States" (Weisbord, 2004:444). It became famous in the industry for its low overhead and high worker productivity "driven by the people who did the work" (ibid.). When the company was sold, corporate policies were implemented that quickly dissolved the participatory work practices. That corporate executives saw after a while that they had made a mistake in dismantling a good thing was of little value because the company was sold again. This time the new owner H. J. Heinz Co., moved to "Heinz-ize" the operation, which meant shutting down half the plant, eliminating the team system, suspending funds for training that made the team system possible and cutting 150 jobs (Kleiner, 1996). Then Heinz, faced with declining productivity, restored training budgets and team meetings and self-management practices, finally acknowledging that the system that had been designed in Topeka had evolved to a much higher level than that in the company's other plants (Kleiner, 1996; Weisbord, 2004). What shall we say about these acts of imposed restructuring or transformation – designed primarily to create or maintain power and control and falsely cut costs – what are we to say about them when they destroyed loss of dignity, autonomy, self-confidence, emotional and physical health, and personhood?

For some, such workplace conditions might be considered an exception, and the acts and structures described as part of "other people's" lives. But for those of us who do not work in a factory, but in a government agency or school, we must ask whether we supervise and manage others in a way that muffles their voices, thereby excluding them from participating in decisions that affect their physical and emotional well-being. In any such workplace, the self that hangs on to pay the rent or send a child to college is willing to spend 40 hours a week, perhaps for 40 years, following orders without ever being asked to open its mouth with a creative thought. Dead before we die, we often take such a way of doing business for granted, see it as a necessary part of daily life, despite its violent and sometimes criminal nature (Niederland, 1968). And, as we have said, we all share collective responsibility for creating such products, workplace structures, and disabling managerial styles. We will discuss alternatives to this way of doing business in Chapter Nine.

Socially Injurious Intimate Relationships

When we look at the relationships in families, we see husbands developing managerial styles as if they were the CEO of a corporation and their spouse was a front-line worker, and parents developing styles that dismantle the competencies children have or desire to have as active participants of their family. Here we will focus on intimate relationships that are structurally violent, as when husbands decide to knowingly physically, psychologically, emotionally, sexually, or spiritually harm their wives by battering them. When these harms occur, we have a collective responsibility to respond. These acts, primarily motivated to create or maintain power, control, dominance, and superiority, lead to the women's loss of dignity, autonomy, self-confidence, emotional and physical health, and personhood. At the extreme, they lead to the deconstruction of self, to spiritual and physical death (Tifft, 1993). We must collectively respond to these actions in order to state that they are unacceptable and must not continue. We have a collective responsibility to meet the self-defined needs of those harmed directly and indirectly by these battering patterns, and if one of these needs is to meet with the person who has battered, we have a responsibility to arrange such a restorative conference. We also have a responsibility to those who have chosen to batter, to help them understand the effects of what they have done and why they have made these decisions; to help them take responsibility for the effects of their actions; and to help them take responsibility for understanding their behavior and for acting to change themselves and how they interact with others so as to better meet their own and others' needs. Moreover, we have a collective responsibility to change the cultural beliefs (e.g., women as inferiors, what it means to be a man/woman in our society [gender]), social distributions (sex inequality in opportunities and remuneration), public policies, and social arrangements (dominance and control, the use of violence) so as to prevent the production and distribution of these violent and harmful patterns of interaction. If we do not collectively respond, we are making the statement that it is acceptable for some persons to thwart the needs and potentialities of others, to disrespect them, to disallow their voices and presence, and to physically and spiritually injure them. If we do not take the responsibility to change these violent arrangements and beliefs so as to prevent such social harms, we are stating that these arrangements are acceptable, and that the lives, potentialities, needs, and freedoms of women are not worth protecting or preserving. We would be declaring that inequality, dominance, patriarchy, physical violence and control, marital rape, intimidation, social deprivation/isolation, and humiliation are the patterns of interaction we desire to preserve and pass on to the next generation.

COMPREHENSIVE RESTORATIVE RESPONSES

A comprehensive restorative response to crime and social harm naturally flows from the postulates stated above. Suggestively, it would be composed of the following features and concerns (Tifft, 2000):

1. *Survivor Needs*. Non-restorative responses to crimes and social harms, such as the production of harmful consumer products and battering, often pay little attention to the reasons these specific harms have come to be defined as unacceptable or as crimes. They are, as well, often almost exclusively offender-focused and provide very little support for those who have been harmed, substantially neither including them in the response processes nor addressing their needs. For that matter, ironically, most offender-focused, retributive responses fail to concern themselves with the "offender's" needs. They are, in truth, enacted primarily to legitimate the societal distributions involved and to reconstitute the rightness of the present-day distributions, values, and social arrangements, those sanctified in law. A needs-based restorative response requires us to ad-

dress the thwarted human needs, lost potentialities, lost senses of self-worth, lost freedoms, lost senses of trust, security, and health, and whatever other needs are specified by those harmed. We must reach out to meet the needs of the "victims/survivors" and those related to them who are indirectly harmed to meet their needs. We, all of us, are harmed, as well, for when one of us is harmed we are all harmed. We need to collectively reach out to ourselves in our different communities to better meet our needs for freedom, autonomy, and health and safety. When patterns of battering and the production/distribution of harmful products become far too frequent, become institutionalized patterns that jeopardize our lives, health, freedom, and well-being, we must respond to change these patterns of living.

2. *Prevention.* Often our collective responses do not contain a proactive, needs-based, primary prevention, public health, social structural/before-the-act prevention component. When this prevention component is missing, the prevalence of the undesired behavior or pattern is unlikely to be altered. Prevention strategies require that we address alternative social arrangements and cultural value changes that might decrease the prevalence of these harms/crimes. What needs-based social arrangements are we going to create such that our production/distribution arrangements no longer produce harmful products, harmful production processes (that harm workers and the environment), and harmful distributions (that produce poverty)? If the root of the production/distribution of harmful products is identified as the tyrannical nature of our arrangements of production, in that a small number of elite decision makers make these decisions without public participation or oversight, then we must seek to democratize these decision-making processes and make them transparent. If the root lies in the relationship between private ownership of the means of production/distribution and ineffective or collusive public regulatory oversight, then these arrangements and the relation-

ships among them must be changed. If the Food and Drug Administration relies exclusively on the pharmaceutical industry for its scientific evidence regarding the safety of food or drugs, and the agency has dismantled its capacity to conduct independent research or require the undertaking of scientifically credible research projects, then this situation needs to be drastically altered. If, there needs to be citizen oversight of corporate investment, production, and distribution decisions, then perhaps there ought to be consumer advocates or public representatives on corporate decision-making bodies. Or, as some would argue, there ought to be a wholesale dismantling of corporate tyranny, replaced by federations of democratically organized co-operative production and distributive organizations.

Similarly, how are we going to meet the needs of everyone such that battering is no longer a prevalent pattern of interaction among intimates? As stated above, the roots of battering lie in relating hierarchically, in patriarchy, in societal inequalities between men and women, in the dictum of getting into power and controlling others, and in the cultural acceptance of violence and female inferiority. Battering is about freedom, autonomy, and well-being. Beyond developing restorative justice responses for meeting the needs of those enveloped in "battering relationships," we need to develop coordinated community responses that reach out to expose children and adults to known ways of relating that are non-hierarchical and non-violent. We need to teach children and adults that differences, injustices, and conflicts can be addressed and temporarily "resolved" in a number of different manners that embody and foster human dignity and respect. We need to demonstrate to others that it is possible to relate as intimates on the basis of equality, but that this involves organizing family/intimate life differently (Sullivan and Tifft, 2004). We also need to begin to organize the worlds of work and learning differently to support participatory decision making, and egalitarian, violence-free, healthy relationships.

3. *Legitimating Just Social Arrangements.* The preceding section clearly raises questions concerning the social arrangements/distributions and cultural values that are being upheld through our collective responses. Collective responses always uphold an order and are organized to secure a specific set of relationships, beliefs, and desired ways of living. Whether or not the collective response is restorative, we need to know exactly what social arrangements and distributions are being defined as legitimate or just, and what values and beliefs are being fostered by these responses. We need to inquire whether or not either the response or the arrangements upheld constitute crimes or harms. We would argue, for example, that collective responses or omissions that have upheld slavery, apartheid, preemptive war, colonial occupation, marital rape, battering, ethnic cleansing, and cultural genocide, and those that uphold political-economic arrangements that consign people to death, despair, and poverty, are themselves crimes and socially injurious. We would argue that imprisoning those who harm others, or holding a "restorative conference" and reintegrating "offenders" and "victims" to social conditions such as those listed above, would be socially injurious. A conference that reintegrated those bound up in battering to a relationship without physical violence, but that is nevertheless patriarchal, autocratic, and gender-based, would in our vision not constitute a restorative justice response.

4. *Enacting Just Collective Responses.* Proposed collective responses to those who have harmed others, such as court-ordered treatment or physical confinement, may themselves be social harms or crimes. If we return to the illustrations given above (i.e., interaction patterns among intimates that yield battering and economic relationships that yield socially harmful products), these harms were defined as actions or arrangements that physically and spiritually injure, and/or thwart the needs, development, potentiality, health, and dignity of others.

From a needs-based perspective, we need to propose and develop responses that are not themselves harms. Those harmed ought not to be further victimized by our collective response, by being ignored, cooled-out, or re-victimized in their inclusion and participation in our response. Those who have harmed need to be provided with support and the opportunity to understand the harms they have "caused," to take responsibility to enter a dialogue concerning the "victim's/survivor's" feelings and needs, and to help create an altered personal relationship if there was a prior relationship. They need to be helped to accept personal responsibility for self-change and to address their own needs (Zehr and Mika, 1998). Applying these ideas to present-day state responses, we need to inquire whether or not, for example, capital punishment, stark and structurally violent prison living conditions, or excessively long prison confinements fit the definition of "crime" and the reasons given for defining acts as "socially injurious." If these responses meet these definitions or criteria, they are themselves violent harms and social injuries, and are therefore, unacceptable. Asking questions similar to those asked in the prior section, what cultural values are embodied or fostered by our response, for example, to "murder" or "homicide"? Do our current responses communicate that life is precious and sacred? Or, do they communicate that life is not sacred and that an individual life is expendable or acceptably utilized to send a message that the state will respond to life-taking with life-taking. Similar questions must be asked of the conditions of incarceration, electronic monitoring, coerced rehabilitation, and restorative conferencing.

5. *Response Correspondence.* Our current-day collective responses are often substantively unrelated to the nature of the social harm and non-responsive to the nature of the larger structural and cultural contexts within which the decision to harm others was made. Moreover, our "why" explanations or "cause" understandings are usually out of sync or have nothing

to do with the substantive nature of the response. For example, incarceration of the decision makers in our harmful product distribution illustration addresses neither the immediate and long-run trust, safety, health, support, and security needs of those specifically harmed, nor our needs as a community to be reasonably sure that others in similar corporate circumstances will not make similarly injurious decisions. Furthermore, an incarceration response to corporate harms or to battering not only fails to address the collective responsibility issues discussed above, it dodges the necessity for changing the social arrangements and cultural structures that "foster," "produce," or "encourage" these choices. Requiring corporate decision makers or those who have battered to participate in "community service" for a certain number of hours (e.g., working in a soup kitchen or nursing home or doing charity work for a community agency) has no substantive connection with either the specific motivation for the harm – for knowingly distributing harmful products or battering (e.g., corporate market share and profit position preservation; exercising dominance and control) – or with the specific nature of these crimes.

As we have already discussed what we see as a reasonable and restorative response to harmful product production-/distribution and battering, let us briefly select a different, more common, economic, street crime – a bus stop robbery of an elderly man by a much younger man – to illustrate what we would see as a positive restorative response. A needs-based response to this bus stop robbery would entail meeting the elderly man's needs for the restoration of trust, the return of his possessions, and perhaps his need to have a restorative conference on his timeline with his attacker to make sense of the incident, to learn why he was selected as the person to be robbed, to allay his fears of being attacked again, to understand what brought his attacker to commit this robbery, to recognize the person who attacked him as human, and to meet his other self-defined needs. It would, as well, involve meeting the "offender's" needs with regard to his reasons for committing the offense. If, for example, he suffered from depression and had also been recently unemployed because the factory where he had worked closed as his work was outsourced to India, we should provide him with occupational retraining and/or work placement in a different factory where the work is neither harmfully organized nor disrespectful of his or others' human dignity. We should aid him to obtain help for his mental sufferings and a chance to meet with the elderly man he harmed so that he might better grasp why and how his behavior was highly unacceptable, why we are responding to his harm, and why he ought to take clearer responsibility for his decision and not repeat it. We should also provide him with the knowledge of realistic alternative responses to his life situation when he feels depressed and if he were to again lose his job. Our restorative response should, as well, address the manner in which employment/unemployment is organized so that unemployment is always only temporary. We should make sure that there is timely notification for impending plant closings and unemployment decision implementations, and we should take the collective responsibility to provide support groups, advisors, and work finders when such circumstances arise. In the short run, there should be full employment with a living wage and the provision of health care and retirement benefits such that the economic basis for economic crimes is greatly diminished. In the long run we must create demonstration projects and organize for totally different, democratic, investment/production/distribution arrangements that far more thoroughly meet our individual and collective needs and far more thoroughly foster restorative justice values.

CHAPTER EIGHT.
The Personal Foundations of
Restorative Justice

Because restorative justice programs seek to meet the unique needs of each person who participates in their healing, reconciliatory processes, those who wish to embrace restorative justice principles as a way to respond to harm must feel at home with social arrangements that are structurally inclusive and that foster the expression of voice, rather than dismiss or muffle it. In the first place, such arrangements do not penalize someone for being in need, but rather regard each person's expression of need as a core part of human growth and development. Psychotherapists, poets, and mystics alike have demonstrated convincingly that we clarify who we are to ourselves and to the world at large through our understanding and expression of our needs (Dupont, 1995; Levertov, 1992; Underhill, 1918). And though the narrative process that promotes such clarification and expression is humanly and personally fulfilling, the unearthing of self that is part of this narrative is invariably painful because it involves the restructuring of self and of our relationships. This is especially true when the narrative process has been set in motion to respond to a harm situation: to free the person harmed from the emotional paralysis that victimhood brings, to enable the person responsible for the harm to acknowledge what was done and show remorse.

When a community's social arrangements are set up to take the narratives of its members seriously – narratives which are always and integrally connected to needs – they restore personhood, facilitate personal initiative, and help de-

velop human competencies (Kropotkin, 1902). And when relationships suffer a breakdown in such a community, the mechanics are already in existence for helping people to be restored. This is true whether we are talking about severed relationships in the family, the school, the workplace, or within the
society as a whole. We saw the restorative process at work in
South Africa, when South Africans established the Truth and
Reconciliation Commission to hear the stories related to their
violent past so that they might unify themselves through the
restoration of the dignity and personhood of all South Africans.
When a community – and again we can say the same for a family, a school, places of work, and the society we live in – is
structured to promote the expression of feelings, an articula-
tion of needs, and the participation of people in the decisions
made to satisfy those needs, personal life develops, or under
adverse circumstances, is restored (Macmurray, 1961). People
feel more connected to each other and are, therefore, less likely
to treat each other exploitatively because they are less likely to
see one another as abstractions, that is, as an objects or com-
modities to be used to serve the interests of power. And that
power might be exercised for reasons of self, the state, the
market, religion, or any social institution that refuses to recognize the centrality of needs. As might be expected, because of
its needs-expressing, needs-meeting imperative, restorative
justice always has to do with dissolving power and confronting
its diverse manifestations. Of course, in the case of the "corrections" component of the criminal justice system, we have already discussed power's manifestation in the form of punishment violence.

We can see that adopting a needs-based restorative perspective on justice, which includes making a commitment to its
practices, does not occur without a transformation in our lives
– oftentimes a significant transformation. That is, it requires a
radical reframing or restructuring of our conception of self and
other, and not just in the abstract, as an idea, but in our political-economy of relationship, that is, in how we feel and think

about others, how we behave toward them, and how we make decisions about them – all of which is intertwined with how inclusive we are toward others. And our inclusivity index always boils down to who we define as having value or worth in relation to ourselves. Hence we must understand how the self we are is intertwined with power.

Constructing Self and Other

Since restorative justice seeks to meet the needs of all involved in its healing processes, those who wish to adopt its principles must first confront the self, that consciousness that hierarchically ranks some people over others and treats the categories created by such rankings as if they were a fact of human nature and inevitable (Sullivan and Tifft, 2004). When we engage in this process, as Norman Brown (1966:142) said, we engage in uncovering "the principle of union, or communion, buried beneath the surface separations, the surface declarations of independence, the surface signs of private property, [so as to uncover] the pathology of the process whereby the normal sense of being a self separate from the external world [others] was constructed." That is, we must get beneath surface distinctions and categories; get beyond the notion (which is indeed a great stumbling block for us all) that says that the definition and satisfaction of my needs is not related to the definition and satisfaction of yours. This is true generally in everyday life, but it is especially true when we are dealing with someone who has harmed us or, looking at it from the other side of the table, someone we have harmed. At the most radical or root level, this means getting beneath the feelings of vengeance, rage, hate, or retribution that a person who has been harmed experiences. It means getting beneath the feelings of hostility, denial, self-protection, blaming the victim, and disengagement that a person who has harmed another experiences. Part of the restorative process entails healing a deep fissure that leads us to refuse to recognize who and what is other in us and that "[t]here is a continual 'unconscious' wandering of other personalities [selves] into ourselves" (Money-Kyrle, 1951:51). That is, we are the other; this is that (Beckett, 1959).

An essential part of the uncovering process we have been talking about also includes getting beneath the justifications we use to claim our privileged status, and to define and enforce our being, our existence, as superior to or more worthy than that of others. What each of us needs to find out is what is the origin and purpose of this hierarchical ordering. What does it do for us since, through such justifications, we not only create a void within ourselves but also create distance between ourselves and others. We develop less of a stake in their well-being, and we close our eyes to the violence that this hierarchical ordering and its subsequent distancing or disengagement give rise to. To claim that *my* story is *the* story of record, and to satisfy my needs without taking into consideration those of others, is indeed very powerful, self-defense-mechanism business, Cain and Abel business, doing the other in for whatever happens to be the *raison du jour*. But in order to dismantle this self-power complex we must simultaneously see how our participation in the compensation/rewards/benefits (distributive justice) system that the power-based self clings to, helps ease the pain we experience when we engage in deficit-creation for others and surplus enhancement for ourselves. And it cannot be denied that such pain exists for, whenever we engage in such warfare, at a certain level of being we know that we are doing violence to others (and ourselves), and experience a heavy guilt for doing so, so much so that we are driven to novo-caine ourselves in a multitude of different ways to deaden its effects. We mentioned a few of these ways earlier.

As might already be evident, no one can hope to achieve a transformation in this orientation toward self and others and in one's perspective on needs, human well-being, and justice simply by reforming or reordering the power-based self through conventional methods, that is, by dressing up the self in a new set of therapeutic or ideological clothes. The power-based self welcomes such veneer transformations ad infinitum because they never touch its core impulses, drives, or governing principles, which are the source of violence. If we wish to make a commitment to restorative justice, to creating a just community in which restorative justice is a cornerstone, we must make a commitment to not reforming but dissolving this power-based self, for, as Norman Brown (1966:149) says: "to have a self is to have enemies, and to be a self is to be at war (the war of every man [sic] against every man). To abolish war, therefore, is to abolish the self; and the war to end war is total war; to have no more enemies, or self." We must get rid of the self that views its existence as property, as real estate, that is owned and whose value fluctuates with the market, promoting the illusion that, "I am my own(ed) self."

In his seminal work, *Discipline and Punish* (1977), the late French psychiatrist, Michel Foucault, examined in great detail the various processes or mechanisms that power-based (punishment violence) social arrangements create and rely on to enforce or reinforce distinctions in "personalities" which, though they offer ego satisfactions, are deadly in the effect they have on one's true self and the true-selves of others. These distinctions serve the function of promoting personal and group superiority or sovereignty of personhood which, in turn, creates hordes of victims along the way. On a geopolitical level, these kinds of distinctions manifest themselves in the nation-state, whose purpose is to distinguish its value from that of others so that it might claim superiority (sovereignty) and then the resources to enforce that superiority (through war, or if that is not profitable, through colonization or state-corporate empire).

Of course, in the eyes of the power-based self that defines its value and the value of others according to the standards and specifications of sovereignty, whether that of the market or the state, a mandate that calls for its dissolution or radical transformation is seen as madness (Brown, 1959). It's tantamount to unilateral disarmament. But, to adhere to the principles of restorative justice requires that one has to not only give up on power as the means to achieve one's ends, but also to give up on ends that are rooted in power. This requires us to abandon living according to the merits-based and rights-based conceptions of social life we spoke about earlier. It means that anyone who is interested in beginning upon the path of abolishing the self as a weapon in the interest of creating restorative relationships or a restorative community and finding happiness, must of necessity enter into a kind of dark night of the soul. To begin to understand how we might enter upon such a journey and withstand the ordeals that it brings (Campbell, 1972; Konner et al., 1988), we might turn to those who seek and have sought to confront our "investment" in a self as an "illusory, separate, and substantial identity." In other words, we might turn to "those [who have been and are] willing to discard [self]" (Brown, 1966:145-146). We have seen (in Chapter One) how Bud Welch, after his daughter was murdered, went through this process and, having come out the other side, was able to embrace Bill McVeigh, and help both McVeigh and himself heal from the tragic losses they experienced.

Transforming the Power-based Self

To find other examples or demonstration projects of the transformation process we are talking about, we can turn to the lives of the mystics of east and west. It is they who best exemplify this journey of discarding self, of transforming the power-based self from the ground up. Indeed, the calling in life of these men and women is to peel away the layers of the power-based self so as to allow those parts of their true self that were once cordoned off, repressed, and marginalized – when they acceded to live according to an ethic of power – to see the light of day (Dürckheim, 1991). They have shown that only by entering into such a process can a person's entire being flourish and one's real self emerge and one find happiness. It is to this process of unfolding that psychotherapist Carl Rogers dedicated his life, by telling the stories of his patients, who said they wished to be freed of the façades they lived behind, facades that their power-based selves created and relied on for self-protection and exploitation of others. Throughout his writings, Rogers (1961, 1980) also recounted the fears people experienced when they gave themselves up to this process. They feared engaging in this unearthing, this archaeology of self, because they feared they would reach a point of being where the self they encountered would be out of control, would go crazy. The dilemma for his patients, for all of us, is that unless we engage this process we will never realize what we seek most or need most in life, what the Danish philosopher Soren Kierkegaard (1941:29) described as "to be that self which one truly is."

The continuing irony in this process is that this true self, this restored self, is a being, a consciousness, of peace and gentleness. It is not out of control, crazy, or monstrous, and it is not the source of the Hobbesian rabble as some have erroneously asserted (Huxley, 1894). But it is "subtle, sparkling, bright, dazzling, glorious, and radiantly awesome like a mirage moving across a landscape in springtime" (Evans-Wentz, 1960:104). In terms of the political-economy of relationship, this transformed self seeks to devote its energies, not to doting on its every whim and fancy, but to taking into account, and helping to meet, the needs of others, to assuaging human pain and suffering. This is what Buddhists mean when they speak of people who seek to become Bodhisattvas to reach this enlightened, true-self state and take the Bodhisattva vow: "However innumerable sentient beings are, I vow to save them./ However inexhaustible the defilements are, I vow to extinguish them./ However immeasurable the *dharmas* are, I vow to master them./ However incomparable enlightenment is, I vow to attain it" (Govinda, 1967:44-48). The core of this vow is relieving the pain and suffering of all sentient beings.

In the face of a harm-done, this self seeks to create a forum in which the stories of those who have suffered loss can emerge, in which those who have suffered can define their needs, and ultimately have their needs met, that is, be restored to their true, and forever-transformed, self. At the highest level, this transformed self is moved to live among others in a way that it no longer seeks something in return for its efforts for it holds no one in debt. A political-economy of reciprocity, and the psychological accounting system that goes along with it, never enters into the equation: *self-enjoyment for the enjoyment of others is the enjoyment of self* (Underhill, 1918; Kropotkin, 1924). In this way, the hold of the deserts-based and rights-based political economies we spoke about in Chapter Five are rendered insignificant.

Those who have committed themselves to the process of confronting their infatuation with power speak of this dissolution process in terms of self-surrender, of a stripping away of self, an emptying of self. It is not uncommon for those men and women who engage and experience this process to reach a point in their development where they can exclaim, "Naught I am, naught I have, naught I lack." This kind of exclamation reflects the highest level of consciousness when one's self-enjoyment is mutually intertwined with others' enjoyment, but lest it appear as a too-far-out and unattainable goal, we need to point out that we all experience this new ground of being to some degree when we take into account the needs of others as our own, when we choose in certain situations to serve them. As indicated earlier, this process of transformation, of examining and dislodging the justifications for treating others as less than one's self, for inflicting loss on them (charging them) in the satisfaction of our own needs, is fraught with great pain, loss, and suffering (Underhill, 1918). A large part of this pain derives from taking an inventory of our self-satisfaction measures and looking at the effect they are having on others. But when we engage in this process with honesty, we develop a sympathy for our ailing self that required so much armament, character armor, for its continuation. We are moved to forgive ourselves for what we have done to ourselves (essentially holding our true selves hostage), and through this process of acknowledgment and remorse are moved to act similarly toward others. We practice not what we preach but what we have experienced and know.

But again, for those who seek to create just relationships and communities and to commit themselves to realizing a sense of justice where the well-being of all is taken into account (justice as equal well-being), such pain and loss are deemed of no account when examined in relation to the personal well-being and community of human concern that is created. By confronting the power-based self directly and the harmful acts this self generates, seekers of restorative community free themselves not only from engaging in acts of punishing self-repression, but also from looking at others in a condescending manner, from measuring themselves in relation to others and for giving preference to their own needs over those of others (Pfeiffer, 1941; Tauler, 1909). In other words, the fundamental fear that we all experience, the fear that there will not be enough to go around and that one's self will dissolve and lose its grip on reality/life, is transformed into a consciousness whose energies allow a person to be present and available to others. The rationale for embracing power-based means for survival is seen for what it is: a violent ruse to maintain one's privileged position among others.

Self-criticism: Self-transformation

But we need to point out that the struggle to dissolve the power-based self is not a once-and-for-all-time event. Aspirants must make a commitment to open the self up to continuous inner scrutiny so that they might gain a continuing assessment of their residual commitment to power and its corollary, disregard for or disengagement from the needs of others. Historically, in religious orders and intentional communities, this process of self-assessment has been regarded as so integrally connected to living a life of justice within community that periods of time were set aside each day for an aspirant to assess his or her growth and well-being as a person. In some monastic communities this process is known as the "examination of conscience" (Jaeger, 1959). Times were set aside each day for the aspirant to look inward and assess progress, and, within the best of circumstances, to do so in a non-neurotic way. The reasoning behind this exercise was that the aspirant, by looking into the self, might "see himself [sic] constantly as God sees him, and to judge himself at every moment, considering not only his actions but also their motives and indeed his inmost desires and thoughts in light of that fear of the Lord which is the beginning of wisdom" (Merton, 1961b:159). In terms of the political-economy of relationship, the aspirant who is the beneficiary of such wisdom recognizes the fundamental value of each person, not in terms of his or her achievements or in terms of his or her position as an equal before the law, but because of each person's needs and the recognition that each person's well-being depends upon how much these needs are taken seriously by others. In practice, it is a move to expend one's available energies in the service of others, rather than centralize or concentrate energies in a self designed for garnering privilege and status and for developing self-satisfying power coalitions (Quinney, 1991).

Those who embrace this process of emptying the self are acutely aware of the devious means the power-based self has at its command to deflect the value of assessment and transformation as it refuses to own up to its infatuation with force and violence and with enchanting others into its service. For centuries, therefore, those who strove to create restorative practices and just communities have taken part in some form of a communal, corrective process, which allows them to open themselves up to the entire community so that the power-based self has no place to hide. In some institutions this reconciliatory process was known as the "Chapter of Faults." In the Oneida community, which flourished during the mid-19th century in New York State, members of the community practiced "mutual criticism." On the one hand, they saw this conferencing process as taking "the place of backbiting in ordinary society" and, on the other, as "the greatest means of improvement and fellowship" (Nordhoff, 1993:289).

Through this process of mutual criticism, community members offered each other feedback. A community member would go before a committee of six or twelve people who were "best acquainted" with the person, or in other instances, before the entire community, to hear what people had to say about them. In the more formal exercises of religious communities, members might kneel with arms outstretched and publicly confess before the community all their faults. And, then, lest the individual be sparing in his or her accounting of the deeds that required attention, after he or she confessed all known faults, members of the community were given an opportunity to supplement what the aspiring holy person missed or excluded. Each member of the community who wished could stand up and tell his brother or sister about a behavior that the community member regarded as sinful, power-based, punishing, self-referencing, or non-restorative. When this process of criticism/self-criticism was finished, the suppliant would ask the community's forgiveness for any harm that his or her deeds had caused any one of them or the community as a whole, and begin upon a period of self-reflection and personal reassessment. We are talking about a process that includes acknowledgment, apology, and forgiveness.

These processes of reconciliatory, restorative criticism/self-criticism are highly formal in nature and have their own list of substantial shortcomings. Some who offered feedback to another did so not to advance that other person's well-being or advantage but their own, and accomplished this through a dismissive mean-spiritedness. The reason that these more formal examples of feedback, criticism, and personal assessment are valuable is that they are forms by which a person, within the context of supportive relationships, might begin to open up to all his or her inner dimensions to others and be restored (Horney, 1942). As we have pointed out elsewhere, this is not an easy process. First of all, when we initially hear about or recognize a new facet of ourselves, we tend to reject it. Our transformed voice seems strange to us; we are as unfamiliar with the new part of our own story as others are. But, when we live among others who are accepting and willing to hear us out, we tentatively accept these new dimensions in earnest (Rogers, 1961). We have begun the process of restoration, of true-self discovery, or more accurately stated, true-self construction.

When we accept this process of radical transformation as part of our lives, indeed embrace it for its restorative essence, we increase our capacity to open up to the larger world which, on the political-economic level, means identifying with the needs and struggles of others. The struggles of people in South Africa, Northern Ireland, Rwanda, Burundi, Iraq, and elsewhere to free themselves of violence become our struggle as well. The struggles of those in our own families, our local schools, our places of work, and in our social hierarchies, become our struggle as well. The more we are able to accept our own hidden dimensions, the closer we come to seeing our own true nature, the more we learn to transfer ourselves "from a centre of self-activity into an organ of revelation of universal being, and to live a life for and oneness with, the larger life outside" (Starbuck, 1901:47). This is indeed a transformative process, for we are less driven to impose our story, our beliefs, and our ways of life on others or to transform them into who we think they ought to be. When an acceptance of self and others begins to take place, we have established a foundation that will enable us to reconcile with each other and to achieve a justice that is restorative when things go awry. We can then achieve equal well-being for all involved because we have a basis for understanding who we and everyone else is.

Behind the Mask of Self

The late-19th and early-20th century German philosopher, Gustav Landauer, saw the integral connection between our inner world and the world around us. He saw that "the deeper we climb down into the tunnels of our individual life, all the more are we in a real community with the race, humanity, the animal world, and finally, if we withdraw from conceptual thoughts and sensate appearances and sink into our most hidden depths, we are participants in the whole unending world. For this world lives in us, it is our origin, that is, it is continuously working in us; otherwise we cease to be what we are. The deepest part of our individual selves is that which is most universal" (Landauer, 1929:59-60; see also Lunn, 1973:132). This is the paradox of paradoxes in that, as we approach the deepest level of our inner being, we discover a self, become a self that is inextricably intertwined with others (Macmurray, 1933). And we develop an awareness that it was always that way, our power-based consciousness having blocked its realization. David Spangler (*Community Directory*, 1995:36) saw this and pointed out that, "Community is not something that is created when people come together and live together, rather it is something that is preexistent and we can awaken to it. There is never a time when we are not in community, and our practice is to awaken to that experience of communion."

The realization of this primordial sense of community, or connectedness of all sentient beings to life and one another which Spangler is alluding to, is made possible because of the way the process of stripping ourselves of power works on the imagination. Through the selfless presence that the unveiling process fosters, the aspirant's imagination projects the more whole self into the life circumstances of others so as to experience on a feeling level how those others experience life, and then to incorporate the concerns of these others into one's own life. The boundaries between inside and outside, between self and other, disintegrate as we come to realize, or experience that "reality is not things...in simple location. Reality is energy or instinct" (Brown, 1966:155). It is this energy which flows through us all by which we are connected to each other so that we ask: "You and I, are we not the same?... Sometimes I cannot tell myself from other people. It seemed to me as though I no longer existed in my own person alone, as though I were one with the all" (Brown, 1966:160).

But it is the imagination that first awakens this deeper and inescapable sense of connectedness in us. As psychoanalyst Melanie Klein (1964:66) says: "In the depths of the mind, the urge to make people happy is linked with a strong feeling of responsibility and concern for them, which manifests itself in genuine sympathy with other people and in the ability to understand them, as they are and as they feel." But we should emphasize that the life of the imagination and the sympathy or empathy with others it brings is not part of a "let's pretend" game, the way some people view imagination. The imagination is a real and active force in effecting transformation in ourselves and in how we go about creating a future. As the American poet William Carlos Williams (1970:120) commented: "the imagination is an actual force comparable to electricity or steam, it is not a plaything but a power that has been used from the first to raise understanding."

In his study of mutual aid as a factor in the successful evolution of both the animal and human species, Peter Kropotkin found much evidence of how the imagination, once activated, helps us to restructure our lives. He saw that the more enlivened a person's imagination is, "the better you can picture to yourself what any being feels when it is made to suffer, and the more intense and delicate will your moral sense be. The more you are drawn to put yourself in the place of the other person, the more you feel the pain inflicted upon him [sic], the insult offered him, the injustice of which he is a victim, the more will you be urged to act so that you may prevent the pain, insult, or injustice" (1968:95). In other words, the active imagination, when it is based in the kind of ground of being that is afforded by, or is, the true-self, the positive, non-power-based self, opens the self up to the possibility of radical, structural change. In terms of what we've been talking about in this book, it's the self opening up to meeting the needs of others (Kropotkin, 1970:30). The co-founder of the Catholic Worker movement, Dorothy Day, who experienced this change in every pore of her being, said that it comes through the kind of "solitude and hunger and weariness of spirit" that we alluded to earlier. During her first days of solitary confinement in jail, her perceptions, her feeling structure, had been transformed to the point that, as she says (Day, 1970:9): "I suffered not only my own sorrow but the sorrows of those about me. I was no longer myself. I was man [sic]. I was no longer a young girl, part of a radical movement seeking justice for those oppressed. I was the oppressed. I was that drug addict, screaming and tossing in her cell, beating her head against the wall. I was that shoplifter who for rebellion was sentenced to solitary. I was that woman who had killed her children, who had murdered her lover." A connection with others at this level of identity is both restorative and reparative in nature and surely a foundation for love.

The Wealth of Restorative Justice

As we can see, such a transformative experience within ourselves and in our relationships with others is reflected in a radical change in the political-economy of relationship we live by, our social ethic. We live with a radically altered sense of worth – ours and that of others – which translates into the value we assign to all aspects of our lives: power, money, status, prestige, and wealth. We see the relationship between these entities and human enjoyment. On a very basic level, we come to understand the 19th-century philosopher John Ruskin's assessment of money, power, riches, and our drive to accumulate and possess more than we need. "What is really desired under the name of riches," Ruskin says, "is, essentially, power over men [sic]" (1903-1912, vol. XVII:44-45, 46). Such an insight suggests that wealth, defined as money, power, control, and surplus as opposed to enjoyment, leads to an impoverishment of self and our relationships with others, other life forms, and our natural environment. It fosters a neurosis that says that true connectedness with others can be achieved through power and by distancing ourselves or disengaging ourselves from others, and that self-worth and enjoyment can be enhanced by diminishing the lives, the enjoyment, and the worth of others. These are the beliefs of *Homo Economicus*. Heavily entangled in a money, power, surplus, status, prestige complex – in hierarchies – and knowing at one level the degree of devastation that embracing such a complex yields, this version of the human being must hide behind a mask of self. Unable or unwilling to acknowledge the harm he or she is doing and to show sincere remorse for these acts, this person forfeits the possibility of a restorative life. Restoration of others is impossible without self-restoration (Sullivan, 1980).

To accept the logic of *Homo Economicus* ("economic man"), and to simultaneously wish to embrace restorative principles in our lives, as we have said, casts us in a terrible bind. To escape this bind in the direction of a needs-based justice, we realize that we must adopt a political-economy of relationship based on some other definition of wealth and well-being than that immersed in deserts-based and rights-based distributive and participatory power relations. That is we must look upon wealth as energy expended in the growth and development of one another and in the restoration of each other when we fail one another (see Chapter Seven).

At a critical juncture in his life, the great 20th-century inventor, artist, and philosopher R. Buckminster Fuller discovered the true nature of wealth and how essential such wealth is for the successful evolution of the species, of the human community, everywhere. "Money is not wealth," Fuller concluded: "Wealth is the accomplished technological ability to protect, nurture, support, and accommodate all growful needs of life" (Fuller, 1981:xxvi). He was getting at the economic foundations of a needs-based society. And in such a society, we can measure how rich we are, personally and collectively, according to how we direct our life energy, our actions, technological and otherwise, to meet the needs of all people – in our families, our schools, our places of work, in the world. Anything less is a sham. And from our discussion thus far, we should all be attuned to the rash of justifications and consequences that emerge when we commit ourselves to other paths, for example, power paths. So, we already have the beginnings of a process of the examination of conscience.

Put into the context of narrative and restorative justice, the "technological ability to protect, nurture, support, and accommodate all growful needs of life" means that we begin with listening to the stories of others, not some, but all others. There will, for a time, be some people who do not have a right to have their stories told and heard, and there will, for awhile, be some people whose stories will be judged as not worthy of being told or heard, but both of these sets of persons, in order to become the selves they truly are, need to have their stories told and heard, and need to have the needs that are embodied in or derive from these stories met. Whether we choose to speak of a restorative community in terms of place, as a complex of relationships, or as an experience in which individuals make themselves available to each other in the interest of healing and self-enjoyment, that community, if it is to be called restorative and just, must be based in a political-economy that protects, nurtures, supports, and accommodates the growful needs of all (Mounier, 1971).

To embrace and to begin to live this kind of social ethic will require a kind of fearlessness because the personal and institutional social ethic of political and economic power runs contrary to it at every turn. The global corporate market, and the imperial nation-state configurations that protect and benefit from these power-based interests will seek to dismiss, muffle, or snuff out voices and narrative stories that run contrary to their developments. It was from an understanding of what we are up against in these social circumstances that led India's great poet and Nobel Laureate for Literature, Rabindranath Tagore (1861-1941) to write:

> Let me not pray to be sheltered from dangers
>
> but to be fearless in facing them.
>
> Let me not beg for the stilling of my pain
>
> but for the heart to conquer it.
>
> Let me not look for allies in life's battlefield
>
> but to be my own strength.
>
> Let me not crave in anxious fear to be saved
>
> but hope for patience to win my freedom.

CHAPTER NINE.
Restorative Justice as a Transformative Process

Although differences exist over where restorative justice had its beginnings and which restorative justice practices best foster healing when people are faced with the pain and suffering of harm, all of us who embrace the spirit of restorative justice agree that, at its core, restorative justice is a process that is concerned about meeting human needs. We also agree that it is a process of personal healing and human growth which is indiscriminate in its aims in that it seeks to meet the needs, not of some, but of all those who find themselves in a situation of harm. But we must keep in mind that restorative justice did not emerge as a singular correctional practice from the storehouse of corrections, but out of a political philosophy of relationship that says that people interact, develop, and live fully when their needs are voiced and taken seriously by others (Gil, 1999). That is, we develop our potentialities as human beings and enhance our collective well-being when our needs are respected, expressed, listened to, defined with care, and ultimately met (Kropotkin, 1968; Sullivan and Tifft, 2004). A major difficulty many societies are facing in our globalizing market economy is that many of the needs-based practices that prevailed in those societies and enabled them to evolve successfully are being torn from their infrastructure (Putnam, 1993). For example, as the globalizing empire of the United States, facilitated in part by global organizations such as the World Bank and the International Monetary Fund, intervenes in the lives of peoples and countries around the world to impose its brand of political, human well-being ("democracy"), it has also imposed its ethic of deserts-based capitalism and its concomitants: exploitation, commodification, surveillance, and retributive punishment.

As we indicated earlier, when we raise the possibility of establishing a restorative, needs-based economy among friends, family members, and students, a sizeable portion of people in these groups regard such ideas with skepticism at best, a larger portion, as madness. Needs-based values are largely absent from their lives, so it is difficult for them to see how restorative justice could be of any value to "correct" harm situations in the community, let alone serve as a guide for organizing their lives. Hence, we have come to rely on the tail to wag the dog in that we must rely on restorative justice, not only to help people in pain and suffering heal from a harm done, but also to re-educate ourselves, the human community, about how a needs-based way of life helps people develop and mature as persons as well helps societies to evolve. Our interest here, of course, is in looking for ways to apply restorative justice principles to our everyday lives, to reintroduce needs-based polities and economies (Zion, 1998). Some have spoken of this move as an effort to create or restore ourselves to civil society (Strang and Braithwaite, 2001).

But when we talk about the application of restorative justice to our everyday lives, we find ourselves in a sticky wicket of sorts because the question immediately arises: to what extent should those of us who advocate restorative justice principles practice these principles in our everyday lives. And this is not an issue that we can by-pass easily. We are suggesting that it is of little value to talk about restorative justice, and to seek to introduce its practices into the lives of those who find themselves "victims" or "offenders" of a crime or social harm, if we do not relish narrative in our own lives, if we do not confront issues of power in our own lives, if we do not strive to create needs-based relationships wherever we are. Indeed, we are suggesting that the opportunity to create restorative practices does not exist in the future or in select circumstances, as when a municipality decides to adopt a restorative justice demonstration project, but everywhere and any time we engage in social relationships with others. That is, possibilities for growth, healing, and transforming social arrangements exist on all levels, from the most personal up through the most global (Tifft, 1993; Chomsky, 1994b; Brock-Utne, 1985; Gil, 1986). And on a global level, some might refer to such restoration in terms of "sustainable development" (Martin, 2004; Daly, 1996). The choices we make about how to live in and sustain the world we inhabit reflects not only our perspective on justice but also our moral stances in life; and it is through these choices that each of us reveals our essential being to others (Pieper, 1996). Our morality is manifested not in any metaphysical spiritual preferences or through the institutionally-defined religious beliefs we espouse, but in the political-economy we live out among others in community. That is, how healthy we are, how spiritually grounded we are, how moral we are, can be measured by how much we are committed to meeting the needs of all and to living out relationships in which seeking the equal well-being of all is our intention.

Restorative Intimate and Family Relationships

As we look to apply restorative justice principles to our everyday lives then – that is, to create needs-based relationships and ultimately restorative, sustainable communities – perhaps the most logical starting point is our relationships with our intimates: with our partners, and in our child-care and parent-care relationships. It is here that the social revolution begins and is maintained, where we have a continuing choice about how restorative we wish to be in our lives. And it is always our hope that the quality of these relationships will spill over into our preschool, school, day care, eldercare, and work arrangements, and finally throughout the culture (Forsey, 1995). As we develop restorative relationships at the most personal of levels, we find that we are less hampered by the "it can't be done" or "one person can't make a difference" syndromes that can deflate our energies for transforming social relationships on a larger scale. Moreover, as we begin to create relationships in which we regard the stories of others as essential to personal and social well-being, we come to recognize that hierarchy and the exercise of power (see Chapter Six) are not universal qualities of relationship, nor are they necessary components of social life (Barclay, 1982). We discover that we can structure into any sphere of our daily lives an ethic of justice that states that human well-being and enjoyment can be found when we take into account the needs of others as well as our own (D. Sullivan, 1998).

When we begin to think about applying needs-based, restorative values to our intimate relationships, we see that it is possible to relate to a partner without power and condescension, without seeking to achieve and enforce a favored status for our self over that of our partner. In other words, we can establish and flourish in relationships in which there is no overt or hidden hierarchy or domination present. Those enamored of power and with satisfying their own needs at the expense of others live in relational distance with their mates; they maintain separate spheres and parallel lives, a way of life that fosters not-so-subtle resentments between partners that, unless attended to restoratively, fester and eat at the foundation of the relationship. On the other hand, those who work to achieve each other's equal well-being share in "a collaboration of love and labor that produces profound intimacy and mutual respect" (Schwartz, 1994:56; Blumstein and Schwartz, 1985). These partners are friends who "know each other and love each other...they think and feel for one another. Each is the object of the other's thought and affection...and they behave in terms of one another. They make plans together, cooperate, and share their enjoyments and their thoughts" (Macmurray, 1932:179).

In relationships bound by such mutual affection, partners freely share in the work at hand, they share in making key decisions that affect each other's lives, they have equal access to the family's resources (including discretionary funds) according to their needs, and they have equal weight in developing and pursuing their own life plans (Schwartz, 1994; Kinkade, 1994). Of course, such relationships do not emerge in a vacuum or spontaneously, but require considerable creativity, attentiveness, "conscious and sustained effort" (Conze, 1967:81). They require each partner to be available to the other, which, at a minimum, means taking responsibility for generating real conversation and warmth, for listening to one another, for developing an awareness of one's own needs combined with the desire and effort to articulate these needs to the partner in a peaceful way (Mounier, 1971; Macmurray, 1961). This, of course, takes practice because many people, when they first begin to express their needs, feel vulnerable and mask such vulnerability by being confrontational. Finally, it should be pointed out that each person's needs, work, plans, desires, and overall value are not based on how educated a person is, what kind of employment or social position he or she has, or how much money a person earns, but in his or her uniqueness and dignity as a person (Schwartz, 1994). Value derives primarily through needs because it is through the discovery and meeting of one's needs that each person can be responsive to the needs of the other, and vice versa.

In families that include children and older relatives, a grandparent for example, partnering that is needs-based requires that both caregivers relinquish the traditional "good provider" and "exclusive caretaker" roles that have historically composed gender, and have left women responsible for nearly all home-work and home responsibilities, and correspondingly, left men with little or no home responsibilities other than the fiscal solvency of the family. As such, these imposed roles, from which oftentimes there is no relief, only serve to create and exacerbate relational distance, resentment, and disengagement among partners, as well as between them and other members of the family (Bernard, 1986). Women/mothers have been left doing nearly all the family's relational work as well as the routine, commonplace tasks, such as preparing and serving meals, washing the dishes and clothes, taking an ailing parent to the doctor's office, changing a child's diaper, bathing the children, listening to everyone's concerns and handling everyone's daily conflicts – all the work related to meeting the primary needs of all the family's members. Fathers/men have been left with the tasks of occasionally playing and sometimes disciplining the children and performing non-routine home-work tasks.

In contrast, when it comes to "family work," in the needs-based, egalitarian family, young and old alike must be given every opportunity to share in completing the home-work and participating in the making of decisions and "rules" or guidances that affect all family members (Piercy, 1976). Children especially need to know that they are appreciated as co-creators of the family dynamic, not as subjects in a parental dynasty that reinforces stratification, while older family members must be encouraged to participate in the family's activities to the best of their abilities to their dying day. Sharing the family work without gender or age designations brings about mutual experiences and understanding, a shared responsibility for getting things done. At the same time, while all members of the family have access to family resources and energies, they also understand that the primary caregivers also have needs. Here, as elsewhere, the importance of open communication, listening to each other's stories, concerns, and wishes cannot be overestimated.

But maintaining such structures requires constant attentiveness to each person's needs and realities, and to the root of "problems" when they rise (Schumacher, 1998). Only then can the genesis of a "family problem" or "personal trouble" be addressed, the incidence of troublesome behavior decreased, and more supportive arrangements or processes developed for meeting the re-clarified needs of each: children, parents, and grandparents alike (Brazelton, 1992). And when parents remain open to the observations and criticisms of their children and elderly parents, when they can get to the core of what the children are saying, complaining about, or even clamoring for, they foster mutual respect, trust, and mutual understanding. Everybody is listened to, presents their concerns and tries to come up with new ways of alleviating the conflict or problem. They thus are freed from the constraints of hierarchy, non-reflective authority, and patterns of behavior that dismiss the unique needs of all (Berry, 1996). Imposed discipline and punishment vanish by self- and other-awareness, by mutual understanding, by bonded, supportive cooperation, and by shared collective responsibility for the quality of life lived within the family.

Restorative Places of Work

But families that strive to take into account the needs of all their members, themselves require external structural support to help them sustain such a home-based political economy (Kossek and Ozeki, 1999). It is essential, therefore, that the work arrangements that these family members are a part of outside the home be organized in ways that allow, indeed encourage, them to take care of each other when some family member is in particular need, for example, when a child becomes unexpectedly ill or a parent has had a heart attack and must be hospitalized (Burke, 1989; Elizur, 1992; Galinsky & Johnson, 1998; Hill et al., 2001). Places of work that treat those who work there as persons with lives beyond the confines of the assembly line, shop, office, or boardroom, differ from those prevalent in large-scale corporate operations that view people as "workers," as economies of scale or, as organizational consultant Emery Trist (1978) has noted, as "spare parts" to inspect, surveil, and micro-manage as if they were incompetents or "infants." Clearly these latter perceptions do not stimulate arrangements that embody respect, human dignity, and well-being. This leads us to say a few things about transforming places of work into restorative venues (Greenberg, 1996; Sullivan and Tifft, 2004).

– 173 –

First of all, work arrangements that defy human scale and severely limit people's participation in decisions that affect the work they do, and the life of the workplace generally, deny us our fundamental need to have a say in the things that affect our lives. We all seek this, that is, we all desire to be respected as "stakeholders" in the processes of the organizations we are part of. We wish to be part of the narrative process out of which our needs and the needs of the organization are defined (hopefully simultaneously), and to have a say in the decisions about how these needs will be satisfied. To have one's voice heard is the first step in creating a collaborative workplace.

When our voices are dismissed or muffled, and/or when we are treated as spare or interchangeable parts, rather than as resourceful persons whose talents need to be cultivated and supported, we are put on the defensive. We are forced to forgo enjoyable contact with our co-workers and we are forced to forgo the personal satisfaction that comes from tackling tasks with initiative and creativity (Trist, 1978). Moreover, as we discussed in Chapter Seven, when we are excluded from participating in decisions that affect our lives we are forced to forgo our mental well-being and our physical health and safety (Weisbord, 2004; Chen, 2003; Pardo del Val et al., 2002). In fact, studies of Swedish and American male workers have shown that the more influence we have over the work we perform, the less likely we are to contract heart disease (Johnson, 1986; Theorell, 1991; Alfredson et al., 1985; Weisbord, 2004; Nelson, 1983). Furthermore, there is a vast amount of research that indicates that differing organizational climates have a significant effect on "worker" attitudes, satisfaction, and productivity. In light of such findings and of the feedback that "workers" generally give about the ill effects of being excluded from participation in their work lives, some consultants and theorists of organizational behavior have argued that participative management is not a fanciful option that managers and boards of trustees can choose to implement or not, but an "ethical imperative" (Sashkin, 1984:4).

In workplaces that structurally incorporate and embody the kinds of restorative values we have been talking about, we do not witness the exercise of raw power, the use of Kafkaesque surveillance, or the meting out of reprimands and punishments to control those who work there when they are judged as not having acceptably completed their tasks or when they are accused of having violated agreed upon "rules," such as safety rules, performance rules, or respect rules (Fletcher and Rapoport, 1996). Rather, we see a collaborative climate with supervisors, coordinators, team-leaders, or crew-leaders who espouse and act on values that comprise what some describe as "inner leadership" (Bass, 1985; Avolio et al., 1991). In such organizations supervisors are interested in the development and well-being of those they supervise, as well as their own development and well-being (Fairholm, 2003; Bjerke, 1999). Some would say they even inspire others (Bilchik, 2001) as well as foster respect and a degree of trust that ultimately leads to pride in the work and higher performance (And, 1972). Those who work in such environments will tell you that the organization is interested in them as whole persons, which includes, as we mentioned earlier, attending to their real needs to leave work unexpectedly to care for a sick child or parent, to come to work late because of a doctor's appointment, or to take a day off because of a pressing family or personal matter, a religious holiday, or just because one needs to (Plas, 1996; Braham, 1999). It also includes attending to a person's spiritual values when these are self-defined as "the vital, engaging principle in the person, the core of self" (Fairholm, 2003:22).

It is not surprising, therefore, that on some fronts we are currently witnessing an increased sensitivity on the part of some owners and executive decision makers to the impact that the organizational climate, policies, and structure have on personal well-being and quality productivity. They grasp that a workplace whose driving ethic reflects an overarching concern for participatory self-management regardless of organizational position is inconsistent with policies and managerial decision-making arrangements that foster the outright control or manipulation of work situations by bosses or "superiors." Consequently, any threat-based or power-based relationship between supervisors and those they supervise is defined as counterproductive to everyone's physical and emotional health, and to the fiscal health of the organization (Adams and Hansen, 1992; Young, 1992; Turner and Clomp, 1992). Moreover, as we mentioned above, those who have worked toward developing collaborative work arrangements know that truly creative and productive work is done only when those at work fully share in all workplace decisions and processes, when their whole person is valued (Marshall, 1995). This means that, at a minimum, the safety and health care of all workers must be provided for, and that ultimately the needs of all must be taken into account with respect to compensation – regardless of position in the organization or degree of difficulty of the tasks at hand. When this level of equality exists, feelings of envy, greed, and resentment toward those with whom one works are lessened significantly, for each sees and each is seen by the other as a resourceful person to be valued. The workplace becomes transformed from a battlefield where aggressive and passive-aggressive behavior is the order of the day to an enjoyable, collaborative venture. Under work conditions that foster the cooperation and personal well-being of all, everyone has a continuing bevy of positive experiences to carry back home with them to share with their partner and other family members (Hart, 1992; Tifft, 1993; Krimerman and Lindenfeld, 1992; Lindenfeld, 2001).

Again, many who currently own and manage workplaces, if only for reasons of organizational cost-effectiveness and enhanced product or service quality and productivity, increasingly acknowledge how important it is for the organization to respond to the entire life of its "workers" (Kleiner, 1996; Shifley, 2003; Lindenfeld, 2003). They also see that those who live peaceful, joyous, and healthy family lives are able to contribute far more to their workmates on the job and ultimately to the success of the operation (Freudenheim, 1988; Leary, 1988). In fact, they begin to see them not as "workers" or personnel, but as persons (Goodman, 1963). Of course, this is where we left off in our discussion of restorative intimate and family relations – looking at the spillover implications of work arrangements and what people carry home with them from work (Maume and Houston, 2001; Tifft, 1993; Kimbrell, 1992; Sale, 1980). A family that embraces restorative values and ways of living will be hard pressed to maintain these values when its members are denigrated or battered in the workplace, and, conversely, a workplace will be less likely to receive the full talents and energy of those who work there, unless it takes into account the complete lives of its workers and supports restorative-based family life (Wood et al., 2003).

Restorative Schools

Just as we have looked at ways that the family and the workplace might be restructured to reflect restorative values, we now turn our attention to school settings to embrace what a school looks like when it embodies restorative values. And here as well we are talking about the inclusion of restorative values and processes, not only after a harm of some sort has taken place, but structurally and from the outset (Cameron and Thorsborne, 2001; Morrison, 2001). In other words, how would a school be organized so that its "curriculum" fostered self-discipline or self-management in young people such that they were more prone to take into account the needs of others as well as their own? Of course, as in the case of the restoratively-structured family and workplace, such a school must be designed to meet the needs of all. Elsewhere we have spoken about such changes in education in terms of the moral development of children (Tifft et al., 1997), while others have chosen to speak of them in terms of the creation of civil society (Strang and Braithwaite, 2001; Schaefer, 2003).

In many communities, parents, students, administrators, and teachers have demonstrated an interest in creating schools that take into account the needs of all (J. Sullivan, 1998, 2001; Power et al., 1989a; Lickona, 1991a, 1991b). They have become increasingly vocal about the need to move away from a school environment that concentrates on comparing, differentiating, homogenizing, hierarchically ordering, segregating, separating, and excluding students (Foucault, 1977:183; Piaget, 1965; Power et al., 1989a). Those interested in the peaceful development and growth of children are looking for constructive environments in which children are given a chance to interact with and learn from one another, as well as from teachers. They want a world of learning that reflects collaborative learning arrangements (Nevin et al., 1990; Sullivan, 2001). This means that student-learners help select what to learn as part of their experience and preparation in learning how to be in charge of themselves, to be responsible for their own lifelong learning. Instead of worrying about labeling and segregating students, teachers, administrators, and collaborative learners would involve themselves in full-inclusion processes that allow everyone to learn from each others' experiences, mistakes, insights, and accomplishments, and consequently to support everyone in taking responsibility for the quality of life at school (Armstrong, 1987; Sullivan et al., 1987; St. John, 2003).

Spruce Run: An Inclusionary School

As the 21st century moves past the halfway mark of its first decade, needs-based schools are no longer part of someone's utopian wish list; they have been in practice, albeit not in great numbers, for some time. We offer by way of illustration Spruce Run School, an elementary school situated in west central New Jersey. This is a "full inclusion" school architecturally-designed and academically-structured to meet the needs of all – student-learners, teachers, parents, and administrators alike.

We begin with the real-life story of two first graders as they walk into the main office of their Pre-K to Grade 2 school in Clinton Township, where the noted and innovative principal, John Sullivan, served as its chief administrator for nearly two decades. The two six-year olds approach the counter dividing the room and exchange good morning greetings with the school secretary. Across the three-foot-high section of counter, which comes up to their chests, they deliver the attendance sheets, lunch counts, and messages from parents, and then returned to their classrooms. Their ability to complete this simple task would not have been possible the previous summer when this office was being built because the architect's plans had called for the entire counter to be built at a height of four feet, over which most six year olds and those younger would not have been able to see. Architects, state inspectors, and central office administrators had all missed what Sullivan saw and wondered. "This school is for children," he thought, "How will they feel when they come to the office and be unable to see anyone behind the counter?"

During our own school years, we have all been to our school's main office for one reason or another so we know the answer to that question. They would feel like they were out of place, in an unfriendly place, a place not meant for them, a place constructed for big people. And so Sullivan requested that the carpenters be called in and that the counter be adapted to accommodate the physical and psychological needs of the young students for whom this school would be their home away from home for most of their waking day. The lowered counter section told these young learners that this was their place, that they belonged, that the adults at the school respected them and desired to communicate with them face-to-face, and that they could come to the office and communicate with comfort and confidence, without fear.

Age-appropriate adaptations in other physical facilities at the school had also been overlooked, such as the height of toilets, urinals, and sinks. These too were changed. Even the loud, erratic flush of the automatic toilets had to be adjusted because it frightened some of the youngest children. But the vision of Sullivan and his innovative teachers at Spruce Run was not simply to make adaptations and accommodations to address the physical and emotional needs of the children. As a full-inclusion school, a school in which all students with a full range of abilities and "disabilities," learn in age-appropriate regular classes (Forest and Pearpoint, 1992), they practiced a philosophy whereby everyone within the school's walls was a member of a community of learners (Barth, 1990). This was a place where it was acknowledged that all children and adults have gifts and talents to give. Sullivan and the Spruce Run teachers believed that the school must flex to meet the needs of students, not the reverse. This community of learners was committed to the success of all students. Failure was not a possibility.

What made this pedagogy all the more remarkable was that all 540 students who lived within this school district's boundaries could attend their neighborhood school if they wished and no one in any of the schools was to learn in segregated classrooms. Here, only 5% of the students were classified as "disabled," whereas nationwide close to 10% of all school-age children are "serviced" in special education, a percentage that continues to grow. Indeed in some places more than 20% of the students in a given district are classified as having "learning disabilities," and two-thirds of the 10% nationwide so classified (more than 5 million students) attend separate classrooms either in the same school as others in their neighborhoods, or at a school that is often a considerable distance from their neighborhood (National Center for Education Statistics, 2002). This, of course, has implications for those students and their families now, as well as when they move on to higher education, because the number of students with "learning disabilities" entering college, for example, has more than doubled from 15% to 32% (Kid Source, 2004).

Certainly to create a needs-based, inclusionary school is a challenge. Many adaptations and accommodations have to be made for all student-learners to be stretched toward their full potential, toward being successful. As an inclusionary school, Spruce Run flexed to meet the needs of the learner and did not segregate him/her to another place to be "fixed," or until he/she had adapted sufficiently to return to Spruce Run. In effect, Spruce Run, as an inclusionary school embodied a perspective on human community, that is, a just, restorative community (Power et al., 1989a, 1989b). Yet, most schools and most states, as pointed out, are clearly more committed to an arrangement of separate, parallel educational experiences for both regular and special education students. Whereas the national average for students with all disabilities being placed in general education classes is 33%, the range among the states in the U.S. is from 3% to 91% (Kid Source, 2004). How is it that some states and districts include almost all students in their regular classroom settings, while others include so very few?

Restorative School Environments

In the past decade or so, we have seen a growing body of evidence depicting the efforts of parents and school officials to transform the school environment and culture to insure inclusion and success for all learners. At one time, for example, a student in a wheelchair would have been unable to enter the school or go to a classroom on the second floor. Such students are no longer prevented from doing so because physical structural accommodations (ramps and elevators) have become commonplace, indeed, are now required by law. But such changes, once implemented, require little personal attention and little change in the social organization of the school, and little change in personal beliefs and attitudes of those in the school's learning community. But this is not the case when we consider major transformational changes in the educational structure, administration, faculty, curriculum, classroom culture, learning materials, and teaching methodology within a school. These changes are of a different ilk. They require personal transformation and commitment on the part of all who work there and are part of the school's learning community. They require adaptations and accommodations in one's beliefs, attitudes, and practices; they require taking risks, working collaboratively, and an openness to entirely different classroom dynamics. And such requirements do not come without a price (Thousand and Villa, 1989). Hence, we must look upon the "mainstreaming of failures" not as an indication that those children with disabilities are inherently incapable of "success" in regular classrooms, but rather, that such "failures" are the result of inappropriate social organizational arrangements, internecine politics, or a lack of will and/or skill on the part of those responsible for implementing these programs (Bogdan, 1983; Wang, 1989). In the inclusionary school, social organizational changes and changes in personal and professional orientations have led to major transformations in the school's learning environments. And once in place, such transformations do not persist of their own accord, but require a constant monitoring of visionary energies to place equal value on every student-learner's responsibility to learn (Schein, 1985; Hoy, 1986).

When we look at how most schools and their curricula are structured, we see a tragic drama talking place. Typically classrooms in the traditionally organized school accommodate the "average" student and largely neglect the needs of those who deviate from the norm, whether the deviation be academic, social, physical, or emotional in nature (Hallahan and Kaufman, 1992). The standard way by which an advanced- or slower-learning student's needs are met is via a separate classroom or separate school. But even in those classrooms, a new "bell curve" (normal distribution) is established and students at the extremes are once again neglected. Marginalization is institutionalized and perpetuated.

In these typical traditional schools, we have teachers who have been trained in a teaching style that accommodates the average to high-average student. This teaching style is universally an "in-front-of-the-classroom" lecture presentation, with students sitting as passive listeners/consumers at their desks. There is heavy reliance on the overhead projector, chalkboard, Power Point charts, and textbooks or learning materials that have been market-projected to meet the needs of the greatest number of typical students. Advanced students either already know much of what is presented in these texts, or master their contents rather quickly while the "slow" or "disadvantaged" learner, as he or she is labeled, has difficulty getting through these same materials (J. Sullivan, 1998, 2001). The assessing quiz or test comes too late for the first group, too soon for the latter. Success comes to those whose learning style combination is primarily auditory or linguistic. Those students whose learning style or mode is primarily kinesthetic, tactile, or visual, those who primarily need to move, who primarily need to touch and feel, or who primarily need to see how things work, are not offered much of an opportunity to learn these materials via the learning mode combination that best fits them. Consequently, they do not find much success in the required performances. Obviously, all of these multiple combinations of learning modes or styles need to be presented and available, but far too often they are not (Gardner, 1991). We ourselves might have struggled in such a classroom, so we know why so many students become bored with or dislike school and why so many drop out and learn to not enjoy learning.

Since schools and classrooms do not generally accommodate individual student needs, they are not positive, safe, invigorating, joyful places for those with "challenges," again, whether they be physical, mental, or emotional. They are not positive, safe, trustful, dignifying places for those without challenges either. The child who is active and cannot sit still does not fit and is often resented by the teacher, the parents of other students, and the other students, as well, because he/she is disrupting the learning of these "typical" students (J. Sullivan, 1998, 2001). The sad part is that the challenged child's needs are often viewed as competing with and often monopolizing the attention and draining the energies of the teacher, energies that could be utilized to meet the needs of the others in the class. The same goes for the student who is very social or the one who wants to learn and express his/her learning through creative activities or through different modes of learning, such as drawing or music. The most common route taken to meet the needs of those student learners who have trouble "performing" in the traditional rational-linguistic modes is to label them as remedial, at-risk, learning disabled, attention deficit-hyperactive, gifted and talented, emotionally disturbed, etc., and to separate them into alternative classrooms or schools. Schools that do not segregate are often heralded by education officials as helping students to learn to work and live with differing or individuated others or learning how to live and work with others different from themselves when they become grown-ups. But, more regularly, especially when segregated, children are learning about labeling, segregating, differentiation in space, and stratification (Stainback et al., 1989). Some say we should expect our schools not to mirror the docilizing, disciplinizing, needs-denying processes that are present in other institutions in our society but, in fact, the traditional school agenda and the non-inclusionary school are organized to reproduce an experience that reflects these processes and stratifications (J. Sullivan, 1998, 2001; Gil, 1998).

Understandably, getting schools to meet the needs of children, and in particular the needs of challenged children, has been a long uphill fight. Only recently, has the research on inclusive, restorative classrooms begun to show that students and teachers can work together in regular classrooms to meet these needs and do so without either labels or separation (Villa and Thousand, 1995). The idea that all students must study the same curriculum, learn at the same pace and by the same learning mode/teaching style, and proceed through school by grade levels, has seen its day. But a stumbling block to moving toward creating effective schools, including inclusionary schools, is the disbelief that all students can learn. Of course, it would be hard to find a school whose administrators and staff would claim that they don't believe all students can learn. But the organizational structure and culture of many of their schools tell us what their true beliefs are, beliefs that prevent such a conviction from being realized. Schools like Spruce Run, which back up these espoused beliefs with real action, ensure that all students succeed and provide the necessary support systems to make such success a reality. A social climate is fostered within which, "The drive is no longer the teacher's but the children's own... The teacher is at last with the stream and not against it, the stream of children's inexorable creativeness" (Ashton-Warner, 1963:93). In such schools we also see high expectations for achievement by all students, visionary leadership, parental participation, collegiality and collaboration, encouraged staff development, and the establishment of a caring, communal environment. When these qualities are present, students achieve high on standardized tests and perform well according to other organizational effectiveness indicators (Brophy and Good, 1986; Edmonds, 1979; Stedman, 1987; Thousand and Villa, 1989).

As we mentioned earlier, in the section on the restorative workplace, a supervisor's or executive's vision of excellence – in the case of the school, the principal's vision – becomes a reality in accord with his or her ability to build trust, collegiality, and collaborative teamwork within the school community (Hoy, 1986, 1991; Mintzberg, 1979). At Spruce Run, the principal does not have to scrutinize or micro-manage teacher behavior nor restrict it through strict rules and regulations. Teachers and others can be seen working in small groups and interacting frequently, in the course of planning learning programs for each student-learner, trying out new ideas, learning modes and materials, attempting to brainstorm on how to solve problems, assessing effectiveness, and sharing what they have learned at a conference or skills workshop. Moreover, traditional bureaucratic conflict is all but eliminated in such a collaborative environment as teachers form an "adhocracy," an organization of professionals who try out decisions to address the diverse needs of each unique child as they arise. The flow of ideas is far more horizontal than hierarchical. These needs-oriented teachers reshape a perhaps once static curriculum guide into thematic units relevant to all children, provide a variety of hands-on activities, stimulating materials, and technology to replace or supplement textbooks and workbooks, and provide learning experiences such as cooperative learning, mode-specific and multiple mode-learning centers, and student-generated research projects, all of which makes grotesquely obsolete the in-front-of-the-room mode of "instruction." The collaborative, person-centered teacher at Spruce Run is no longer "the sage on stage, but one of a group of guides on the side."

As we might expect in a school such as Spruce Run, the assessment measures for gauging student progress or growth have changed radically. The traditional grading system – which is competitive and stratifying of selves, and which diminishes for some the self-motivation to learn – has been replaced with an authentic assessment program that involves students in the assessment of their own accomplishments. In very practical terms, their accomplishments are collected in portfolios (Tucker, 1985; Shriner et al., 1989). In assessing the work in these portfolios and elsewhere, teachers and students jointly review understandable criteria for excellence and students evaluate their work according to these criteria and set goals for group learning projects. In this way each learner can enjoy a common learning theme while doing a self-chosen individualized project at his or her own pace and through their own modes of learning. Performance is measured against a self-established standard, not in comparison with the performances of others. When such needs-based inclusionary schools are implemented throughout a school district, those who rely on student achievement information to make employment or college admission decisions will have to individually assess a personal-best works portfolio, rather than make hiring or admission choices based on grades or nationally standardized test abstractions. Authentic portfolios better indicate the quality of each person's performance and potentiality. Creating genuine portfolios generates pride in one's work and reinvigorates enthusiasm to discover more about one's relationship to the world and the others in it.

At Spruce Run and in other collaborative classrooms, teachers involve students in making decisions affecting their "academic performance," but they also involve them in celebrations of individual and collective accomplishments. Furthermore, they involve them in learning how to define and respond to the injustices, conflicts, and the disruptive problems of classmates. In these kinds of social arrangements, we are less likely to see serious harms, bullying, and the demonization of students regarded as "bullies," "weirdos" or "nerds" for, through their collaboration on all that affects each other's lives, the students develop a greater empathy and feel for one another (Emde et al., 1987; Gibbs, 1991; Hoffman, 1987). Administrators and teachers who work in such environments know by experience that resolving disruptions or injustice issues are best addressed through finding alternative needs-meeting or learning modes. If, for example, one class member finds him/herself unable to sit still in a group that is listening to a story being read by the teacher, it might be decided that everyone would be better accommodated if this class member listened to the rest of the story elsewhere – on a CD-ROM, computer, or headphone set in class. Or, if this did not work out, he/she might find a different activity that he/she would undisruptively enjoy until the story activity had been completed.

Seriously unacceptable conduct in the context of such an inclusionary school is not seen as school rule breaking – a violation of the institution – but rather, a violation of relationships among those at school and perhaps in the wider community. This means that when a serious harm within these relationships occurs, that a participatory learning framework can be initiated that attempts to teach and model how to deal with conflict in social relationships. Through such an experience, social or relational bonds can be reconstructed and strengthened (Morrison, 2001). As these relationships need to be explored and repaired, this is an opportunity to attempt to problem-solve, to explore how the organizational climate, the classroom culture, the student-learners' individualized learning programs, the pedagogy, the specific materials being studied, and the modes of learning, all might be involved in the relational situation, and be changed. Moreover, there is the need to explore how the life chances of the principal student-learners involved might be improved, and how everyone might begin to relate differently so as to reduce the chance that such an occasion will again arise (Cameron and Thorsborne, 2001:183-184). If some of these relational conflicts involve a student-learner's difficulties in coming to terms with intentionality, or with harm acknowledgment and responsibility displacement, then these issues must be addressed as learning issues at school and perhaps in the home. This would mean that the learning of students at school may extend to a need to develop education programs for their parents (Braithwaite et al., 2003).

In this context, the disciplinary, deserts-based, rewards/punishment "classroom management" approach of the traditional school is thoroughly replaced with innovative prophylactic peacemaking or restorative justice programs (Prothrow-Stith, 1987; Prothrow-Stith and Weissman, 1991). These programs seek to create a classroom climate and a school culture that encourages and supports the peaceful resolution of conflict, and beyond this approach, to create peace-building education and action programs that situate student-learners' whole lives (not just their school lives) in the structurally violent arrangements of the larger society. They seek to transform these violent social arrangements so as to create a more just society, a more meaningful future for these students' parents, for themselves, for their children, and for us all (Galtung, 1976; Berlowitz, 1994). Hence, needs-based, inclusionary schools have a restorative ethical base at their core.

The Restorative Reality

When we look at the transformative power of restorative schools and of the restorative families and places of work we discussed earlier, we see that they are the foundation blocks of restorative communities, communities that give short shrift to power-based social arrangements especially those designed to respond to violence with counterviolence (Morris, 1995; Pugh, 1995; Mika, 1992, 1993). These restorative institutions reflect a political economy in which the well-being of all is a primary concern, not only in specific interpersonal encounters, but structurally as well. What is achieved through restorative justice efforts as we have defined them, therefore, is not only the healing of intimate connections that have been severed by a harm-done, but also the reinforcement of social arrangements that take into account the needs of all (Sullivan and Tifft, 1998). In such arrangements, we are less likely to feel a need to rely on power to secure our future or to inflict loss upon another as a corrective or preventive measure because the power-based self that thrives at the expense of others is offered a chance to surrender. By participating in these processes, each person is moved not only to take the risk of experiencing the self he or she truly is, but also to become a presence to others that serves as the foundation of social life without power, that takes the other unto oneself so as to become a seamless All.

As we strive to create the kinds of restorative communities we have been talking about, we have to wonder what kind of progress is realistically possible without radical changes in our current deserts-based, global market economy and in our rights-based nation-state polity, which is currently hell-bent on enlarging its imperialistic empire to dominate the internal dynamics of other nation-states and world social relations. These institutions reflect a political-economy that undermines collaborative, restorative, needs-based relationships through their continuous marginalization of peoples and fragmentation of communities (North American Congress on Latin America, 1993). We have to continue to raise this question because even seemingly well-intentioned market reforms "have undermined the basis of functioning democracy, leaving people isolated, 'each for oneself'" (Chomsky, 1994b:184).

To move in the direction of the restorative, sustainable, needs-based communities we have been talking about, we also need to pay increasing attention to the importance of place, not only by creating just social arrangements where we live, but also by paying attention to the requirements of the natural environment we live in and cultivate (Vitek and Jackson 1996). At the most elemental level, this includes taking into account the true cost of things (D. Sullivan, 1986-1987), which includes preserving and restoring the conditions that insure a sustainable agriculture (Jackson, 1980). On the political-economic level, it means creating communities that are sustainable and cost-effective. Of course, as we have suggested, this also entails creating social environments in which young people are taught to respect and develop character and moral intelligence rather than transnational market craftiness (Coles, 1997; D. Sullivan, 1982). Only when we engage the environment according to its needs structure can we begin to understand how to protect our continuing supply of safe food, clean air, pure water, nurtured children, and creative, caring adults.

And contrary to what many believe today, the answer to building communities that are restorative will not be found in cookie-cutter designs, such as that developed by the Disney Corporation for its managed community of Celebration, Florida (Wilson, 1995; Frantz and Collins, 1999). Such market-envisioned, profit-driven communities are a twist in the logic of what is required to live with and among each other sanely, joyfully. Those who peddle such communities commit an act of hubris of the highest order, one that is symptomatic of the current neurosis we all suffer from when we buy into such market-generated fantasies of well-being. This neurosis thrives on the continuing belief that, on the one hand, we lack the competence to overcome relational distance and create community for ourselves, and on the other, that community is a place or a commodity that can be packaged, retailed, purchased, and consumed. But such a belief and its underlying hubris will persist only as long as we refuse to journey to that part of our inner being where the roots of restorative community thrive. Beginning upon this journey then is the first and most pressing requirement for living restoratively. How fortunate we are that each of us has the capability to meet that requirement now, wherever we are, and without purchasing a thing. And even more wonderful is that the invitation to begin this journey is never withdrawn.

EPILOGUE

As editors of the international journal, *Contemporary Justice Review*, several years ago we grew concerned about the kinds of issues that university students, in particular those who studied criminal justice and criminology, were exploring about justice. As others had done before us, we couched our concerns in terms of "justice literacy," what people should know and take into consideration in order to grasp the full landscape of justice issues. For us, this also included the principles that enable us to live justly. Our initial question was: were there certain books, authors, and ideas that one ought to examine in order to talk intelligently about justice? We felt so committed to this topic that we put the collected comments and concerns about literacy of eight scholars from around the United States – some writing in collaboration with others – into a double issue of the journal (volume 1, issues 2-3). We called the issue "Justice Literacy: What Every Student of Justice Needs to Know (And Speak Intelligently About) Before Graduation." We wanted students to be able to gauge how broad and deep an understanding they had of the effects that differing conceptions of justice have on human well-being. What social arrangements and cultural ideas do they believe foster or preserve such well-being and how do they think the human community should respond to situations when someone has upset that well-being, specifically when someone has harmed another, and sometimes in gruesome ways?

To some extent, we were aware that in posing questions of justice in this way, we were begging the question in the sense that we knew and even postulated in the Editors' Note at the beginning of the issue that "every person who walks into a university classroom, indeed every person (and from a very early age), knows all he or she needs to know about justice"

(Sullivan et al., 1998b:180). We knew this to be the case because, year after year, the students who walked into our classrooms, and indeed every person we met and talked to about such matters, "ha[d] already experienced hurts, injustices, and harms in some way, ha[d] developed his or her own view of what constitute[d] a harm or injustice-done, and kn[ew] what constitute[d] a suitable response to such harms and injustices in the form of justice-done" (ibid.). In other words, each person we encountered could be said to be "quite learned regarding his or her own 'theory of crime' and 'system of justice' for defining and resolving harm situations in which he or she (or another) was involved" (ibid.). Yet many people had only vague ideas about how a society within which they would like to live might be organized and how disputes and harms might be resolved in such a society. In contrast, some others had ideas about how their just society might be organized and how crimes ought to be reacted to, but these ideas were so fixed that they appeared to be nailed to the floor of their hearts.

For us, questions about justice are not rhetorical questions. Indeed, we believe people should have a basic competency to (at the very least) acknowledge that their desired ways of living and interacting with others leads to violence and great harm (to others and themselves). We also believe that people should have a ready competency to not knowingly commit violence against others. At best, they should acknowledge that how we interact with one another greatly affects our individual and collective well-being, and that an understanding of this may lead some to knowingly, willingly serve others, to listen to them, to understand them, and even to act to meet their needs. What we see almost invariably is that students (and people from every walk of life) are able to speak with authority about issues of justice in the sense that they can see what's wrong with the world and know a way to correct it. And yet, they remain inordinately unaware of the political-economic foundations upon which these views of justice rest. They remain ignorant of, and even willingly unreflective about, the assumptions upon which they base their existence and relationship with others. Consequently they remain to a considerable degree knowing avoiders of the effects that their "system of justice" has, not only on who they are and can be as persons, but also who others are allowed to be. And when we talk about a system of justice (social justice, distributive justice, participatory justice, and harm-responding justice) that constrains or coerces people to be, and act, and think a certain way, we are dealing with issues of power, of interpersonal and structural violence. And in the case of the latter, we are talking about violence that is structured into our lives, about power, which translates into violence on both of these levels.

Any worthwhile exploration of justice requires, therefore, that we examine where our point of view comes from and where it is situated along the political-economic spectrum of deserts-based, rights-based, and needs-based political-economies. Very quickly this translates into how we treat others, interact with them, and generally relate to them day to day. Is one's point of view grounded in a deserts-based (what one has achieved?) economy, or is it grounded in a rights-based (who one is under the law) economy, or is it based on need (who one is as a person)? If we can say there is such a thing as a justice-literacy quotient (a JLQ, if you will), it derives from how well we understand the nature of this spectrum and how well we are able to situate ourselves on it, that is, pinpoint where our core values and relationships with others reside.

And this inquiry is not a mere academic exercise. Once we decide where our core values are situated, we are in effect making a statement about who we are, about what we value, and about where we place others in relation to ourselves. In effect, we are taking a moral stand, making a set of moral choices. At this point we can indeed speak with authority about justice and justice issues because we are speaking from personal experience and with a certain understanding of how our choices and decisions are having an impact on the lives of others (and ourselves). We now know when we are being a source of well-being for others and when we are being a source of pain and suffering for them. This perspective on justice literacy is very different from the way that most others interested in this topic engage it. Though these other perspectives may provide a list of books to be read or ideas to be explored, they rarely get to the underlying core or root issues, the issues that define who one person is in relation to others, who we are in relation to those we meet each day. These are the issues that indicate whether we'll get someone else a plate of food at a picnic before we get our own; whether we'll attend to the needs of a pestering child before our own; whether we'll respond to the needs of our partner or friend the way they would like to be responded to; whether we'll work with others to organize our places of work and learning so as to meet the needs of everyone there; and whether we'll organize with others to confront power, engage in challenging all modes of stratification, and build peaceful alternatives to existing structures of inequality and injustice. This is everyday life stuff and the kind of stuff that we began this book with in the very first sentence.

If we can claim to have done anything in this book, it is to have explored the possibilities of a restorative justice that is transformative, a justice that allows us to rebuild from the ground up, not only the way we relate to others but also the social arrangements through which we live with and among others in our everyday lives. As we (Tifft and Sullivan) have explored these issues with one another and multitudinous others over the years, we have offered you the opportunity to explore the ethical dimensions of your life, your everyday practice of justice, and to declare where you stand on these issues, on the spectrum of values. As we have seen, these get to the core of your self, to how much you embrace power, to whether you treat others condescendingly, whether you look for the possibilities of equality in different situations, whether you seek to create community and willfully collaborate with earth and other life forms. We have also offered each of you the opportunity to explore all the things that have to do with whether you feel cheated or harmed or a "winner" in life, within the way things are set-up in our present society. We have offered you as well an opportunity to explore the reasons you experience life as you do, and how you respond to your observations, insights, and positions on this. If you accept (or have accepted) this challenge, difficult though it may be, from now on your statements about justice, in word and in deed, will reflect how great a desire you have to live in a society in which everyone's essential needs are met. How magnanimous a challenge. It is the kind of society that the co-founder of the Catholic Worker Movement, Peter Maurin, used to talk about. He said it was a society in which it is easier for people to be good, one in which we can more easily enjoy each other's company. To create this kind of society is our daily intention, our daily prayer. It is the reason we wrote this book. We thank you for grappling with these issues just as we have, from the ground up, or in any which way it turned out for you.

REFERENCES AND BIBLIOGRAPHY

Abel, C. F., & Marsh, F. A. (1984). *Punishment and restitution: A restitutionary approach to crime and the criminal.* Westport, CT: Greenwood Press.

Achilles, M. (2004). Will restorative justice live up to its promise to victims? In H. Zehr & B. Toews (Eds.), *Critical issues in restorative justice* (pp. 65-73). Monsey, NY: Criminal Justice Press.

Achilles, M., & Amstutz, L. S. (2003, Winter). Victim services and victim offender mediation programs: Can they work together? *Conciliation Quarterly*, 22(1), 6-8.

Achilles, M., & Zehr, H. (2001). Restorative justice for crime victims: The promise, the challenge. In G. Bazemore & M. Schiff (Eds.), (2001). *Restorative community justice: Repairing harm and transforming communities* (pp. 87-99). Cincinnati, OH: Anderson Publishing Co.

Adams, F. T., & Hansen, G. B. (1992). Education for ownership and participation. In L. Krimerman & F. Lindenfeld (Eds.), *When workers decide: workplace democracy takes root in North* America (pp. 135-140). Philadelphia: New Society Publications.

Adler, C., & Wundersitz, J. (Eds.). (1994). *Family conferencing and juvenile justice: The way forward or misplaced optimism?* Canberra: Australian Institute of Criminology.

Alfredson, L., Spetz, C. L., & Theorell, T. (1985). Type of occupation and near future hospitalization for myocardial infarction and some other diagnoses. *International Journal of Epidemiology*, 14, 378-388.

Allers, U. (1992, February). Peace and conflict resolution initiatives in U.S. Schools. *Justicia: Newsletter of Greater Rochester Community of Churches Judicial Process Commission*, pp. 3-4.

Alter, S (1999). *Apologising for serious wrongdoing: Social, psychological and legal considerations.* Report for the Law Commission of Canada, 1999. Available online at: http://www.lcc.gc.ca/en/themes/mr/ica/-2000/html/apology.asp

Amnesty International. (1998, October). *United States of America: Rights for all. On the wrong side of history: Children and the death penalty in the USA* (AMR 51/58/98). New York: Author.

Amstutz, L. S. (2004). What is the relationship between victim service organizations and restorative justice? In H. Zehr & B. Toews (Eds.), *Critical issues in restorative justice* (pp. 85-93). Monsey, NY: Criminal Justice Press.

And, D. E. (1972). Trust and managerial problem solving. *Administrative Science Quarterly*, 17, 229-239.

Andrews, A. B. (1992). *Victimization and survivors services: A guide to victim assistance*. New York: Springer Publications.

Angus, L., Levitt, H., & Hardke, L. (2000). Narrative processes and psychotherapeutic change: An integrative approach to psychotherapy research and practice. *Journal of Clinical Psychology*, 55(10), 1255-1270.

Armstrong, T. (1987). *In their own way: Discovering your child's personal learning style*. Los Angeles: Tarcher.

Arnove, A. (2000, October). Challenging Iraq sanctions: An interview with Kathy Kelly from Voices in the Wilderness. *Z Magazine*, 13(10), 40-43.

Aron, A. (1992). Testimonio: A bridge between psychotherapy and sociotherapy. *Refugee Women and Their Mental Health*, 13, 173-189.

Armstrong, T. (1987). *In their own way: Discovering your child's personal learning style*. Los Angeles: Tarcher.

Arrigo, B. A. (2000). Social justice and critical criminology: On integrating knowledge. *Contemporary Justice Review*, 3(1), 7-37.

Arrigo, B., & Williams, C. R. (2003). Victim vices, victim voices, and impact statements: On the place of emotion and the role of restorative justice in capital sentencing. *Crime & Delinquency*, 49(4), 603-626.

Ashton-Warner, S. (1963). *Teacher*. New York: Simon and Schuster.

Asma, D. (2000). Objectifying evil: Courtroom construction of the accused as other. *Contemporary Justice Review*, 4(1), 7-40.

Austin, R. D. (1993). Freedom, responsibility and duty: ADR and the Navajo Peacemaker Court. *The Judges Journal*, 32(8), 47-48.

Avolio, B. J., Waldman, D. A., & Yammarino, F. J. (1991). Leading in the

1990's: The four I's of transformational leadership. *Journal of European Industrial Training*, 15, 9-16.

Axelrod, S. (1996). What's wrong with behavior analysis? *Journal of Behavioral Education*, 6, 247-256.

Axelrod, S., & Hall, R. V. (1999). *Behavior modification: Basic principles.* Austin, TX: Pro-Ed.

Ban, P. (1996). Implementing and evaluating family group conferences with children and families in Victoria, Australia. In J. Hudson, A. Morris, G. Maxwell & B. Galaway (Eds.), *Family group conferences: Perspectives on policy and practice* (pp. 140-151). Monsey, NY: Criminal Justice Press.

Barclay, G. & Tavares, C. (2002). *International comparisons of criminal justice statistics 2000.* London: Home Office, Research, Development, and Statistics Directorate.

Barclay, H. (1982). *People without government: An anthropology of anarchism.* London: Kahn & Averill with Cienfuegos Press.

Barstow, D. (2003, December 21). A trench caves in: A young worker is dead. Is it a crime? Retrieved January 10, 2005 from: http://www.nytimes.com/2003/12/21/national/21OSHA.html?hp=&pag ewanted=print&position=

Barstow, D., & Bergman, L. (2003a, January 8). At a Texas foundry, an indifference to life. Retrieved January 10, 2005 from: http://www.nytimes.com/2003/01/08/national/08PIPE.html?ex=11055 06000&en=aef50b52ebc0708b&ei=5070

Barstow, D., & Bergman, L. (2003b, January 9). Family's profits, wrung from blood and sweatshop. Retrieved January 10, 2005 from: http://www.nytimes.com/2003/01/09/national/09PIPE.html?ex=11055 06000&en=157ff7284b9bda51&ei=5070

Barstow, D., & Bergman, L. (2003c, January 10). Deaths on the job, slaps on the wrist. Retrieved January 10, 2005 from: http://www.nytimes.com/2003/01/10/national/10PIPE.html?ex=11055 06000&en=66faba2d0198b789&ei=5070

Barth, R. (1990). *Improving schools from within.* San Francisco: Jossey-Bass.

Bass, B. M. (1985). *Leadership and performance beyond expectations.* New York: The Free Press.

Baumeister, R. F. (1997). *Evil: Inside human violence and cruelty.* New York: W. H. Freeman.

Baumeister, R. F., & Bratslavsky, E. (2000). Victim thinking. In J. H. Harvey, & E. D. Miller (Eds.), *Loss and trauma: General and close relationship perspectives* (pp. 86-101). Philadelphia: Brunner-Routledge.

Baumeister, R. F., Stillwell, A., & Wotman, S. R. (1990) Victim and perpetrator accounts of interpersonal conflict: Autobiographical narratives about anger. *Journal of Personality and Social Psychology,* 59, 994-1005.

Bazemore, G., & Schiff, M. (Eds.). (2001). *Restorative community justice: Repairing harm and transforming communities.* Cincinnati, OH: Anderson Publishing Co.

Beattie, J. H. M. (1957). Informal judicial activity in Bunyoro. *Journal of African Administration,* 9, 188-195.

Beck, A. J., & Karberg, J. C. (2001, March). Prison and jail inmates at midyear 2000. Washington, DC: National Criminal Justice Reference Service (http://virlib.ncjrs.org/Statistics.asp).

Becker, D., Lira, E. Castillo, M. I., Gómez, E., & Kovalskys, J. (1995). Therapy with victims of political repression in Chile: the challenge of social reparation. In N. J. Kritz (Ed.), *Transitional justice: How emerging democracies reckon with former regimes* (pp. 583-591). Washington, DC: United States Institute of Peace Press.

Becket, L. C. (1959). *Neti˙ Neti (Not this˙ Not that).* London: John M. Watkins.

Beirne, P., & Messerschmidt, J. (2000). *Criminology* (3rd ed.). Boulder, CO: Westview Press.

Bergman, L., Rummel, D., & MacIntyre, L. (2003). A dangerous business. In N. Docherty & D. Rummel (Producers), *Frontline.* Boston: WGBH.

Berlowitz, M. J. (1994). Urban educational reform: Focusing on peace education. *Education and Urban Society,* 27(1), 82-95.

Bernard, J. (1986). The good provider role: Its rise and fall. In A. S. Skolnick & J. H. Skolnick (Eds.), *Family in transition* (5th ed.), (pp. 125-144). Boston: Little, Brown.

Berry, W. (1996). Conserving communities. In W. Vitek & W. Jackson (Eds.), *Rooted in the land: Essays on community and place* (pp. 76-84). New Haven: Yale University Press.

Bilchik, G. S. (2001, March/April). Leaders who inspire. *Health Forum Journal*, 10-15,

Bjerke, B. (1999). *Business leadership and culture: National management styles in the global economy*. Cheltenham, UK: Edward Elgar.

Bluehouse, P., & Zion, J. (1993). *Hoozhooji Naat'aanii*: The Navajo justice and harmony ceremony. *Mediation Quarterly*, 10(4), 327-336.

Blumstein, P., & Schwartz, P. (1985). *American couples: Money, work, sex*. New York: Pocket Books.

Bogdan, R. (1983). A closer look at mainstreaming. *Educational Forum*, 47, 425-434.

Bolton, M. M. (2004, October 1). Diocese $5.2M mediation effort gets calls: Handling of priest sex-abuse victims draws some criticism. *Albany Times Union*. Retrieved December 1, 2004 from: http://www.timesunion.com/AspStories/story.asp?category=ALBANY&storyID=290802&BCCode=&newsdate=10/1/2004&tacodalogin=no

Boraine, A. (2001). *A country unmasked: Inside South Africa's Truth and Reconciliation Commission*. New York: Oxford University Press, 2001.

Boyes-Watson, C. (2000). Reflections on the purist and maximalist models of restorative justice. *Contemporary Justice Review*, 3(4), 441-450.

Braham. J. (1999, February 1). The spiritual side. *Industry Week*, 48-56.

Braithwaite, J. (1989). *Crime, shame and reintegration*. New York: Cambridge University Press.

Braithwaite, J. (1994). Conditions of successful reintegration ceremonies. *The British Journal of Criminology*, 34, 139-171.

Braithwaite, J. (2000). Decomposing a holistic vision of restorative justice. *Contemporary Justice Review*, 3(4), 433-440.

Braithwaite, J. (2003). Principles of restorative justice. In A. von Hirsch, J. Roberts, A. Bottoms, J. Roach & M. Schiff (Eds.), *Restorative justice and criminal justice: Competing or reconcilable paradigms?* (pp. 1-20). Oxford: Hart.

Braithwaite, J. & Strang, H. (2001). Introduction: Restorative justice and civil society. In H. Strang & J. Braithwaite (Eds.), *Restorative justice and civil society* (pp. 1-13). Cambridge, UK: Cambridge University Press.

Braithwaite, V., Ahmed, E., Morrison, B., & Reinhart, M. (2003). Researching the prospects for restorative justice practice in schools: The "Life in School Survey" 1996-9. In L. Walgrave (Ed.), *Repositioning Restorative Justice* (pp. 169-190). Cullompton, Devon, UK: Willan Publishing.

Branch, K. M. (1992). Participative management and employee and stakeholder involvement. In G. Széll (Ed.), *Concise Encyclopedia of Participation and Co-Management* (chapter 10). New York: Walter de Gruyter.

Brazelton, T. B. (1982). *Becoming a family.* New York: Dell Publishing.

Brazelton, T. B. (1992). *To listen to a child: Understanding the normal problems of growing up.* Redding, MA: Addison-Wesley.

Bringing them Home, Report of the National Inquiry into the Separation of Aboriginal and Torres Strait Islander Children from Their Families. (1997, April). Sydney, Australia: Human Rights and Equal Opportunity Commission (http://www.austlii.edu.au/au/special-/rsjproject/rsjlibrary/hreoc/stolen/).

Brison, S. (2002). *Aftermath: Violence and the remaking of self.* Princeton: Princeton University Press.

Brock-Utne, B. (1985). *Educating for peace: A feminist perspective.* New York: Pergamon Press.

Brodeur, P. (1974). *Expendable Americans.* New York: Viking Press.

Brophy, J. E. & Good, T. L. (1986). Teacher behavior and student achievement. In M. C. Wittrock (Ed.), *Handbook of research on teaching* (3rd ed.). New York: MacMillan.

Brown, N. O. (1959). *Life against death: The psychoanalytical meaning of history.* Hanover, NH: Wesleyan University Press.

Brown, N. O. (1966). *Love's body.* New York: Random House.

Burford, G., & Hudson, J. (Eds.). (2000). *Family group conferencing: New directions in community-centered child and family practice.* New York: Aldine de Gruyter.

Burke, R. J. (1989). Some antecedents and consequences for work, family conflicts. In E. B. Goldsmith (Ed.), *Work & family: Theory, research, and applications* (pp. 287-302). Newbury Park, CA: Sage.

Burnside, J., & Baker, N. (Eds.). (1994). *Relational justice: Repairing the breach.* Winchester, UK: Waterside Press.

Burton-Rose, D., Pens, D., & Wright P. (1998). *The celling of America: An inside look at the U.S. prison industry.* Monroe, ME: Common Courage Press.

Bush, R. & Folger, J. (1994). *The promise of mediation: Responding to conflict through empowerment and recognition.* San Francisco, CA: Jossey-Bass Publishers.

Cahil, T. (2000, October 15). Visual profiling. *Albany Times Union,* p. 15.

Cameron, L., & Thorsborne, M. (2001). Restorative justice and school discipline: Mutually exclusive? In H. Strang & J. Braithwaite (Eds.), *Restorative justice and civil society* (pp. 180-194). Cambridge: Cambridge University Press.

Campbell, J. (Ed.). (1972). *Man and transformation: Papers from the Eranos Yearbooks.* Princeton, NJ: Princeton University Press.

Chen, M-S. (2003). Workers' participation and their health and safety protection in China's transitional industrial economy. *International Journal of Occupational and Environmental Health,* 9, 368–377.

Childe, G. (1954). *What happened in history.* Baltimore, MD: Penguin Books.

Childres, R. (1965). Compensation for criminally inflicted personal injury. *Minnesota Law Review,* 50, 271-283.

Chomsky, N. (1994a). *Keeping the rabble in line: Interviews with David Barsamian.* Monroe, ME: Common Courage Press.

Chomsky, N. (1994b). *World orders old and new.* New York: Columbia University Press.

Chomsky, N. (2000, May 12). *U.S. Colombia policy.* Paper presented at Roxbury Community College.

Christie, N. (1977). Conflict as property. *The British Journal of Criminology,* 17, 1-14.

Christie, N. (1993). *Crime control as industry: Towards gulags western style?* New York: Routledge.

Chupp, M. (1989). Reconciliation procedures and rationale. In M. Wright & B. Galaway (Eds.), *Mediation and criminal justice: Victims, offenders and community* (pp. 56-68). London: Sage Publications.

Cienfuegos, A. J., & Monelli, C. (1983). Testimony of political repression as a therapeutic instrument. *American Journal of Orthopsychiatry,*

53, 43-51.

Clark, R. (1999). The "celling" of America, the political economy of force, and the violence of economic sanctions in international relations. *Contemporary Justice Review*, 2, 5-22.

Clear, T. (1994). *Harm in American penology: offenders, victims, and their communities*. Albany, NY: State University of New York Press.

Cobban, H. (2002). The legacies of collective violence: The Rwandan genocide and the limits of law. *Boston Review* (http://www.bostonreview.net/BR27.2/cobban.html).

Cobban, H. (2004). Healing Rwanda: Can an international court deliver justice? *Boston Review* (http://www.bostonreview.net/BR28.6-/cobban.html).

Cohen, S. & Smyme, S. L. (Eds.). (1985). *Social support and health*. Orlando, FL: Academic Press.

Coles, R. (1995). *Listening to children: A moral journey with Robert Coles*. PBS Home Video: Social Media Productions.

Coles, R. (1997). *The moral intelligence of children*. New York: Random House.

Coles, R. (1999). *The secular mind*. Princeton, NJ: Princeton University Press.

Collins, R. L., Taylor, S. E., & Skokan, L. A. (1990). A better world or a shattered vision: Changes in life perspectives following victimization. *Social Cognition*, 8, 263-285.

Community directory: A guide to cooperative living. (1995). Langley, WA: Fellowship for Intentional Community.

Consedine, J. (1995). *Restorative justice: Healing the effects of crime*. Lyttelton, NZ: Ploughshares Publications.

Conze, E. (1967). *Buddhist thought in India: Three phases of Buddhist philosophy*. Ann Arbor, MI: University of Michigan Press.

Crain, W. C. (1985). *Theories of Development* (pp. 118-136). Englewood Cliffs, NJ: Prentice-Hall.

Criminal Justice Review Group. (2000). *Review of the criminal justice system in Northern Ireland*. Belfast: Her Majesty's Stationery Office.

Cunneen, C. (1998). Community conferencing and the fiction of indigenous control. *The Australian and New Zealand Journal of Criminol-*

ogy, 30(3), 292-311.

Cunneen, C. (2001). Reparations and restorative justice: Responding to the gross violations of human rights. In H. Strang & J. Braithwaite (Eds.), *Restorative justice and civil society* (pp. 83-98). Cambridge: Cambridge University Press.

Cushing, R. & Welch, B. (1999, March). *"Not in Our Name": Homicide survivors speak out against the death penalty.* Paper presented at the Human Rights Initiative Brown Bag Lunch, Kennedy School of Government, Harvard University.

Dakof, G. A., & Taylor, S. E. (1990). Victims' perceptions of social support: What is helpful from whom? *Journal of Personality and Social Psychology*, 58, 80-89.

Daly, H. (1996). *Beyond growth: The economics of sustainable development.* Boston, MA: Beacon Press.

Daly, K. (2001). Conferencing in Australia and New Zealand: Variations, research findings and prospects. In A. Morris & G. Maxwell (Eds.), *Restorative justice for juveniles: Conferencing, mediation and circles* (pp. 59-84). Oxford, UK and Portland, OR: Hart Publishing.

Daly, K. (2002). Restorative justice: The real story. *Punishment and Society*, 4, 55-79.

Daly, K. (2003a). Making variation a virtue: Evaluating the potential and limits of restorative justice. In E. Weitekamp & H. Kerner (Eds.), *Restorative justice in context: International practice and directions* (pp. 23-50). Cullompton, Devon, UK: Willan Publishing.

Daly, K. (2003b). Mind gap: Restorative justice in theory and practice. In A. von Hirsch, J. Roberts, A. Bottoms, K. Roach, & M. Schiff, (Eds.) *Restorative justice and criminal justice: Competing or reconcilable paradigms?* (pp. 219-236). Oxford: Hart Publishing.

Daly, K., & Hayes, H. (2001). Restorative justice and conferencing in Australia. *Trends and Issues*, No. 186, Australian Institute of Criminology, Canberra. Retrieved December 5, 2004 from: http://www.aic.gov.au/publications/tandi/tandi186.html

Daly, K. & Immarigeon, R. (1998). The past, present, and future of restorative justice: Some critical reflections. *Contemporary Justice Review*, 1, 21-45.

Danieli, Y. (1981). On the achievement of integration in aging survivors of the Nazi Holocaust. *Journal of Geriatric Psychiatry,* 14(2), 191-210.

Danieli, Y. (1992). Preliminary reflections from a psychological perspective. In T. Van Boven, C. Flinterman, F. Grünfeld, & I. Westendorp (Eds.), *Seminar on the right to restitution, compensation and rehabilitation for victims of gross violations of human rights and fundamental freedoms* (pp. 196-213). Maastrict: Netherlands Institute of Human Rights.

Danner, M. (2004, October 7). Abu Ghraib: The hidden story. *The New York Review of Books*, 51(15), 40-44.

Davis, R.C., & Smith, B. E. (1994). Victim impact statements and victim satisfaction: An unfulfilled promise?" *Journal of Criminal Justice*, 22 (1), 1-12.

Day, D. (1970). *Meditations: Selected and arranged by Stanley Vishnewski*. New York: Paulist Press.

Death Penalty Moratorium Implementation Project, American Bar Foundation (2004). Retrieved November 27, 2004 from: http://www.abanet.org/moratorium/latesttrend.html#un

De Jonge, K. (2001, January). *Interim report on research on Gacaca jurisdictions and it preparations*. Kigali: Penal Reform International.

Delens-Ravier, I. (2003). Juvenile offenders' perceptions of community service. In L. Walgrave (Ed.), *Repositioning restorative justice* (pp. 149-166). Cullompton, Devon, UK: Willan Publishing.

Denzin, N. K. (1984). Toward a phenomenology of domestic, family violence. *American Journal of Sociology*, 90, 483-513.

DiCristina, B. (1995). *Method in criminology: A philosophical primer*. Albany, New York: Harrow and Heston.

Didion, J. (1992). *After Henry*. New York: Simon & Schuster.

Dignan, J. (2000). *Restorative justice options from North Ireland*. Belfast: Her Majesty's Stationery Office.

Dignan, J. & Marsh, P. (2001). In A. Morris & G. Maxwell (Eds.), *Restorative justice for juveniles: Conferencing , mediation and circles* (pp. 85-102). Oxford and Portland, OR: Hart Publishing.

Dignan, J., & Sorsby, A. (1999). *Resolving neighbour disputes through mediation in Scotland*. Edinburgh: Scottish Office Central Research Unit.

Duff, R. A. (2002). Restorative punishment and punitive restoration. In L. Walgrave (Ed.), *Restorative justice and the law* (pp. 82-100). Cullompton, Devon, UK: Willan Publishing.

Dugan, M. (July, 1996). A nested theory of conflict. *A Leadership Journal: Women in Leadership-Sharing the Vision*, 1(1), 9-20.

Dupont, J. (Ed.). (1995). *The clinical diary of Sándor Ferenczi*. Cambridge, MA: Harvard University Press.

Dürckheim, K. (1991). *The Japanese cult of tranquility*. York Beach, ME: Samuel Weisner.

Dyck, D. (2000). Reaching toward a structurally responsive training and practice of restorative justice. *Contemporary Justice Review*, 3(3), 239-265.

Edmonds, R. (1979). Some schools work and more can. *Social Policy*, 9(5), 28-32.

Elias, Robert. (1986). *The politics of victimization: Victims, victimology and human rights*. New York: Oxford University Press.

Elizur, D. (1992). Work and nonwork relations: The corical structure of work and home life relationship. *Journal of Organizational Behavior*, 12, 313-322.

Ellsberg, R. (1983). *By little and by little: The selected writings of Dorothy Day*. New York: Alfred A. Knopf.

Emde, R., Johnson, W. F., & Easterbrooks, M. A. (1987). The Do's and Don'ts of early moral development: Psychoanalytic tradition and current research. In J. Kagan & S. Lamb (Eds.), *The emergence of morality in young children* (pp. 245-276). Chicago: University of Chicago Press.

Englebrecht, C. (2004). *Revisiting the victims' rights movement: A review of the movement and its implications for our understanding of the "victim."* Unpublished manuscript.

Enright, R. (2001). *Forgiveness is a choice: A step-by-step process for resolving anger and restoring hope*. Washington, DC: Apa Lifetools.

Enright, R. D. & North, J. (1998). *Exploring forgiveness*. Madison: University of Wisconsin Press.

Epstein, S. S. (1980). The asbestos "Pentagon Papers." In M. Green & R. Massie, Jr. (Eds.), *The big business reader* (pp. 75-81). New York: Pilgrim Press.

Evans, R. (1998). *Housing plus and urban regeneration: what works, how, why, and where*. London: Housing Corporation.

Evans-Wentz, W. Y. (Ed.). (1960). *Bardol Thödöl: The Tibetan book of the dead; or the after-death experiences on the Bardo Plane, according to Lama Kazi Dawa-Sanday's English rendering*. Oxford: Oxford University Press.

Fairholm, G. W. (2003). *The techniques of inner leadership: Making inner leadership work*. Westport, CT: Praeger.

Fay, G. R. (2004, August). *AR 15-6 Investigation of the Abu Ghraib Detention facility and 205^(th) Military Intelligence Brigade*. Washington, DC: U.S. Department of Defense.

Feinberg, J. (1970). The nature and value of human rights. *Journal of Value Inquiry*, 4, 243-257.

Feinberg, J. (1998). Justice and personal desert. In L. P. Pojman & O. McLeod (Eds.), *What do we deserve?: A reader on justice and deserts* (pp. 70-83). Oxford: Oxford University Press.

Fellner, J. (2004). *Torture is a management failure*. New York: Human Rights Watch (http://hrw.org/english/docs/2004/09/24/usdom9387.-htm).

Fenzel, L. M. (1989). Role strains and the transition to middle school: Longitudinal trends and sex differences. *Journal of Early Adolescence*, 9, 211-226.

Ferrell, J. (1999). Anarchist criminology and social justice. In B. Arrigo (Ed.), *Social justice / Criminal justice: The maturation of critical theory in law, crime and deviance* (pp. 91-108). Belmont, CA: West/Wadsworth.

Flanigan, B. (1992). *Forgiving the unforgivable*. New York: Macmillan.

Flanigan, B. (1996). *Forgiving yourself*. New York: Macmillan.

Flaste, R. (1977, October 28). Teach kindness: There's a lesson in it for parents. *The New York Times*, p. 18.

Fletcher, J., & Rapoport, R. (1996). Work-family issues as a catalyst for organizational change. In S. Lewis & J. Lewis (Eds.), *The work-family challenge* (pp. 142-158). London: Sage.

Forest, M. & Pearpoint, J. C. (1992). Putting all kids on the map. *Educational Leadership*, 50(2), 26-31.

Forman, T. (Producer), & Klug, R. (Director). (1999). *My daughter's killer*

(48 Hours). New York: CBS.

Forsey, H. (1995). Community as crucible. In *Communities directory: A guide to cooperative living* (pp. 27-30). Langley, WA: Fellowship for Intentional Community.

Foucault, M. (1977). *Discipline and punish: The birth of the prison.* New York: Pantheon.

Frank, N. K. & Lynch, M. J. (1992). *Corporate crime: corporate violence. A primer.* Albany, NY: Harrow and Heston.

Frantz, D., & Collins, C. (1999). *Celebration, U.S.A.: Living in Disney's brave new town.* New York: Henry Holt and Company.

Fraser, S. & Norton, J. (1996). Family group conferencing in New Zealand child protection work. In J. Hudson, A. Morris G. Maxwell & B. Galaway (Eds.), *Family group conferences: Perspectives on policy and practice* (pp. 37-48). Monsey, NY: Criminal Justice Press.

Freudenheim. M. (1988, August 23). Employees act to stop family violence. *New York Times*, p. A1.

Fuller, R. B. (1981). *Critical path.* St. Martin's: New York.

Galaway, B. & Hudson, J. (Eds.). (1996). *Restorative justice: International perspectives.* Monsey, NY: Criminal Justice Press.

Galaway, B., Hudson, J. & Novack, S. (Eds.). (1980). *National assessment of adult restitution programs.* Final Report. Duluth, MN: University of Minnesota.

Galinsky, E., & Johnson, A. A. (1998). *Reframing the business case for work-life initiatives.* New York: Families and Work Institute.

Galtung, J. (1969). Violence, peace and peace research. *Journal of Peace Research*, 6(3), 167-191.

Galtung, J. (1976). Peacekeeping, peacemaking and peacebuilding. In J. Galtung (Ed.), *Peace, war, and defense* (pp. 282-305). Copenhagen: Christian Ejlers.

Gardner, H. (1991). *The unschooled mind: How children think and how schools should teach.* New York: Basic Books.

Garland, D. (2001). *The culture of control: Crime and social order in contemporary society.* Oxford, UK: Oxford University Press.

Gaster, T. H. (1961). *Thespis: Ritual, myth and drama in the ancient Near East.* New York: Anchor Books.

Gibbs, J. C. (1991). Toward an integration of Kohlberg's and Hoffman's theories of morality. In W. L. Kurtines & J. L. Gewitz (Eds.), *Handbook of moral development and behavior: Volume 1: Theory* (pp. 183-222). Hillsdale, NJ: Lawrence Erlbaum.

Gibbs, J. L. (1963). The Kpelle moot: A therapeutic model for the informal settlement of disputes. *Journal of the International African Institute*, 33, 1-10.

Gil, D. G. (1986). Sociocultural aspects of domestic violence. In M. Lystad (Ed.), *Violence in the home* (pp. 124-149). New York: Brunner/Mazel.

Gil, D. G. (1987). Individual experience and critical consciousness: Sources of change in everyday life. *Journal of Sociology and Social Welfare*, 14, 5-20.

Gil, D. G. (1989). Work, violence, injustice, and war. *Journal of Sociology and Social Welfare*, 16, 39-53.

Gil, D. G. (1996). Preventing violence in a structurally violent society: Mission impossible. *American Journal of Orthopsychiatry*, 66, 77-84.

Gil, D. G. (1998). *Confronting injustice and oppression: Concepts and strategies for social workers*. New York: Columbia University Press.

Gil, D. G. (1999). Understanding and overcoming social-structural violence. *Contemporary Justice Review* 2(1), 23-35.

Gobodo-Madikizela, P. (2003). *A human being died that night: A South African story of forgiveness*. New York: Houghton Mifflin.

Goffman, E. (1961). *Asylums*. Garden City, NY: Anchor Books.

Goodman, P. (1961). *Growing up absurd: Problems of youth in the organized system*. New York: Random House.

Goodman, P. (1963). *People or personnel: Decentralizing and the mixed system*. New York: Random House.

Goodwin, L. (2000, May 25). New school order: The cops in the hall. *Metroland News Weekly*, pp. 14-17.

Gopnik, A. (2000, October 2). Food fight. *The New Yorker*, 64-71.

Gordon, D. M. (1973). Capitalism, class, and crime in America. *Crime & Delinquency*, 19(2), 163-186.

Gourevitch, P. (1998). *We wish to inform you that tomorrow we will be killed with our families: Stories from Rwanda*. New York: Farrar, Straus and Giroux.

Govier, T. (2002). *Vengeance and forgiveness*. New York: Routledge.

Govinda, L. A. (1967). *Foundations of Tibetan mysticism: According to the esoteric teachings of the great mantra OM MANI PADME HUM*. London: Rider & Company.

Graber, L., Keys, T, & White, J. (1996). Family group decision-making in the United States: The case of Oregon. In J. Hudson, A. Morris, G. Maxwell & B. Galaway (Eds.), *Family group conferences: Perspectives on policy and practice* (pp. 180-194). Monsey, NY: Criminal Justice Press.

Greenberg, J. (1996). *The quest for justice in the workplace*. Thousand Oaks, CA: Sage.

Griffiths, C. T., & Hamilton, R. (1996). Sanctioning and healing: restorative justice in Canadian aboriginal communities. In B. Galaway & J. Hudson (Eds.), *Restorative justice: International perspectives* (pp. 175-191). Monsey, NY: Criminal Justice Press.

Gutlove, P., & Thompson, G. (2003). *Psychological healing: A guide for practitioners*. Cambridge, MA: Institute for Resource and Security Studies.

Hallahan, D., & Kaufman, J. (1982). *Exceptional children*. Englewood Cliffs, NJ: Prentice Hall.

Hampton, J. (1988). Forgiveness, resentment and hatred. In J. G. Murphy & J. Hampton (Eds.), *Forgiveness and mercy* (pp. 35-87). Cambridge: Cambridge University Press.

Harding, J. (1989). Reconciling mediation with criminal justice. In M. Wright & B. Galaway (Eds.), *Mediation and criminal justice: Victims, offenders and community* (pp. 27-43). London: Sage Publications.

Harris, M. K. (1998). Reflections of a skeptical dreamer: Some dilemmas in restorative justice theory and practice. *Contemporary Justice Review, 1*, 57-69.

Harris, N. (2003). Evaluating the practice of restorative justice: The case of family group conferencing. In L. Walgrave (Ed.), *Repositioning restorative justice* (pp. 121-135). Cullompton, Devon, UK: Willan Publishing.

Hart, E. (1992). Salsedo press: Community roots, quality printing. In L. Krimerman & F. Lindenfeld. (Eds.), *When workers decide: Workplace democracy takes root in North America* (pp. 13-20). Philadelphia: New Society Publications.

Harter, S., Whitesell, N.R., & Kowalski, P. (1992). Individual differences in the effects of educational transitions on young adolescents' perceptions of competence and motivational orientation. *American Educational Research Journal, 29,* 777-808.

Hartwell, M. B. (2000). The Role of Forgiveness in Reconstructing Society After Conflict. *Journal of Humanitarian Assistance.* Retrieved November 27, 2004 from: http://www.jha.ac/articles/a048.htm

Harvey, J. H., & Miller, E. D. (Eds.). (2000). *Loss and trauma: General and close relationship perspectives.* Philadelphia: Brunner-Routledge.

Hassall, I. (1996). Origin and development of family group conferences. In J. Hudson, A. Morris, G. Maxwell & B. Galaway (Eds.), *Family group conferences: Perspectives on policy and practice* (pp. 17-36). Monsey, NY: Criminal Justice Press.

Hatamiya, L. T. (1993). *Righting a wrong: Japanese Americans and the passage of the Civil Liberties Act of 1988.* Stanford, CA: Stanford University Press.

Hayes, H. & Daly, K. (2003). Youth justice conferencing and re-offending. *Justice Quarterly, 20,* 725-764.

Hayner, P. B. (2001). *Unspeakable truths: Confronting state terror and atrocity.* New York: Routledge.

Henry, S., & Lanier, M. M. (Eds.). (2001). *What is crime? Controversies over the nature of crime and what to do about it.* Lanham, MD: Rowman and Littlefield.

Henry, S., & Lanier, M. M. (2001a). The prism of crime: Toward an integrated definition of crime. In S. Henry and M.M. Lanier (Eds.), *What is crime? Controversies over the nature of crime and what to do about it* (pp. 227-243). Lanham, MD: Rowman and Littlefield.

Herbst, P. K. R., (1992). From helpless victim to empowered survivor: Oral history as a treatment for survivors of torture. *Refugee Women and Their Mental Health, 13,* 141-154.

Herman, E., & Chomsky, N. (1988). *Manufacturing consent: The political economy of the mass media.* New York: Pantheon.

Herman, J. L. (1997). *Trauma and recovery.* New York: Basic Books.

Hill, E. J., Hawkins, A. J., Ferris, M. & Weitzman, M. (2001). Finding an extra day a week: The positive influence of perceived job flexibility and work and family life balance. *Family Relations, 50*(1), 49-58.

Hirsch, S. (2002). Victims for the prosecution: A survivor of the embassy bombings on the limits of victim impact testimony. *Boston Review*, 27(5), 21-25.

Hocking, F. (1965). Human reactions to extreme emotional distress. *Medical Journal of Australia*, 2(12), 477-483.

Hoffman, M. L. (1987). The contribution of empathy to justice and moral judgement. In N. Eisenberg & J. Strayer (Eds.), *Empathy and development* (pp. 47-80). New York: Cambridge University Press.

Horney, K. (1942). *Self-analysis*. New York: Norton & Company.

Horwitz, Tony. (1994, December 4). Jobs to nowhere. *Albany Times Union*, p. A3.

Hoy, W. (1986). *Effective supervision*. New York: Random House.

Hoy, W. (1991). *Educational administration*. New York: McGraw-Hill.

Hudson, J., Morris, A., Maxwell, G., & Galaway, B. (1996a). Introduction. In J. Hudson, A. Morris, G. Maxwell & B. Galaway (Eds.), *Family group conferences: Perspectives on policy and practice* (pp. 1-16). Monsey, NY: Criminal Justice Press.

Hudson, J., Morris, A., Maxwell, G., & Galaway, B. (Eds.). (1996b). *Family group conferences: Perspectives on policy and practice*. Monsey, NY: Criminal Justice Press.

Human Rights Watch. (2003, September). *Ill-equipped: U.S. prisons and offenders with mental illness*. (Index # 1564322904.) New York: Author.

Huxley, T. (1894). *Evolution and ethics and other essays*. London: Macmillan and Co.

Illich, I. (1977). *Toward a history of needs*. New York: Pantheon.

International Centre for Prison Studies. (2003). *Prison brief for United States of America* (http://www.prisonstudies.org/).

Irwin, J., & Austin, J. (1994). *It's about time: America's imprisonment binge*. New York: Oxford University Press.

Jackson, W. (1980). *New roots for agriculture*. San Francisco: Friends of the Earth.

Jacob, B. R. (1970). Reparation or restitution by the criminal offender to his victim: Applicability of an ancient concept in the modern correctional process. *The Journal of Criminal Law, Criminology and Police*

Science, 61, 152-167.

Jaeger, H. (1959). L'Examen de conscience dans les religions non-Chretiennes et avant le Christianisme. *Numen* 6, 175-233.

James, O. (1995). *Juvenile justice in a winner-loser-culture: Socioeconomic and familial origins of the rise of violence against the person.* London: Free Association Books.

Jamieson, K. H. (1996). *Packaging the presidency: A history and criticism of presidential campaign advertising.* New York: Oxford.

Janoff-Bulman, R., & Berger, A. R. (2000). In J. H. Harvey, & E. D. Miller (Eds.), *Loss and trauma: General and close relationship perspectives* (pp. 29-44). Philadelphia: Brunner-Routledge.

Johnson, J. V. (1986). *The impact of workplace social support, job demands and work control upon cardiovascular disease in Sweden.* (Report No. 1.) Stockholm: Division of the Social Psychology of Work, Department of Psychology, University of Stockholm.

Johnstone, G. (Ed.). (2002). *Restorative justice: Ideas, values, debates.* Cullompton, Devon, UK: Willan Publishing.

Johnstone, G. (2004). How, and in what terms, should restorative justice be conceived? In H. Zehr & B. Toews (Eds.), *Critical issues in restorative justice* (pp. 5-16). Monsey, NY: Criminal Justice Press and Cullompton, Devon, UK: Willan Publishing.

Kamel, R., & Kerness, B. (2003). *The prison inside the prison: Control units, supermax prisons, and devises of torture.* Philadelphia: American Friends Service Committee.

Kaplan, B., & Johnson, D. (1964). The social meaning of Navajo psychopathology. In A. Kiev (Ed.), *Magic, faith, and healing: Studies in primitive psychiatry today* (pp. 203-229). Glencoe: The Free Press.

Kaplan, R. M., Patterson, T. L., Kerner, D., Grant, I., & the HIV Neurobiological Research Center (1997). Social support: Cause or consequence of poor health outcomes in men with HIV infection? In G. R. Pierce, B. Lakey, I. G. Sarason, & B. R. Sarason (Eds.), *Sourcebook of social support and personality* (pp. 279-301). New York: Plenum.

Karp, D. R. (2000). Sociological communitarianism and the just community. *Contemporary Justice Review*, 3(2), 153-173.

Kennedy, M. (1970). Beyond incrimination: Some neglected facets of the theory of punishment. *Catalyst*, 5, 1-16.

Kerstenberg, M. (1980, August). Discriminatory aspects of the German restitution law and practice. In Y. Danieli (Chair), *Nazi Holocaust effects*. Session presented at the meeting of the First World Congress of Victimology, Washington, DC.

Kid Source (2004). *Getting ready for college advising high school students with learning disabilities*. Retrieved December 18, 2004 from: http://www.kidsource.com/Heath/gr.html

Kierkegaard, S. (1941). *The sickness unto death*. Princeton: Princeton University Press.

Kimbrell, A. (1992). Time for men to pull together. *Utne Reader*, May/June, pp. 66-74.

Kinkade, K. (1994). *Is it utopia yet?: An insider's view of Twin Oaks community in its 26th year*. Louisa, VA: Twin Oaks Publishing.

Klein, M. (1964). Love, guilt and reparation. In M. Klein & J. Riviere (Eds.), *Love, hate and reparation* (pp. 57-119). New York: W. W. Norton & Company.

Kleiner, A. (1996, June 3). *Fast company*, p. 44.

Kleinig, J. (1971) The concept of desert. *American Philosophical Quarterly, 8*, 71-78.

Knopp, F. H. (1996). *A primer on the complexities of traumatic memory of childhood sexual abuse: A psychobiological approach*. Brandon, VT: Safer Society Press.

Kohn, A. (1993). *Punished by rewards: The trouble with gold stars, incentive plans, A's, praise, and other bribes*. Boston: Houghton Mifflin.

Kohn, A. (1996). *Beyond discipline: From compliance to community*. Alexandria, VA: Association for Supervision and Curriculum Development.

Konner, J., & Perlmutter, A. H. (Executive Producers), & Moyers, B. (Executive Editor). (1988). *Joseph Campbell and the Power of Myth; with Bill Moyers* [Film]. (Available from The Voyage Company, Santa Monica, CA.)

Kossek, E., & Ozeki, C. (1999). Bridging the work-family policy and productivity gap: A literature review. *Community, Work and Family, 2*(1), 7-32.

Kozol, J. (1991). *Savage inequalities: Children in America's schools*. New York: Crown.

Kozol, J. (1996). *Amazing grace: The lives of children and the conscience of a nation*. New York: Crown.

Kozol, J. (2000). *Ordinary resurrections: Children in the years of hope*. NY: Crown.

Kozol, J. (2002, June 10). Benign neglect. *The Nation* (http://www.-thenation.com/docprint.mhtml?i=20020610&s=kozol).

Krimerman, L., & Lindenfeld, F. (1992). Drawing in and reaching out: Strategies to strengthen the workplace democracy movement. In L. Krimerman & F. Lindenfeld. (Eds.), *When workers decide: Workplace democracy takes root in America* (pp. 239-246). Philadelphia: New Society Publications.

Kris, E. (1952). *Psychoanalytic explorations in art*. New York: International Universities Press.

Kritz, N. J. (Ed.). (1995). *Transitional justice*. Washington, DC: United States Institute of Peace Press.

Kropotkin, P. (1902). *Mutual aid: A factor in evolution*. London: Heinemann.

Kropotkin, P. (1924). *Ethics: Origin and development*. New York: Mother Earth Publications.

Kropotkin, P. (1968). *The conquest of bread*. New York: Benjamin Blom.

Kropotkin, P. (1970). Authority. In R. N. Baldwin (Ed.), *Kropotkin's revolutionary pamphlets*. Cambridge, MA: Harvard University Press.

Krystal, H., & Niederland, W. G. (1968) Clinical observations on the survivor syndrome. In H. Krystal (Ed.), *Massive psychic trauma* (pp. 327-348). New York: International Universities Press.

Kushner, H. S. (1996). *How good do we have to be? A new understanding of guilt and forgiveness*. New York: Little, Brown and Company.

LaBarre, W. (1964). Confession as cathartic therapy in American Indian tribes. In A. Kiev (Ed.), *Magic, faith, and healing: Studies in primitive psychiatry today* (pp. 36-49). Glencoe: The Free Press.

Ladd, J. (1957). *The structure of a moral code: A philosophical analysis of ethical discourse applied to the ethics of Navajo Indians*. Cambridge, MA: Harvard University Press.

Lakoff, R. (2001). Nine ways of looking at apologies: The necessity of interdisciplinary theory and method in discourse analysis. In D. Schiffrin, D. Tannen, & H. E. Hamilton (Eds.), *Handbook of discourse analysis* (pp. 199-214). Cambridge, MA: Basil Blackwell.

Lamont, J. (1994). The concept of desert in distributive justice. *Philosophical Quarterly*, 44, 45-64.

Landauer, G. (Ed.). (1929). *Briefen* (2 vols.). M. Buber (Ed.). Frankfurt: Verlag Rütten & Loening.

Landtman, G. (1938). *The origin of the inequality of the social classes.* London: Kegan Paul, Trench, Trubner & Co. Ltd.

Lane, R. E. (1986). Market justice, political justice. *American Political Science Review*, 80, 383-402.

Lanier, M., & Henry, S. (2004). *Essential criminology* (2nd ed.). Boulder, CO: Westview Press.

Laster, R. E. (1970). Criminal restitution: A survey of its past history and an analysis of its present usefulness. *University of Richmond Law Review*, 5, 80-98.

Leary, W. E. (1988, August 5). U.S. urged to fight infant mortality. *New York Times*, p. D17.

Lederach, J. P. (1997). *Building peace: Sustainable reconciliation in divided societies.* Washington, DC: Endowment of the United States Institute for Peace.

Lee, M. (2000, April 3). April 3, 2000 - Inner City Press Bronx Report. Retrieved January 13, 2005 from: http://www.gothamgazette.com-/commentary/comm.29.shtml

Leebaw, B. (2001). Restorative justice for political transitions: Lessons from the South African Truth and Reconciliation Commission. *Contemporary Justice Review*, 4(3), 267-289.

Lemonne, A. (2003). Alternative conflict resolution and restorative justice: A discussion. In L. Walgrave (Ed.), *Repositioning restorative justice* (pp. 43-63). Cullompton, Devon, UK: Willan Publishing.

Leon, S. (2000, October 12). The censored candidate. *Metroland*, 23(41), 12-14, 16.

Levertov, D. (1992). *New & selected essays.* New York: New Directions Books.

Levi, D. L. (1997). Note: The role of apology in mediation. *New York University Law Review*, 72 (5), 1165-1210.

Levine, M., & George, P. S. (1992, March). Shyness and the modern middle school. *Middle School Journal*, 23(4), 30-32.

Lewis, N. A. (2004, November, 30). Red Cross finds detainee abuse in Guantánamo: US rejects accusations. *The New York Times*, pp. A1, A19.

Lewis, S. (2003). Flexible working arrangements: Implementation, outcomes, and management. *International Review of Industrial and Organizational Psychology*, 18, 1-28.

Lickona, T. (1991a). *Educating for character: How our schools can teach respect and responsibility*. New York: Bantam.

Lickona, T. (1991b). An integrated approach to character development. In J. S. Benninga (Ed.), *Moral character, and civic education in the elementary school* (pp. 67-83). New York: Teachers College Press.

Liebmann, M. (1998). *Community and neighbour mediation*. London: Cavendish.

Lilles, H. (2001). Circle sentencing: Part of the restorative justice continuum. In A. Morris & G. Maxwell (Eds.), *Restorative justice for juveniles: Conferencing, mediation and circles* (pp. 161-182). Oxford UK and Portland, OR: Hart Publishing.

Lindenfeld, F. (2001). Worker ownership at Algoma Steel. *Humanity and Society*, 25(1), 3-17.

Lindenfeld, F. (2003). Commentary on "The organization of work as a factor in social well-being." *Contemporary Justice Review*, 6(2), 127-131.

Lofton, B.P. (2004). Does restorative justice challenge systemic injustices? In H. Zehr & B. Toews (Eds.), *Critical issues in restorative justice* (pp. 377-386). Monsey, NY: Criminal Justice Press and Cullompton, Devon, UK: Willan Publishing

Longclaws, L., Galaway, B., & Barkwell, L. (1996). Piloting family group conferences for young aboriginal offenders in Winnipeg, Canada. In J. Hudson, A. Morris, G. Maxwell & B. Galaway (Eds.), *Family group conferences: Perspectives on policy and practice* (pp. 195-205). Monsey, NY: Criminal Justice Press.

Love, C. (2000). Family group conferencing: Cultural origins, sharing, and appropriation – A Maori reflection. In G. Burford & J. Hudson (Eds.), *Family group conferencing: New directions in community-centered child and family practice* (pp. 15-30). New York: Aldine de Gruyter.

Lunn, E. (1973). *Prophet of community: The romantic socialism of Gustav Landauer*. Berkeley: University of California Press.

Maag, J. W. (1996). *Parenting without punishment*. Philadelphia: The Charles Press.

Maag, J. W. (1997). Parenting without punishment: Making problem behavior work for you. *Reclaiming Children and Youth: Journal of Emotional and Behavioral Problems*, 6(3), 176-179.

Maag, J. W. (2001). Rewarded by punishment: Reflections on the Disuse of Positive Reinforcement in Schools. *Exceptional Children*, 67(2), 173-186.

Mackey, V. (1997). *Restorative justice: Toward nonviolence*. Louisville, KY: Presbyterian Criminal Justice Program.

Macmurray, J. (1932). *Freedom in the modern world*. London: Faber and Faber.

Macmurray, J. (1933). *Interpreting the universe*. London: Faber and Faber.

Macmurray, J. (1961). *Persons in relation*. New York: Harper and Brothers.

Madrid v. Gomez, 889 F.Supp. 1146, 1261 (N.D. California, 1995).

Mare, R. D., & Winship, C. (1984). The paradox of lessening racial inequality and greater joblessness among black youth: enrollment, enlistment, and employment, 1964-1981. *American Sociological Review*, 49, 39-55.

Marsh, P., & Crow, G. (1996). Family group conferences in child welfare services in England and Wales. In J. Hudson, A. Morris, G. Maxwell & B. Galaway (Eds.), *Family group conferences: Perspectives on policy and practice* (pp. 152-166). Monsey, NY: Criminal Justice Press.

Marshall. E. M. (1995). *Transforming the way we work: The power of the collaborative workplace*. New York: Amacom.

Martin, D. (1981). *Battered wives*. San Francisco: Volcano Press.

Martin, E. (2004). Sustainable development: Postmodern capitalism, and environmental policy and management in Costa Rica. *Contemporary Justice Review*, 7(2), 153-169.

Martin-Baro, I. (1990, March 23). Reparations: Attention must be paid. *Commonweal*, 184-186.

Mauer, M. (1990). *Young black men and the criminal justice system.* Washington, DC: The Sentencing Project.

Mauer, M. (1992). *Americans behind bars: One year later.* Washington, DC: The Sentencing Project.

Maume, D., & Houston, P. (2001). Job segregation and gender differences in work-family spillover among white collar workers. *Journal of Family and Economic Issues*, 22(2), 171-189.

Maxwell, G., & Morris, A. (1996). Research on family group conferences with young offenders in New Zealand. In J. Hudson, A. Morris, G. Maxwell & B. Galaway (Eds.), *Family group conferences: Perspectives on policy and practice* (pp. 88-110). Monsey, NY: Criminal Justice Press.

Maxwell, G. M., & Morris, A. (1999). *Understanding reoffending.* Final report (unpublished). Institute of Criminology, Victoria University of Wellington.

Maxwell, G. & Morris, A. (2001). Family group conferencing and reoffending. In A. Morris & G. Maxwell (Eds.), *Restorative justice for juveniles: Conferencing, mediation and circles* (pp. 243-281). Oxford and Portland, OR: Hart Publishing.

Maxwell, G. & Morris, A. (2004). What is the place of shame in restorative justice? In H. Zehr & B. Toews (Eds.), *Critical issues in restorative justice* (pp.133-142). Monsey, NY: Criminal Justice Press and Cullompton, Devon, UK: Willan Publishing.

Maxwell, G., Morris, A., & Anderson, T. (1999) *Community panel adult pre-trial diversion: Supplementary evaluation.* Wellington: Institute of Criminology, Victoria University of Wellington.

McCold, P. (2000). Toward a holistic vision of restorative juvenile justice: A reply to the maximalist model. *Contemporary Justice Review*, 3(4), 357-414.

McCold, P. (2003). A survey of assessment research on mediation and conferencing. In L. Walgrave (Ed.), *Repositioning restorative justice* (pp. 67-120). Cullompton, Devon, UK: Willan Publishing.

McCold, P. (2004). What is the role of community in restorative justice theory and practice? In H. Zehr & B. Toews (Eds.), *Critical issues in restorative justice* (pp. 155-172). Monsey, NY: Criminal Justice Press and Cullompton, Devon, UK: Willan Publishing.

McCold, P., & Stahr, J. (1996, November). *Bethlehem police family group conferencing project.* Paper presented at the annual meeting of the American Society of Criminology; Chicago, IL.

McCold, P., & Wachtel, B. (1998a). Community is not a place: A new look at community justice initiatives. *Contemporary Justice Review, 1*, 71-86.

McCold, P. & Wachtel, B. (1998b). *Restorative policing experiment: The Bethlehem Pennsylvania police family conferencing project.* Pipersville, PA: Community Service Foundation.

McCullough, M. E., Sandage, S. J., & Worthington, E. L. (1997). *To forgive is human; How to put your past in the past.* Downers Grove, IL: InterVarsity Press.

McEvoy, K., & Mika, H. (2002). Restorative justice and the critique of informalism in Northern Ireland. *The British Journal of Criminology, 42*(3), 534-562.

McEvoy, K., & Mika, H. (2001). Policing, punishment and praxis: Restorative justice and nonviolent alternatives to paramilitary punishments in Northern Ireland. *Policing and Society, 11*(3/4), 359-382.

Mendez, J. (1991). Review of the book *A miracle, a universe: Settling accounts with torturers. New York Law School Journal of Human Rights, 8*, 8.

Mendez, J. (1997). Accountability for past abuses. *Human Rights Quarterly, 19*, 255-282.

Merton, T. (1961a). Chant to be used in processions around a site with furnaces. In M. McClure, L. Ferlinghetti, & D. Meltzer (Eds.), *Journal for the protection of all beings: A visionary and revolutionary review* (pp. 5-7). San Francisco: City Lights Books.

Merton, T. (1961b). *Mystics and Zen masters.* New York: Dell Publishing Company.

Messmer, H., & Otto, H-U. (Eds.). (1992). *Restorative justice on trial: Pitfalls and potentials of victim-offender mediation – international research perspectives.* Dordrecht, The Netherlands: Kluwer.

Michalowski, R. J. (1985). *Order, law, and crime: An introduction to criminology.* New York: Random House.

Mika, H. (1989). *Cooling the mark out? Mediating disputes in a structural context.* Paper presented at the North American Conference on Peacemaking and Conflict Resolution, Montreal, Quebec.

Mika, H. (1992). Mediation interventions and restorative justice: Responding to the astructural bias. In H. Messmer and H-U. Otto. (Eds.), *Restorative justice on trial: Pitfalls and potentials of victim-offender mediation – international research perspectives* (pp. 559-567). Dordrecht, The Netherlands: Kluwer.

Mika, H. (1993). The practice and prospect of victim-offender programs. *SMU Law Review,* 46(2), 191-206.

Mika, H. (2002). *Evaluation of Northern Ireland community-based restorative justice schemes.* Belfast: Atlantic Foundations.

Mika, H. (2002). Evaluation as peacebuilding?: Transformative values, processes, and outcomes. *Contemporary Justice Review,* 5(4), 339-349.

Mika, H., Achilles, M., Halbert, E., Stutzman, L. S., & Zehr, H. (2002). *Taking victims and their advocates seriously: A listening project.* Akron, PA: Mennonite Central Committee.

Miles, Jeffrey. M. (1995). The role of the victim in the criminal process: Fairness to the victim and fairness to the accused. *Criminal Law Journal,* 19(4), 193-203.

Miller, D. (1976). *Social justice.* Oxford: Oxford University Press.

Miller, D. (1999). *Principles of social justice.* Cambridge, MA: Harvard University Press.

Milovanovic, D., & Henry, S. (2001). Constitutive definition of crime: Power as harm. In S. Henry & M. M. Lanier (Eds.), *What is crime? Controversies over the nature of crime and what to do about it* (pp. 165-178). Lanham, MD: Rowman and Littlefield.

Mimica, J., & Agger, I. (2000). NGO perspectives: An evaluation of psychological projects and a retrospective. In D. Ajdukovic & M. Ajdukovic (Eds.), *Mental health care of helpers* (pp. 251-259). Zagreb, Croatia: Society for Psychological Assistance.

Minow, M. (1998). *Between vengeance and forgiveness: Facing history after genocide and mass violence.* Boston, MA: Beacon Press.

Mintzberg, H. (1979). *The structuring of organizations.* Englewood Cliffs, NJ: Prentice Hall.

Monet, G. (Producer). (1997). *Confronting evil* [Film]. (Available from HBO Studio Productions, 120A E23rd Street, New York, NY 10010.)

Money-Kyrle, R. E. (1951). *Psychoanalysis and politics.* New York: W. W. Norton and Company.

Moore, D. B., & O'Connell, T. (1994). Family conferencing in Wagga Wagga: A communitarian model of justice. In C. Adler & J. Wundersitz (Eds.), *Family conferencing and juvenile justice: The way forward or misplaced optimism?* (pp. 45-86). Canberra: Australian Institute of Criminology.

Morris, A., & Maxwell, G. (1993). Juvenile justice in New Zealand: A new paradigm. *Australian & New Zealand Journal of Criminology*, 26, 72-90.

Morris, A. & Maxwell, G. (1997). *Family group conferences and convictions*. Occasional Paper No. 5, Institute of Criminology, Victoria University of Wellington, New Zealand.

Morris, A. & Maxwell, G. (Eds.). (2001). *Restorative justice for juveniles: Conferencing, mediation and circles*. Oxford and Portland, OR: Hart Publishing.

Morris, A., Maxwell, G., Hudson, J., & Galaway, B. (1996). Concluding thoughts. In J. Hudson, A. Morris, & B. Galaway (Eds.), *Family group conferences: Perspectives on policy and practice* (pp. 221-234). Monsey, NY: Criminal Justice Press.

Morris, C. (2003, October). *Legal consequences of apologies in Canada*. Draft working paper presented at the workshop on "Apologies, Non-Apologies, and Conflict Resolution," Victoria, BC, Canada.

Morris, R. (1994). *A practical path to restorative justice*. Toronto: Rittenhouse.

Morris, R. (1995). Not enough! *Mediation Quarterly*, 12, 285-291.

Morrison, B. (2001). The school system: Developing its capacity in the regulation of a civil society. In H. Strang & J. Braithwaite (Eds.), *Restorative justice and civil society* (pp. 195-210). Cambridge, UK: Cambridge University Press.

Mott Haven-Longwood Asthma Resource Manual. (2005). Health Force and The Mott Haven-Longwood Childhood Asthma Partnership, New York City Department of Health. Retrieved January 13, 2005 from: http://www.asthma-nyc.org/healthforce/resourcemanual.html#CONTENTS

Mounier, E. (1971). *Personalism*. Notre Dame: University of Notre Dame Press.

Müller-Fahrenholz, G. (1997). *The art of forgiveness: Theological reflections on healing and reconciliation*. Geneva: World Council of

Churches Publications.

Nader, L., & Todd, Jr., H. F. (Eds.). (1978). *The disputing process – law in ten societies*. New York: Columbia University Press.

National Center for Education Statistics. (2002). Inclusion of students with disabilities in regular classrooms. In *The Condition of Education 2002* (NCES 2002–025). Washington, DC: U.S. Department of Education. Retrieved December 18, 2004 from: http://nces.ed.gov/programs-/coe/2002/section4/indicator28.asp

Neier, A. (1990, February 1). What should be done about the guilty? *New York Review of Books*, 32-34.

Neimeyer, R. A., & Levitt, H. M. (2000). In J. H. Harvey, & E. D. Miller (Eds.), *Loss and trauma: General and close relationship perspectives* (pp. 401-412). Philadelphia: Brunner-Routledge.

Nelson, B. (1983, April 3). Bosses face less risk than bossed. *New York Times*, p. E16.

Nevin, A., Thousand, J., Paolucci-Whitcomb, P., & Villa, R. (1990). (Broadcast on February 4, 1999.) Collaborative consultation: Empowering public school personnel to provide heterogeneous schooling for all. *Journal of Educational and Psychological Consultation*, 1, 41-67.

New Zealand Department of Social Welfare. (1984). *Daybreak*. Wellington, NZ: Author.

Niederland, W. G. (1968). An interpretation of the psychological stresses and defenses in concentration-camp life and the late after effects. In H. Krystal (Ed.), *Massive psychic trauma* (pp. 60-70). New York: International Universities Press.

Nielsen, M. O. (1996). A comparison of developmental ideologies: Navajo Nation Peacemaker Courts and Canadian Native Justice Committees. In B. Galaway & J. Hudson (Eds.), *Restorative justice: International perspectives* (pp. 207-223). Monsey, NY: Criminal Justice Press.

Nordhoff, C. (1993). *American utopias*. Stockbridge, MA: Berkshire House. (Original work published as *The communistic societies of the United States* in 1875.)

North American Congress on Latin America (NACLA). (1993, February 4). *Report on the Americas; A market solution for the Americas?* XXVI.

Northey, W. (1992). Justice is peacemaking: A biblical theology of peacemaking in response to criminal conflict. *New Perspectives on Crime and Justice*, Issue #12. Akron, PA: Mennonite Central Committee, Office of Criminal Justice.

Nutter, R., Hudson, J., & Galaway, B. (1989). *Community service and victim offender contact: An annotated and cross referenced bibliography.* Washington: DC: National Institute of Corrections.

O'Mahoney, D., Chapman, T., & Doak, J. (2002). *Restorative cautioning: A study of police based restorative cautioning in Northern Ireland.* Northern Ireland Office, Research and Statistical Series, Report 4. Northern Ireland Statistics and Research Agency.

Paliwala, A. (1982). Law and order in the village: Papua New Guinea's village courts. In C. Sumner (Ed.), *Crime, justice and underdevelopment* (pp. 192-227). London: Heinemann.

Pardo del Val, M., Martínez Pérez, J. F., & Dasí Rodríguez, S. (2002). *Participative management and organizational culture.* Paper presented at the European Academy of Management, EURAM, Stockholm, Sweden.

Pavlich, G. (2004). What are the dangers as well as the promises of community involvement? In H. Zehr & B. Toews (Eds.), *Critical issues in restorative justice* (pp. 173-183). Monsey, NY: Criminal Justice Press and Cullompton, Devon, UK: Willan Publishing.

Peacemakers Trust (2003). *Apologies, non-apologies and conflict resolution* (http://www.peacemakers.ca/education/newdirectionsApology-2003.html).

Peachey, D. (1989). The Kitchener experiment. In M. Wright & B. Galaway (Eds.), *Mediation and criminal justice* (pp. 14-26). London: Sage Publications.

Pence, E. (1983). The Duluth domestic abuse intervention project. *Hamline Law Review*, 6, 247-275.

Pence, E. (1987). *In our best interest: A process for personal and social change.* Duluth: Minnesota Program Development.

Pence, E. (1989). *The justice system's response to domestic assault cases: A guide for policy development* (Rev. ed.). Duluth: Domestic Abuse Intervention Project, Minnesota Program Development.

Pennell, J., & Burford, G. (1996). Attending to context: Family group decision making in Canada. In J. Hudson, A. Morris, G. Maxwell & B. Galaway (Eds.), *Family group conferences: Perspectives on policy and practice* (pp. 206-220). Monsey, NY: Criminal Justice Press.

Penner, L. A., Dovidio, J. F. & Albrecht, T. L. (2000). Helping victims of loss and trauma: A social psychological perspective. In J. H. Harvey, & E. D. Miller (Eds.), *Loss and trauma: General and close relationship perspectives* (pp. 62-85). Philadelphia: Brunner-Routledge.

Pepinsky, H. E. (1995). Peacemaking primer. *Peace and Conflict Studies*, 2, 32-53.

Pepinsky, H. (1998). Empathy works, obedience doesn't. *Criminal Justice Policy Review*, 9, 141-167.

Peterson, S. (2000). *Me against my brother: At war in Somalia, Sudan, and Rwanda*. New York: Routledge.

Pfeiffer, F. (1941). *Meister Eckhart* (R. Blakney, Trans.). New York: Harper & Brothers.

Pfohl, S. (1994). *Images of deviance and social control: A sociological history*. New York: McGraw-Hill.

Piaget, J. (1965). *The moral judgement of the child* (C. M. Gabain, Trans.). New York: Free Press. (First published in 1932.)

Pieper, J. (1966). *The four cardinal virtues*. Notre Dame, IN: University of Notre Dame Press.

Pierce, G. R., Lakey, B., Sarason, I. G., & Sarason, B. R. (Eds.). (1997). *Sourcebook of social support and personality*. New York: Plenum.

Piercy, M. (1976). *Woman on the edge of time*. New York: Fawcett Crest.

Plas, J. M. (1996). *Person-centered leadership: An American approach to participatory management*. London: Sage.

Polk, K. (1994). Family conferencing: Theoretical and evaluative questions. In C. Adler & J. Wundersitz (Eds.), *Family conferencing and juvenile justice: The way forward or misplaced optimism?* (pp. 123-140). Canberra: Australian Institute of Criminology.

Power, F. C., Higgins, A., & Kohlberg, L. (1989a). The habit of the common life: Building character through democratic community schools. In L. Nucci (Ed.), *Moral development and character education: A dialogue* (pp. 125-143). Berkeley, CA: McCutchan.

Power, F. C., Higgins, A., & Kohlberg, L. (1989b). *Lawrence Kohlberg's approach to moral education*. New York: Columbia University Press.

Pranis, K. (2001). Restorative justice, social justice, and the empowerment of marginalized populations. In G. Bazemore & M. Schiff

(Eds.), *Restorative community justice: Repairing harm and transforming communities* (pp. 287-306). Cincinnati, OH: Anderson Publishing Co.

Prejean, H. (1993). *Dead man walking: An eyewitness account of the death penalty in the United States.* New York: Vintage Books.

Presser, L. (2003). Remorse and neutralization among violent male offenders. *Justice Quarterly, 20,* 801-825.

Prothrow-Stith, D. (1987). *Violence prevention curriculum for adolescents.* Newton, MA: Education Development Center.

Prothrow-Stith, D., & Weissman, M. (1991). *Deadly consequences.* New York: Harper Collins.

Proudhon, P-J. (1888). *System of economic contradictions, or, the philosophy of poverty.* Boston: Benjamin Tucker.

Pugh, T. (1995). *Restorative justice: Four community models.* Saskatoon Community Mediation, Saskatoon, SK; and the Mennonite Central Canada Victim Offender Ministries, Clearbrook, BC.

Putnam, R. (1993). *Making democracy work: Civic traditions in modern Italy.* Princeton: Princeton University Press.

Quinney, R. (1975). *Criminology: Analysis and critique of crime in America.* Boston: Little, Brown and Company.

Quinney, R. (1991). The way of peace: On crime, suffering and service. In H. E. Pepinsky & R. Quinney (Eds.), *Criminology as peacemaking* (pp. 3-13). Bloomington: Indiana University Press.

Quinney, R. (2000). *Bearing witness to crime and social justice.* Albany, NY: State University of New York Press.

Reiman, J. (2003). *The rich get richer and the poor get prison: Ideology, class, and criminal justice* (7th Ed.). Boston: Allyn and Bacon.

Rhodes, L. (2004). *Total confinement: Madness and reason in the maximum security prison.* Berkeley, CA: University of California Press.

Riggs, D. S., & Kilpatrick, D. (1990). Families and friends: Indirect victimization by crime. In A. J. Lurigio, W. G. Skogan, & R. C. Davis (Eds.), *Victims of crime: Problems, policies, and programs* (pp. 120-138). Newbury Park, CA: Sage Publications

Rimer, S. (2001, April 25). Victims not of one voice on execution of McVeigh. *The New York Times,* pp. A1, A16.

Ritzer, G. (2000). *The McDonaldization of society* (New Century Ed.). Thousand Oaks, CA: Pine Forge Press.

Roberts, A. R. (1990). *Helping crime victims: Research, policy, and practice.* Newbury Park, CA: Sage Publications.

Roberts, A. W., & Masters, G. (1998). *Group conferencing: Restorative justice in practice.* Minneapolis, MN: University of Minnesota Center for Restorative Justice and Mediation.

Roche, D. (2002). Restorative justice and the regulatory state in South African townships. *The British Journal of Criminology,* 42(3), 514-533.

Roche, D. (2003). *Accountability in restorative justice.* Oxford: Oxford University Press.

Rogers, C. R. (1961). *On becoming a person.* Boston: Houghton Mifflin.

Rogers, C. R. (1980). *A way of being.* Boston: Houghton Mifflin.

Ruiz v. Johnson, 37 F.Supp.2d 855, 914 (S.D. Texas, 1999).

Ruskin, J. (1903-1912). *Works of John Ruskin* (Vol. XVII). E. T. Cook & A. Wedderburn (Eds.). London: G. Allen & Unwin.

Sachs, A. (1998, December 18). *Post-apartheid South Africa: Truth, reconciliation and justice.* The Fourth D. T. Lakdawala Memorial Lecture. Delhi: Institute of Social Sciences.

Safer, J. (1999). *Forgiving and not forgiving: A new approach to resolving intimate betrayal.* New York: Avon Books.

Salasin, S. E. (1986). Introduction: A blow of redirection. In S. Heiderbach (Ed.), *Invisible wounds: Crime victims speak* (pp. 1-3). New York: Harrington Park Press.

Sale, K. (1980). *Human scale.* New York: Coward, McCann and Geoghegan.

Santora, M. (2002, October 7). After son's suicide, mother is convicted over unsafe home. *The New York Times,* pp. B1, B5.

Sashkin, M. (1984). Participative management is an ethical imperative. *Organizational Dynamics,* 12(4), 4-22.

Scarry, E. (1985). *The body in pain: The making and unmaking of the world.* New York: Oxford University Press.

Schaefer, D. (2003). A disembodied community collaborates in a homicide:

Can empathy transform a failing justice system? *Contemporary Justice Review*, 6(2), 133-142.

Schafer, S. (1960). *Restitution to victims of crime*. London: Stevens and Sons Limited.

Schafer, S. (1965). Restitution to Victims of Crime – An old correctional aim modernized. *Minnesota Law Review*, 50, 243-254.

Schein, E. H. (1985). *Organizational culture and leadership: A dynamic view*. San Francisco: Jossey-Bass.

Schlesinger, J. K. R., Brown, H., Fowler, T. K., & Horner, C. A. (2004, August). *Final Report of the Independent Panel to Review DoD Detention Operations* (The Schlesinger Report). Washington, DC: U.S. Department of Defense.

Schlosser, E. (1998, December). The prison-industrial complex. *The Atlantic Monthly*, pp. 51-77.

Schneider, C. D. (2000). What it means to be sorry: The power of apology in mediation. *Mediation Quarterly*, 17, 1-15.

Schoffner, M., & Williamson, R.D. (2000). Facilitating student transitions into middle school. *Middle School Journal*, March, pp. 47-52.

Schultz, L. G. (1965). The violated: A proposal to compensate victims of violent crime. *St. Louis University Law Journal*, 10, 238-250.

Schultz, T. W. (1961). Investment in human capital. *American Economic Review*, 51, 1-17.

Schumacher, J. (1998). Questions for students of justice. *Contemporary Justice Review*, 1(2-3), 213-241.

Schwartz, P. (1994). Modernizing marriage. *Psychology Today*. September/October, pp. 54, 56, 58-59, 86.

Sheffer, S. (2001). *Beyond retribution*. http://www.mvfr.org/ShowObject.jsp?object_id=35

Shibutani, T. (1970). On the personification of adversaries. In T. Shibutani (Ed.), *Human conflict and conflict behavior* (pp. 223-233). Englewood Cliffs, NJ: Prentice Hall.

Shifley, R. (2003). The organization of work as a factor of social well-being. *Contemporary Justice Review*, 6(2), 105-126.

Shriner, J. G., Ysseldyke, J., & Christenson, S. (1989). Assessment procedures for heterogeneous classrooms. In S. Stainback, W. Stainback, and M. Forest (Eds.), *Educating all students in the mainstream of regular education* (pp. 159-182). Baltimore, MD: Paul H. Brookes.

Sibomana, A. (1997). *Hope for Rwanda* (C. Tertsakian, Trans.). London, Pluto Press.

Siegel, B. (1989). *Peace, love, & healing: Bodymind communication and the path to self-healing; An exploration.* New York: Harper & Row.

Silver, R. L. (1982). *Coping with an undesirable life event: A study of early reactions to physical disability.* Unpublished doctoral dissertation, Northwestern University, Evanston, IL.

Silverman, S. W. (1996). *Because I remember terror, father, I remember you.* Athens: University of Georgia Press.

Simmons, R. G., & Blythe, D. A. (1987). *Moving into adolescence: The impact of pubertal change and school context.* Hawthorne, NY: Aldine De Gruyter.

Simpson, C. (1994). *Science of coercion.* New York: Oxford.

Skelton, A. (2002). Restorative justice as a framework for juvenile justice reform: A South African perspective. *The British Journal of Criminology, 42*(3), 496-513.

Sklar, H. (1994). *Scapegoating the poor.* Boulder: David Barsamian.

Social Exclusion Unit (1998). *Bringing Britain together: A national strategy for neighborhood renewal.* Command Paper 4045. London: Her Majesty's Stationery Office.

Social Exclusion Unit (2001). *A new commitment to neighbourhood: Neighborhood action strategy plan.* London: Her Majesty's Stationery Office.

Social Exclusion Unit (2004). Creating sustainable communities. Office of the Deputy Prime Minister. Retrieved January 12, 2005 from: http://www.socialexclusionunit.gov.uk/page.asp?id=10

Southerland, M. D., Collins, P. A. & Scarborough, K. E. (1997). *Workplace Violence: A Continuum From Threat to Death.* Cincinnati: Anderson Publishing Co.

Stainback, W., Stainback, S., & Slavin, R. E. (1989). Rationale for merger of regular and special education. In S. Stainback, W. Stainback, and M. Forest (Eds.), *Educating all students in the mainstream of regular education* (pp. 15-26). Baltimore, MD: Paul H. Brookes.

Starbuck, E. D. (1901). *The psychology of religion: An empirical study of the growth of religious consciousness*. London: Walter Scott.

Stauber, J., & Rampton, S. (1995). *Toxic sludge is good for you: Lies, damn lies and the public relations industry*. Monroe, ME: Common Courage Press.

Stedman, L. C. (1987). It's time we changed the effective schools formula. *Phi Delta Kappa*, 69(3), 215-224.

Steinbeck, J. (1939). *The grapes of wrath*. NY: The Viking Press

Stewart, T. (1996). Family group conferences with young offenders in New Zealand. In J. Hudson, A. Morris, G. Morris & B. Galaway (Eds.), *Family group conferences: Perspectives on policy and practice* (pp. 65-87). Monsey, NY: Criminal Justice Press.

St. John, P. A. (2003). The songs teachers teach are not necessarily the songs children sing: The boy who would be an airplane. *Contemporary Justice Review*, 6(1), 47-53.

Stone, S. S., Helms, W. A., & Edgeworth, P. (1999). *The impact of juvenile court mediation on recidivism*. Unpublished paper. University of West Georgia.

Stowe, S. (2002, October 7). A boy alone, treated as if he were "nothing." *The New York Times*, p. B5.

Strang, H. (2001). Justice for victims of young offenders: The centrality of emotional harm and restoration. In A. Morris & G. Maxwell (Eds.), *Restorative justice for juveniles: Conferencing, mediation and circles* (pp. 183-194). Oxford and Portland, OR: Hart Publishing.

Strang, H. (2002). *Repair or revenge: Victims and restorative justice*. Oxford, UK: Clarendon Press.

Strang, H. (2004). Is restorative justice imposing its agenda on victims? In H. Zehr & B. Toews (Eds.), *Critical issues in restorative justice* (pp. 95-105). Monsey, NY: Criminal Justice Press.

Strang, H., Barnes, G., Braithwaite, J. & Sherman, L. (1999). *Experiments in restorative policing: A progress report on the Canberra Reintegrative Shaming Experiments (RISE)*. Canberra: Law Program, Research School of Social Sciences, Australian National University (www.aic.gov.au/rjustice/rise/index.html).

Strang, H., & Braithwaite, J. (2001). *Restorative justice and civil society*. Cambridge: Cambridge University Press.

Strubbe, M. A. (1990). Vulnerable years: Early adolescents and stress. *Michigan Middle School Journal* 14 (2), 4, 19-23.

Stuart, B. (1992). Circle sentencing: Mediation and consensus – "turning swords into ploughshares." Restorative justice in the third decade: retrospective and prospective. *Accord* 14(1), 9-13.

Stuart, B. (1994). *Alternative dispute resolution in action in Canada: Community center circles*. Unpublished paper. Whitehorse, Yukon: Yukon Territorial Court.

Stuart, B. (1996). Circle sentencing: Turning swords into ploughshares. In B. Galaway & J. Hudson (Eds.), *Restorative justice: International perspectives* (pp. 193-206). Monsey, NY: Criminal Justice Press.

Sullivan, D. (1980). *The mask of love: Corrections in America; toward a mutual aid alternative*. Port Washington, NY: Kennikat Press.

Sullivan, D. (1982). Mutual aid: The social basis of justice and moral community. *Humanity and Society*, 6, 294-302.

Sullivan, D. (1986-1987). The true cost of things: The loss of the commons and radical change. *Social Anarchism*, 6, 20-26.

Sullivan, D. (1998). Living restorative justice as a lifestyle: An interview with Fred Boehrer. *Contemporary Justice Review*, 1, 149-146.

Sullivan, D., & Boehrer, F. (1999). The "celling" of America, the political economy of force, and the violence of economic sanctions in international relations: An interview with Ramsey Clark. *Contemporary Justice Review*, 2, 5-21.

Sullivan, D., Sanzen, P., & Callaghan, K. (1987). The teaching and studying of justice: Fostering the unspeakable vision of cooperation. *Crime and Social Justice*, 29, 128-135.

Sullivan, D., & Sullivan, K. (1998, November). *The political economy of just community: A radical interpretation*. Paper presented at the annual meeting of the American Society of Criminology, Washington, DC.

Sullivan, D., & Tifft, L. (1998a). Criminology as peacemaking: A peace-oriented perspective on crime, punishment, and justice that takes into account the needs of all. *The Justice Professional*, 11, 5-34.

Sullivan, D., & Tifft, L. (1998b, March). *A social structural alternative to the punishment response: Toward a regrounding of the imagination in a needs-based economy*. Paper presented at the annual meeting of the

Academy of Criminal Justice Sciences, Albuquerque, NM.

Sullivan, D., & Tifft, L. (1998c). The transformative and economic dimensions of restorative justice. *Humanity and Society*, 22, 38-54.

Sullivan, D., & Tifft, L. (2000a). The requirements of just community: An introduction that takes into account the political economy of relationship. *Contemporary Justice Review*, 3(2), 121-152.

Sullivan, D., & Tifft, L. (2000b). *Restorative justice as a transformative process: The application of restorative justice principles to our everyday lives.* Voorheesville, NY: Mutual Aid Press.

Sullivan, D., & Tifft, L. (2004). What are the implications of restorative justice for society and our lives? In H. Zehr & B. Toews (Eds.), *Critical issues in restorative justice* (pp. 387-400). Monsey, NY: Criminal Justice Press.

Sullivan, D., Tifft, L., & Cordella, P. (1998a). The phenomenon of restorative justice: some introductory remarks. *Contemporary Justice Review*, 1, 7-20.

Sullivan, D., Tifft, L., & Cordella, P. (1998b). Editors' introductory remarks: A context for understanding justice literacy. *Contemporary Justice Review*, 1(2-3), 175-187.

Sullivan, J. (1998). Meeting the individual needs of all learners in the inclusion classroom. *The Justice Professional*, 11 (1-2), 175-187.

Sullivan, J. (2001). The school as a community of learners: meeting the needs of all in the inclusion classroom; an interview with John Sullivan. *Contemporary Justice Review*, 4(2), 219-231.

Sumner, C. J. (1987). Victim participation in the criminal justice system. *The Australian and New Zealand Journal of Criminology*, 20, 195-217.

Taft, L. (2000). Apology subverted: The commodification of apology. *Yale Law Journal*, 109, 1135-1160.

Tait, R., & Silver, R. C. (1989). Coming to terms with major negative life events. In J. S. Uleman & J. A. Bargh (Eds.), *Unintended thought* (pp. 351-382). NY: Guilford.

Tallack, W. (1900). *Reparation to the injured: And the rights of the victims of crime to compensation.* London: Wertheimer, Lea & Co.

Tannen, D. (2001). *I only say this because I love you: Talking to your parents, partner, sibs, and kids when you're all adults.* New York: Ballantine Books.

Tauler, J. (1909) *The inner way: Being 36 sermons for festivals* (2nd ed.). (New Trans. with Intro by Rev A. W. Hutton.) London: Methuen & Co.

Tavuchis, N. (1991). *Mea culpa: The sociology of apology and reconciliation.* Stanford, CA: Stanford University Press.

Taylor, S. (1999). The internment of Americans of Japanese ancestry. In R. Brooks (Ed.), *When sorry isn't enough* (pp. 164-168). New York: NYU Press.

Thomson, D. (2004). Can we heal ourselves? Transforming conflict in the restorative justice movement. *Contemporary Justice Review,* 7(1), 107-116.

Theorell, T. (1991). On cardiovascular health in women: Results of epidemiological and psychosocial studies in Sweden. In M. Frankenhauser, V. Lundberg, & M. Chesney (Eds.), *Women, work and health: Stress and opportunities* (pp. 187-204). London: Plenum.

Thousand, J., & Villa, R. (1989). Enhancing success in heterogeneous schools. In S. Stainback, W. Stainback, and M. Forest (Eds.), *Educating all students in the mainstream of regular education* (pp. 89-103). Baltimore, MD: Paul H. Brookes.

Tifft, L. (1978, November). *The definition and evolution of social justice.* Paper presented at the annual meeting of the American Society of Criminology, Dallas, Texas.

Tifft, L. (1979). The coming redefinitions of crime: An anarchist perspective. *Social Problems,* 26, 392-402.

Tifft, L. (1982). Capital punishment research, policy, and ethics: Defining murder and placing murderers. *Crime and Social Justice,* 17, 61-68.

Tifft, L. (1993). *Battering of women: The failure of intervention and the case for prevention.* Boulder: Westview Press.

Tifft, L. (1994-5). A social harms definition of crime. *Critical Criminologist,* 6(3-4), 9-13.

Tifft, L. (2000). Social justice and criminologies: A commentary. *Contemporary Justice Review,* 3(1), 45-54.

Tifft, L. (2002). Crime and peace: A walk with Richard Quinney. *Crime & Delinquency,* 48(2), 243-262.

Tifft, L., & Markham, L. (1991). Battering women: Battering Central Americans. In H. E. Pepinsky & R. Quinney (Eds.), *Criminology as peacemaking* (pp. 114-153). Bloomington: Indiana University Press.

Tifft, L., & Sullivan, D. (1980). *The struggle to be human: Crime, criminology, and anarchism.* Over-the-Water, Sanday, Orkney, Scotland: Cienfuegos Press.

Tifft, L., & Sullivan, D. (2001). A needs-based social harms approach to defining crime. In S. Henry & M. Lanier (Eds.), *What is crime? Controversies over the nature of crime and what we should do about it* (pp. 179-203). New York: Rowman and Littlefield.

Tifft, L., & Sullivan, D. (2005, forthcoming). Needs-based, anarchist criminology. In S. Henry, & M. Lanier (Eds.), *The essential criminology reader.* Boulder, CO: Westview Press.

Tifft, L., Sullivan, J., & Sullivan, D. (1997, November). *Discipline as enthusiasm: An entry into the recent discussion on the moral development of children.* Paper presented at the annual meeting of the Association for Humanist Sociology, Pittsburgh, PA.

Toews, B., & Katounas, J. (2004). Have offender needs and perspectives been adequately incorporated into restorative justice? In H. Zehr & B. Toews (Eds.), *Critical issues in restorative justice* (pp. 107-118). Monsey, NY: Criminal Justice Press.

Tobolowsky, P. M. (1999). Victim participation in the criminal justice process: Fifteen years after the President's Task Force on Victims of Crime. *New England Journal on Criminal and Civil Confinement, 25* (1), 21-105.

Toews, B. & Katounas, J. (2004). Have offender needs and perspectives been adequately incorporated into restorative justice. In H. Zehr & B. Toews (Eds.), *Critical issues in restorative justice* (107-118). Monsey, NY: Criminal Justice Press and Cullompton, Devon, UK: Willan Publishing.

Tonry, M. (2004). *Thinking about crime: Sense and sensibility in American penal culture.* New York: Oxford University Press.

Trist, E. L. (1978). Adapting to a changing world. In G. E. Sanderson (Ed.), *Readings in quality of working life* (pp. 10-20). Ottawa: Labour Canada.

Truth and Reconciliation Commission of South Africa. (1998-1999). *Report* (Vols. 1-5). Cape Town: Juta & Co. and New York: Grove's Dictionaries; (the full report can also be found at www.truth.org.za).

Tucker, J. (1985). Curriculum-based assessment: An introduction. *Exceptional Children*, 52, 199-204.

Turner, C., & Clomp, C. (1992). Building bridges: Linking education and community economic development. In L. Krimerman & F. Lindenfeld. (Eds.), *When workers decide: Workplace democracy takes root in North America* (pp. 144-147). Philadelphia: New Society Publications.

Umbreit, M. (1988). *Victim understanding of fairness: Burglary victims in victim offender mediation.* Minneapolis, MI: Citizens Council on Crime and Justice.

Umbreit, M. (1988). Violent offenders and their victims. In M. Wright & B. Galaway (Eds.), *Mediation and criminal justice: Victims, offenders and community* (pp. 99-112). London: Sage Publications.

Umbreit, M. (1995a). The development and impact of victim-offender mediation in the United States. *Mediation Quarterly*, 12, 263-276.

Umbreit, M. (1995b). *Mediating interpersonal conflicts: A pathway to peace.* West Concord, MI: CPI Publishing.

Umbreit, M. (1996). Restorative justice through mediation: The impact of programs in four Canadian provinces. In B. Galaway & J. Hudson. (Eds.), *Restorative justice: International perspectives* (pp. 373-385). Monsey, NY: Criminal Justice Press.

Umbreit, M., & Stacey, S. (1996). Family group conferencing comes to the U.S.: A comparison with victim-offender mediation. *Juvenile and Family Court Journal*, 47(2), 29-38.

Umbreit, M. S., Vos, B., Coates, R. B., & Brown, K. A. (2003). *Facing violence: The path of restorative justice and dialogue.* Monsey, NY: Criminal Justice Press.

Umbreit, M., & Zehr, H. (1996). Restorative family group conferences: Differing models and guidelines for practice. *Federal Probation*, 60(3), 24-29.

Underhill, E. (1918). *Mysticism: A study in the nature and development of man's spiritual consciousness.* London: Methuen & Co.

University of the State of New York, Board of Regents. (1989). *New York State Regents policy statement on middle-level education and schools with middle-level grades.* Albany, NY: Author.

Updegraff, J. A., & Taylor, S. E. (2000). In J. H. Harvey, & E. D. Miller

(Eds.), *Loss and trauma: General and close relationship perspectives* (pp. 3-28). Philadelphia: Brunner-Routledge

Vandeginste, S. (2001). Rwanda: Dealing with genocide and crimes against humanity in the context of armed conflict and failed political transition. In N. Biggar (Ed.), *Burying the past: Making peace and justice after civil conflict* (pp. 251-285). Georgetown: Georgetown University Press.

Van Ness, D. & Strong, K. H. (1997). *Restoring justice*. Cincinnati: Anderson Publishing.

Viadero, D. (1993, September 12). Special school reduces "distractions" for 9th graders. *Education Week*, p. 12.

Villa, R. A., & Thousand, J. (Eds.). (1995). *Creating an inclusive school*. Alexandria, VA: Association for Supervision and Curriculum Development.

Villa-Vicencio, C. (1999). A different kind of justice: The South African Truth and Reconciliation Commission. *Contemporary Justice Review*, 1(4), 407-428.

Villa-Vicencio, C., & Verwoerd, W. (Eds.). (2000). *Looking back reaching forward: Reflections on the Truth and Reconciliation Commission of South Africa*. Capetown: University of Cape Town Press.

Vitek, W., & Jackson, W. (1996). *Rooted in the land: Essays on community and place*. New Haven: Yale University Press.

Vock, D.C. (2002). Deadly equation: The decision to impose the state's ultimate sanction is greatly affected by where the murder occurs and the race of the victim. *Illinois Issues on line*. Retrieved November, 26, 2004 from: http://illinoisissues.uis.edu/features/2002june/death.html

Walgrave, L. (1995) Restorative justice for juveniles: Just a technique or a fully fledged alternative? *The Howard Journal of Criminal Justice*, 34(3), 228-249.

Walgrave, L. (2000). How pure can a maximalist approach to restorative justice remain?: Or can a purist model of restorative justice become maximalist? *Contemporary Justice Review*, 3(4), 415-432.

Walgrave, L. (Ed.) (2003). *Repositioning restorative justice*. Cullompton, Devon, UK: Willan Publishing.

Wang, M. (1989). Accommodating student diversity through adaptive instruction. In S. Stainback, W. Stainback, and M. Forest (Eds.), *Edu-*

cating all students in the mainstream of regular education (pp. 159-182). Baltimore, MD: Paul H. Brookes.

Weisbord, M. R. (2004). *Productive workplaces revisited: Dignity, meaning, and community in the 21ˢᵗ century*. San Francisco: Jossey-Bass.

Weitekamp, E. (2001). Mediation in Europe: Paradoxes, problems and promises. In A. Morris & G. Maxwell (Eds.), *Restorative justice for juveniles: Conferencing, mediation and circles* (pp. 145-160). Portland, OR: Hart Publishing.

Welch, M. (2003). Force and fraud: A radically coherent criticism of corrections as industry. *Contemporary Justice Review*, 6(3), 227-240.

Weschler, L. (1995). A miracle, a universe: Settling accounts with torturers. In N. J. Kritz (Ed.), *Transitional justice: How emerging democracies reckon with former regimes* (pp. 491-499). Washington, DC: United States Institute of Peace Press.

Wigfield, A., & Eccles, J. (1994). Children's competence, beliefs, achievement values, and general self-esteem: Change across elementary and middle school. *Journal of Early Adolescence*, 14(2), 107-138.

Williams, G., et al. (1959). Compensation for victims of criminal violence, A round table. *Journal of Public Law*, 8(1), 191-253.

Williams, W. C. (1970). *Imaginations*. New York: New Directions.

Wilson, C. (1995, October 18). Celebration puts Disney in reality's realm. *USA Today*, p. A1.

Wolfgang, M. (1965). Victim compensation in crimes of personal violence. *Minnesota Law Review*, 50, 223-241.

Wood, S., DeMenezes, L., & Lasaosa, A. (2003). Family-friendly management in the UK: Testing various perspectives. *Industrial Relations*, 42(2), 221-250.

Wright, M., & Galaway, B. (Eds.). (1989). *Mediation and criminal justice: Victims, offenders and community* . London: Sage Publications.

Wright, M. (1991). *Justice for victims and offenders*. Philadelphia, PA: Open University Press.

Wright, R. (1940). *Native son*. New York: Harper & Row, Publishers.

Wright, R. (2000). The ethics of living Jim Crow: An autobiographical sketch. In J. C. Oates & R. Atwan (Eds.), *The best American essays of the century* (pp. 159-170). New York: Houghton Mifflin.

Wundersitz, J., & Hetzel, S. (1996). Family conferencing for young offenders: The South Australian experience. In J. Hudson, A. Morris, G. Morris & B. Galaway (Eds.), *Family group conferences: Perspectives on policy and practice* (pp. 65-87). Monsey, NY: Criminal Justice Press.

Yantzi, M., & Worth, D. (1976). *The developmental steps of the victim/offender reconciliation project.* Unpublished paper, Kitchener, Ontario, on file with authors.

Yazzie, R. (1994). "Life Comes From It": Navajo justice concepts. *New Mexico Law Review*, 24, 175-190.

Yazzie, R. (1996, April 10). *Navajo peacemaking.* Paper presented at the conference entitled "Mediation: Coming of Age & Coming Together," Salt Lake City, Utah.

Yazzie, R. (1997, November). *The Navajo Response to Crime.* Paper presented at the meeting of The American Judicature Society on "A National Symposium on Sentencing: The Judicial Response to Crime"; San Diego, CA.

Yazzie, R, (1998). Navajo peacemaking: Implications for adjudication-based systems of justice. *Contemporary Justice Review*, 1(1), 123-131.

Yazzie, R. (1999, April). *Blanketed by law: How Indians are affected by more laws than all other Americans.* Paper presented at "Trial Survival: a Southwest Symposium to Begin the New Century," Flagstaff, AZ.

Yazzie, R., & Zion, J. (1996). Navajo restorative justice: The law of equity and harmony. In B. Galaway & J. Hudson, J. (Eds.), *Restorative justice: International perspectives* (pp. 157-174). Monsey, NY: Criminal Justice Press.

Young, K. (1992). Working better: Employee participation groups at Weirton Steel. In L. Krimerman & F. Lindenfeld (Eds.), *When workers decide: Workplace democracy takes root in North America* (pp. 141-143). Philadelphia: New Society Publications.

Young, M. A. (1995). *Restorative community justice: A call to action.* Washington, DC: National Organization for Victim Assistance.

Young, R. (2001). Just cops doing "shameful" business? Police-led restorative justice and the lessons of research. In A. Morris & G. Maxwell (Eds.), *Restorative justice for juveniles: Conferencing , mediation and circles* (pp. 195-226). Oxford and Portland, OR: Hart Publishing.

Zehr, H. (1989). VORP dangers. *Accord, A Mennonite Central Committee Canada publication for Victim Offender Ministries*, 8, 3.

Zehr, H. (1990). *Changing lenses.* Scottsdale, PA: Herald Press.

Zehr, H. (1995). Reflections on family group conferencing, New Zealand-style. Restorative justice in the third decade: Retrospective and prospective. *Accord*, 14, 1-2.

Zehr, H., & Toews, B. (2004). *Critical issues in restorative justice.* Monsey, NY: Criminal Justice Press and Cullompton, Devon, UK: Willan Publishing.

Zehr, H., & Mika, H. (1998). Fundamental concepts of restorative justice. *Contemporary Justice Review*, 1, 47-55.

Zion, J. W. 1983). The Navajo peacemaker court: Deference to the old and accommodations to the new. *American Indian Law Review*, 11, 89-109.

Zion, J. W. (1997). *The dynamics of Navajo peacemaking.* Paper presented at the 39th annual conference of the Western Social Science Association, Albuquerque, NM.

Zion, J. W. (1998). The use of custom and legal tradition in the modern justice setting. *Contemporary Justice Review*, 1(1), 133-48.

Zion, J. W. (1999). Monster slayer and born for water: The intersection of restorative and indigenous justice. *Contemporary Justice Review*, 2(4), 359-382.

Zion, J. W., & Zion, E. B. (1993). *Hozho' Sokee* – stay together nicely: Domestic violence under Navajo common law. *Arizona State Law Review*, 25, 407-426.

About the Authors

Larry Tifft and Dennis Sullivan have been collaborating on writing and activist projects about justice since they first taught together at the University of Illinois-Chicago in 1972. In 1980, their *The Struggle To Be Human: Crime, Criminology, and Anarchism* was published in the Orkney Islands, the first pacifist-anarchist treatise to appear on crime, punishment, and justice. This was followed by Dennis's *The Mask of Love: Corrections in America; Toward a Mutual Aid Alternative* the same year. In 1993, Larry's *Battering of Women: The Failure of Intervention and the Case for Prevention* was published and, in 1997, Dennis's *The Punishment of Crime in Colonial New York: The Dutch Experience in Albany During the Seventeenth Century* appeared. Dennis and Larry have also written many articles together. In the past several years, they founded and currently serve as editors of the international journal *Contemporary Justice Review,* and both were instrumental in establishing the Justice Studies Association, an international association of scholars, practitioners, and activists committed to restorative and social justice. Larry teaches at Central Michigan University, and Dennis is an Adjunct Professor of Criminal Justice at the State University of New York University at Albany.